WHO IS GOD?

AND CAN I REALLY KNOW HIM?

JOHN HAY & DAVID WEBB

Biblical Worldview of God and Truth: Who Is God? And Can I Really Know Him?

Published by
Apologia Educational Ministries, Inc.
1106 Meridian Plaza, Suite 220/340
Anderson, Indiana 46016
www.apologia.com

Manufactured in the USA
Sixth Printing: January 2017

ISBN: 978-1-935495-07-9

Cover Design: Sandra Kimbell
Book Design: Doug Powell

Printed by Bang Printing, Brainerd, MN

TABLE OF CONTENTS

LESSON 5: WHO ARE THE FATHER, THE SON, AND THE HOLY SPIRIT?

LESSON 6: IF GOD CREATED THE WORLD, WHY ISN'T IT PERFECT?

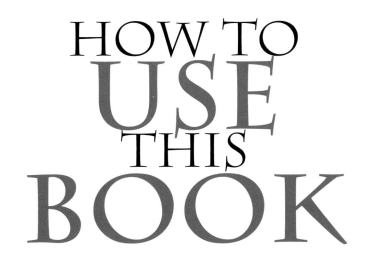

HOW TO USE THIS BOOK

Thank you for choosing the What We Believe series and the first volume, *Who Is God? (And Can I Really Know Him?)*. As with every Apologia textbook, you will find this Bible curriculum easy to use for your whole family. The text is written directly to the student, making it appealing for children from six to fourteen. The material is presented in a conversational, engaging style that will make the study of God's Word exciting and memorable for your students, thereby creating an environment where learning is a joy.

Each lesson contains a great deal of information and is formatted to allow the child to learn at his or her own pace. The course was designed so that you may customize the amount of time you spend on each lesson, depending on your child's interest level and attention span. We do, however, recommend that you present the lessons in order, as each lesson builds on ideas previously discussed. Although most of the lessons can be covered in two-week segments, some will go a little more quickly, while others may take longer. Older students can read and do the activities on their own. Younger students will enjoy an older sibling or parent reading along with them.

Please note that the Bible verses in each lesson are taken primarily from the New International Version (NIV), although a number of translations are employed. For the sake of clarity, the authors have also made extensive use of the International Children's Bible (ICB) and the New Living Translation (NLT) as these versions use vocabulary more accessible to younger students. We recommend, however, that your student use your family's preferred translation for the purpose of memorizing selected passages.

NOTEBOOKING

Notebooking is a fun tool that enables kids to personalize and capture what they have learned in an artful keepsake. In each lesson in this book, you will find a number of passages under the heading "Make a Note of It." In these sections, students are asked to write about what they've learned or about an experience they've had that relates to the lesson. As kids think about their lives in light of the lesson, the spiritual truths of the text will come alive for them and make real-life application easy.

For this purpose, Apologia publishes companion notebooking journals for each book in the series. These full-color, spiral-bound journals include all "Make a Note of It" assignments as well as puzzles, activities, mini books, reading lists, lesson plans, and additional pages for taking notes. Students are encouraged to personalize these journals by filling them with their own words and illustrations.

For younger students—and those who learn best while their hands are busy—we have compiled a 64-page companion coloring book for each of the volumes. Lovingly illustrated, each page depicts a story or teaching from the textbook to reinforce the lessons.

LESSON STRUCTURE

Each lesson in *Who Is God? (And Can I Really Know Him?)* contains several key components.

The Big Idea. Each lesson opens with an introduction to the main topic of the lesson and a brief overview of what the student has learned up to this point.

What You Will Do. This section states the learning objectives for the lesson.

Short Story. Several of the lessons contain a short story featuring characters about the same age as your children. These stories give the student a glimpse into the lives of characters with differing worldviews and integrate concepts taught in the lesson that follows. As the story's characters work through their differences, minister to one another, and seek counsel from the Bible and their parents, students see what a worldview looks like in action.

Think About It. These thought-provoking questions dig deeper into the short stories and can be used to check the student's comprehension. You may choose to supplement or adapt these questions to better suit your child's age and reading level. More than reciting information back about the story itself, these questions probe the student's understanding and provide great dinner-table talking points.

Words You Need to Know. Important vocabulary words in each lesson are defined in the Words You Need to Know section. Kids should write these definitions in their notebooks. These are words that will be used and examined during the lesson and throughout the book. As children familiarize themselves with these words, not only will church services become more meaningful, but kids will be better prepared to express their faith to others.

Hide It in Your Heart. Although the Bible is quoted extensively throughout the book, each lesson identifies two specific Bible memory verses to be written in the child's notebook. The first of these expresses the main theme of the lesson. Your student will know by memorizing this verse that the theme of the lesson is biblical and something God desires us to know. The second pertains to a character trait that you will want your child to internalize and demonstrate as a result of the lesson. These verses are ideal for Bible memorization or copy work. The verses have been chosen carefully for the clarity of the concepts they communicate, but you may prefer to use your family's favorite translation of these verses.

Integrated learning. Throughout the text we have provided interesting articles with an age-appropriate approach to interdisciplinary topics related to the main text. Some of these topics are specifically related to elements in one of the short stories, while others are tied directly to the lesson. These articles are designed to help you and your child to pursue the book's ideas and concepts across the fields of art, math, science, history and more. The beauty of the integrated learning approach is that it gives the student a broader understanding of the main subject while exposing the student to new interests, skills, and experiences.

What Should I Do? This section highlights a specific godly character trait that the child should demonstrate as an appropriate response to what he or she has just learned about God. Here the student is given tools to consider how the lesson applies to his or her own life. Knowing the information provided in each lesson is good, but giving the child tools to put the information to use in daily life creates growth.

Prayer. The main body of each lesson concludes with a prayer that enables the child to acknowledge specific attributes of God and to thank Him for who He is. You may also choose to adapt these prayers for use as a family.

Worldview Study. The final portion of each lesson is part of an ongoing study that introduces the child to the concept of worldview. Worldview studies help us understand how people perceive the world around them. As Christians, we believe certain things about God, humanity, our planet, and the future of mankind that others might consider confusing or even incredible. Understanding why we believe what we believe helps the child to form a worldview that is centered on God's truth as presented in the Bible. When we recognize the components of our own worldview, we can begin to look at other worldviews and understand why others believe as they do. This understanding will help children, as they grow, to communicate effectively with others about the hope that is in us as Christians. This worldview study is presented here in small increments to allow students time to consider what they have learned and to take notice of differing worldviews coming at them from books, radios, TV, movies, the Internet, friends, etc.

House of Truth. Many of the worldview sections end with the addition of a new part of the House of Truth. Intended to be a hands-on memory aid, the House of Truth is a visual model constructed one step at a time. As new concepts are learned, the foundations, walls, and roof of the house are constructed, giving the child a concrete way of thinking about his life within the kingdom of God. In this book, the student will complete the foundation and the first wall of the house. A new wall will be added in the second, third, and fourth volumes of the series.

The House of Truth can be used figuratively, drawn in the student's notebook, or built with items you have on hand. A three-dimensional, build-as-you-go model is also available for purchase separately from Summit Ministries. This colorful, durable House of Truth is constructed block by block as each affirmation of the biblical Christian worldview is developed lesson by lesson. The wooden model forms a visual, tactile framework to help children understand these truths and integrate them into their lives. You can purchase the model at www.summit.org.

LESSON PLAN

Each lesson is designed to be flexible and adaptable to your family's needs. Organize the lessons into a schedule that works for you and your child. Here is a sample lesson plan to consider based on a schedule of two weeks per lesson, three days per week:

WEEK ONE

Day One:
Read "The Big Idea" and "What You Will Do"
Read the Short Story and discuss
Discuss the questions in "Think About It"

Day Two:
Study "Words You Need to Know"
Memorize "Hide It in Your Heart" verses
Read sidebar articles and do activities
Write or draw in notebook about what was studied

Day Three:
Read and discuss first half of the main lesson
Notebook the "Make a Note of It" activities
Write or draw in notebook about what was studied

WEEK TWO

Day Four:
Read and discuss second half of the main lesson
Notebook the "Make a Note of It" activities
Write or draw in notebook about what was studied

Day Five:
Read and discuss "What Should I Do?" for character development
Read and use the prayer for spiritual development
Write or draw in notebook about what was studied

Day Six:
Read and discuss the Worldview Study section
Write or draw in notebook about what was studied
Construct or draw the next phase of the House of Truth

ADDITIONAL TEACHING MATERIALS

A few lessons contain activities that require advance planning. A list of materials for these activities has been provided with each activity. Nearly all the materials are household items or are easily obtained. You will also find the Apologia website to be a valuable source of information and materials to help you in teaching this course.

WHY SHOULD YOU TEACH WORLDVIEW?

When a particular worldview is held by a large number of people, it becomes highly influential, swaying many through media, entertainment, education, and corporate behavior. Some of the more widely held worldviews of the twenty-first century include secular humanism, socialism and Marxism, New Age, postmodernism, and Islam. Not to be excluded is the biblical Christian worldview, the focus of this curriculum.

People develop their worldviews upon beliefs they perceive to be true. Obviously, not all beliefs are true. If they were, we would not see the wide diversity of behaviors that stem from different interpretations of the same reality. For example, the beliefs of secular humanists that permit abortion cannot be equally true with the beliefs of conservative Christians that do not permit abortion. Nor can the beliefs of cosmic humanists that identify all existence as part of a universal consciousness be equally true with the beliefs of Christianity that affirm that creation is dependent upon one transcendent God.

Diverse beliefs about reality fill the marketplace of ideas in the emerging global village. Many ideas are competing for dominance, and this competition is producing conflict and confusion in cultures long held together by traditional worldviews. Christian-based cultures are awakening to find mosques standing next to churches and Bible-based laws swept from the books by a simple majority vote of humanist legislators and judges.

Within this global arena of conflict and change, Christians are faced with at least two critical questions: "How do we know what is true?" and "How must we live our lives in relation to the truth we come to know?" This curriculum is designed to address questions like these. It is based on the biblical Christian worldview, which affirms that truth is absolute and knowable through the revelation of God. It affirms that knowledge of God is the beginning of wisdom and the key to understanding the world around us.

You have the privilege and responsibility of leading your child not only in the paths of truth, but also to a knowledge and fear of the One who is the Truth, Jesus Christ. With the lessons contained in this, the first book in the What We Believe series, you will lay the essential foundational truths upon which the biblical Christian worldview is built: God is truth, and He reveals His truth to people. Lay these stones of foundational truths well. Pray that God will continually reveal and confirm the truths of His Word in the hearts of your student and that your child will respond in obedience to them.

We think you will find this to be an important course of study. Many eternal truths are presented that can change the way your child looks at the world every day. Minor points of doctrinal difference have been avoided in order to focus on the larger issues that make up our faith. As Christians we are asked to be ready to give an account of the hope that is in us. We hope this book brings your faith into clearer focus and your family ever closer to the Lord.

COURSE WEBSITE

The Apologia website contains additional resources to help you teach this course. Visit www.apologia.com/bookextras and enter the following password: Godistruth. Capitalize the first letter, and be sure the password contains no spaces. When you hit "enter," you will be taken to the course website.

NEED HELP?

If you have any questions while using Apologia curriculum, feel free to contact us:

Curriculum Help
Apologia Educational Ministries, Inc.
1106 Meridian Plaza, Suite 220
Anderson, IN 46016
Phone: (765) 608-3280
Fax: (765) 608-3290
E-mail: biblicalworldview@apologia.com
Internet: http://www.apologia.com

WHERE AM I BUILDING MY LIFE?

> HE IS THE ROCK, HIS WORKS ARE PERFECT, AND ALL HIS WAYS ARE JUST. A FAITHFUL GOD WHO DOES NO WRONG, UPRIGHT AND JUST IS HE.

DEUTERONOMY 32:4

THE BIG IDEA

Wise builders know that every house must have a **foundation**. A foundation is usually made of concrete or stone and steel, and its purpose is to hold the house up from underneath. Wise builders also know that the foundation must be built on very solid ground or rock. If the house is built on sand, the building will fall when the sand under the foundation washes away in a storm, or when it shifts during an earthquake.

For the same reason, a person's life must also have a strong foundation. Wise people know that "storms" are a part of life, that we all will face our share of difficulties and disappointments. Therefore wise people build the foundation of their lives on God, whom the Bible calls **the Rock**:

"For who is God besides the LORD? And who is the Rock except our God?" (2 Samuel 22:32)

[God] alone is my rock and my salvation. (Psalm 62:2)

God is like the solid rock, dependable and durable, on which wise people lay the foundations for their houses. You can always count on God and His Word—the Bible—because they always tell us what is true. Whether building houses or building their lives, wise people will follow a good plan, and there is no plan as good as the one found in God's Word.

Yet some people don't follow the best plan for building their houses. More importantly, some people don't follow the best plan for building their *lives*. Some don't know about the instructions God gives us in the Bible for building our lives. Others know about the Bible but choose to ignore it.

Jesus warned us that many people build their lives on sand. This means that they decide what is true in their own minds; they decide for themselves what is right and what is wrong. And when they build their lives without guidance from God, sooner or later their lives start cracking and sliding downward.

Wise builders, however, know that God is the Rock of Truth. That's why they choose to follow the plan God gives us in His Word for building their lives. Instead of building on Sandy Hill, they build in Rocky Canyon.

"There is no one holy like the LORD . . . there is no Rock like our God." (1 Samuel 2:2)

WHAT YOU WILL DO

» You will explore scriptures that explain why you should build your life on the Rock of God and His Word.

» You will identify ways people build their lives on "sand" instead of building on the Rock of God and His Word.

» You will explore scriptures that explain what it means to build a foundation of wisdom for your life.

THE GREAT ARCHITECT

An **architect** is an individual who designs buildings and plans the details related to a building's construction. The word *architect* comes from the Greek word *arkhitekton*, which means "chief builder." The sixteenth-century French theologian John Calvin called God the "Great Architect" and "the Architect of the Universe."

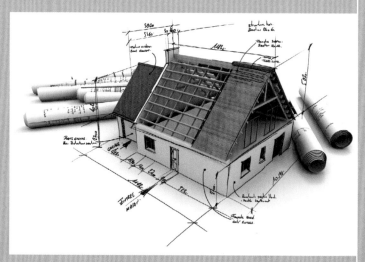

Architects draw their building plans on a document called a **blueprint**. The men and women on a construction crew then follow this blueprint as they build. These plans include many safety features, such as emergency exits and sprinkler systems, designed to protect the people who will work or live in the building.

God has drawn up a plan for building our lives, and His plan includes many important safety features. His blueprint, if followed faithfully, will keep us from all kinds of danger and even show us the way out of difficult situations. It's no wonder this blueprint for living is the best-selling book of all time!

UP SANDY HILL, DOWN ROCKY CANYON

"Dad," Jeremy asked as he gulped down the last of his orange juice, "what time does Ben's flight arrive?"

"I'm not sure. Check it out on the Internet. He's flying on Rocky Mountain Air, flight 380, I think," replied Dad.

"Eleven o'clock, and it's on time," Jeremy said, looking at the website. "Let's get going. I don't want to be late. I haven't seen Ben in over a year."

"You've really missed Ben since we moved out West, haven't you?"

"A whole lot," replied Jeremy. "But we're gonna have a great time this week—you know, hiking, biking, a couple of movies, and lots of staying up late."

"Well, I don't know about staying up late. I think with all those plans, you'll be ready for bed much earlier than you expect," said Dad, laughing.

"I think that's his plane at the gate," shouted Jeremy as he and his dad walked into the waiting area of the airport terminal.

Minutes later, Ben came down the escalator and headed for the baggage claim area.

"Hey, Ben," yelled Jeremy. "We're over here."

As they all exchanged big bear hugs, Ben said, "Thanks, Mr. Simmons, for letting me come for a week this summer. I hope I won't be any trouble."

"I'm sure you won't be any trouble," replied Mr. Simmons. "We're just glad you could come."

After lunch, Jeremy asked, "Ben, you want to see my dad's office? It's downstairs. He's an architect. You know, one of those guys who draws plans for houses and all kinds of buildings. Anyway, he works at home and has a really neat set-up in the basement."

"Sure," replied Ben curiously.

"Tell Ben what you do, Dad," said Jeremy.

"Well, I draw plans—blueprints—you know, diagrams and pictures that tell builders exactly how to build houses and other kinds of buildings. Without blueprints, builders can't build. And without good plans, they sure can't build good, strong buildings."

"Hey, Dad," said Jeremy. "I'm gonna show Ben that house up on Sandy Hill. You remember, the one you drew the plans for."

"Oh, yes. I remember that house very well," said Dad, raising his eyebrows. "And I also remember telling the builder not to build up on Sandy Hill. The ground there is not solid, and after a heavy rain, you can count on mudslides from that hillside."

"Really?" asked Ben.

"Yeah," said Jeremy. "Come on. I'll show you. The bikes are in the garage."

After a slow, hard ride up Sandy Hill, the boys reached the house, or rather, what was left of it.

"Wow! Look at that," exclaimed Ben. "The foundation and walls are all cracked. It looks like the whole house could slide off the hill at any minute."

"Yeah. That's why the signs say 'Keep Out' and 'No Trespassing.' I think the city's gonna tear it down soon. My dad warned them, but the builder thought he knew best. I guess he didn't think my dad was telling him the truth. Anyway, come on, I want to show you another house my dad drew the plans for up in Rocky Canyon. It's a really neat cabin."

The two boys coasted down Sandy Hill and took the bike path along Silver Creek. The hills became steeper as the path wound into Rocky Canyon.

"Cool, huh?" Jeremy said. "This is my favorite place to bike. I like the big pine trees and the sound of the creek. And if you keep your eyes open, you might even see some deer, but hopefully not a bear."

"A bear? Are there bears around here?"

"Yep, but they won't bother you if you stay on the bike path, near the road, and don't try to feed them."

"Don't worry. I'm right behind you!" Ben said nervously.

"There it is," said Jeremy, pointing to the two-story cabin beside Silver Creek. "It's really a neat cabin, and the builder built it just like my dad's plans showed. There's rock under the foundation, so it's gonna be here a long time."

"I bet the guy who built up on Sandy Hill wishes he'd built in Rocky Canyon instead," Ben said.

"I think so too," said Jeremy, looking at his watch. "Hey, we need to start heading home. It's almost time for supper."

As the boys pulled their bikes into the garage, Jeremy hollered, "We're home, Mom! What's for supper?"

"Hamburgers," replied Mrs. Simmons. "How was your ride?"

"Great," exclaimed Ben. "Jeremy showed me the house on Sandy Hill and the cabin in Rocky Canyon. I can't believe someone would go ahead and build a house on Sandy Hill, especially after Mr. Simmons drew good plans and warned the owner about building there."

"Me neither," said Mr. Simmons, who had just come upstairs from his office. "But there are some foolish people in the world. They just don't think it's important to follow good plans for anything, even for building their own lives."

"What do you mean?" asked Ben.

"Well, just like the guy who wouldn't follow my house plans, some people try to build their lives the way *they* want to," replied Mr. Simmons. "They make their own decisions about what's right and wrong and what they want to do. And they ignore a very wise plan that's available to everyone for building their lives."

"What's that plan?" asked Ben.

"It's the plan for our lives that God gives us in the Bible. The Bible is God's Word, and it gives us every detail we need for building strong lives for God. But just like the man who didn't follow my plans and built on Sandy Hill, some people ignore God's Word. They don't build on the rock of God's truth. Instead, they build their lives on the sand of their own ideas. And that's why, sooner or later, they have real problems in their lives."

"And we're going to have a real problem with supper if you don't start cooking the hamburgers before the coals burn out," teased Mrs. Simmons as she handed her husband the platter of buns and hamburger patties.

"Come on, Ben," Jeremy said. "We can watch while Dad's cooking and make our plans for tomorrow. There's a really cool hiking trail up Bear Creek Mountain I want to show you."

"Did you say Bear Creek Mountain?" asked Ben, a little wide-eyed.

"Oh, that's just its name. People haven't seen bears on that trail for years. Besides, I'm gonna show you some really beautiful parts of God's creation. I promise."

THINK ABOUT IT

» How is the cabin in Rocky Canyon different from the house on Sandy Hill? Why does Mr. Simmons expect the Rocky Canyon house to last much longer than the other one?

» Mr. Simmons is an architect. He designed a very nice house but warned the owner not to build it on Sandy Hill. But the owner of the house could choose whether or not to follow Mr. Simmons's plans. What were the consequences? How is this like our relationship with God?

THE PARABLE OF THE WISE AND FOOLISH BUILDERS

Jesus told those who had gathered on the mountainside, "Everyone who hears these words of mine and puts them into practice is like a wise man who built his house on the rock. The rain came down, the streams rose, and the winds blew and beat against that house; yet it did not fall, because it had its foundation on the rock.

"But everyone who hears these words of mine and does not put them into practice is like a foolish man who built his house on sand. The rain came down, the streams rose, and the winds blew and beat against that house, and it fell with a great crash" (Matthew 7:24–27).

Jesus taught many truths using stories called **parables**. These parables are recorded in the New Testament books we call the Gospels—Matthew, Mark, Luke, and John. Jesus' parable of the wise and foolish builders shows us the importance of building our lives on God the Rock and His Word. God and His Word are like the rock under the wise builder's house. When we know and love and obey God's Word, our hearts and minds will be strong like a well-constructed home built on a strong foundation. You see, it's not enough to just *hear* God's words. Jesus says we also need to follow His Word and make it the building plan for our lives.

Why? Because life is not always easy. As the weather changes with the seasons, we enjoy winter wonderlands, followed by the freshness of spring, the warmth of the summer sun, and beautiful autumn colors.

Photo: www.flickr.com, lyng883

THE GREAT PYRAMID OF GIZA

Rising up on a plateau, ten miles west of present-day Cairo in Egypt, is one of the oldest structures in the world. The Great Pyramid of Giza, also known as the Pyramid of Khufu, was completed over a period of about twenty years. Built as a tomb for the Egyptian pharaoh Khufu, the Great Pyramid was constructed from more than two million blocks of limestone weighing over five thousand pounds each. Khufu's pyramid stood as the tallest manmade structure in the world for more than 3,000 years!

The ancient Greeks hailed this amazing feat of engineering as one of the Seven Wonders of the World. Of the seven man-made marvels on the list, five were damaged or destroyed by earthquakes many centuries ago. Another was plundered and burned to the ground. Only the Great Pyramid of Giza lives on today to the delight of millions of visitors every year.

How did the ancient Egyptians build something so huge and enduring in the harsh conditions of the desert? Although the Great Pyramid appears to be built on sand, it is not. The pyramid complex is built on a relatively level area of bedrock, which provides strength and stability.

Where will you build your life—on shifting sands or on the eternal Rock, who is the Lord our God?

But these same seasons sometimes bring with them crippling blizzards, violent thunderstorms, damaging droughts, and devastating hurricanes. Likewise, even the most devoted follower of God will experience the occasional storm in life—fear, temptation, disappointment, failure, and more. But if you have built your life on the Rock, if you have made it a habit to love God and to know and obey His Word, then when the storms of life do hit, you can stand strong.

MAKE A NOTE OF IT

Keep a notebook, or journal, in which you write about what you have learned. When you see the "Make a Note of It" box, you will be asked to record in your notebook your answers to important questions.

For your first entry, think about what sand feels like in your hands and beneath your feet. Write about the experience of walking on a beach or in a sandbox. Now answer these questions: Why wouldn't you want to build your house on top of sand? What kinds of "storms" might come into your life? What will happen if you do not build your life on the Rock of God and His Word?

WORDS YOU NEED TO KNOW

- » **Parable:** A short story that contains biblical truths for our lives
- » **Foundation:** The concrete or stone structure that supports a building from beneath
- » **The Rock of Truth:** God and His Word
- » **Wisdom:** Knowing, loving, and obeying God and applying that knowledge to make good decisions

HIDE IT IN YOUR HEART

"For who is God besides the LORD? And who is the Rock except our God?" (2 Samuel 22:32)

He is the Rock, his works are perfect, and all his ways are just. A faithful God who does no wrong, upright and just is he. (Deuteronomy 32:4)

SEVEN WAYS TO BUILD ON THE ROCK

Wisdom is knowing, loving, and obeying God and applying that knowledge to make good decisions. But what does it look like to know, love, and obey God? Here are seven things you can do to know God better, show your love for Him, and obey His Word.

STUDY AND LEARN THE BIBLE

You probably have several textbooks in your home. But they're not doing much to help you if they're just lying around gathering dust. You get the most good out of a history book by picking it up and studying it and learning the lessons it teaches from thousands of years of human experience. You get the most good out of a math book by studying it and putting its principles into practice. How much more then you should study the Bible, which is an instruction manual for life written by God Himself!

All Scripture is given by God and is useful for teaching and for showing people what is wrong in their lives. It is useful for correcting faults and teaching how to live right. Using the Scriptures, the person who serves God will be ready and will have everything he needs to do every good work. (2 Timothy 3:16–17, ICB)

Make time to read and think about the Word of God every day. When you open the Bible to read it, remember that you are stepping into the very presence of God and that He is now going to speak to you. Every hour you spend studying the Bible is an hour of walking and talking with God.

Commit yourself to memorizing God's Word. Store it away in your mind and heart, and His Word will keep you from sin (Psalm 119:11), protect you from false teaching (2 Timothy 3:13–15), fill your heart with joy (Jeremiah 15:16) and peace (Psalm 85:8), provide you power in prayer (John 15:7), and prepare you to do good (2 Timothy 3:16–17). Throughout this book you will find scripture memory verses in the portions titled "Hide It in Your Heart."

KNOW TRUTH, THINK TRUTH, AND FOLLOW TRUTH

If you spend much of your time listening to music, reading books, and watching movies or TV programs that tell you pretty lies, soon you're going to start believing those lies. And

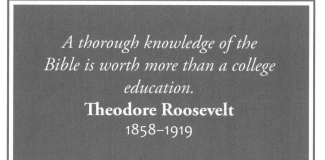

A thorough knowledge of the Bible is worth more than a college education.
Theodore Roosevelt
1858–1919

then you will begin behaving according to these false beliefs. The Bible warns us against such lies and tells us to instead focus on the truth as revealed in God's Word:

> *Don't copy the behavior and customs of this world, but let God transform you into a new person by changing the way you think. Then you will learn to know God's will for you, which is good and pleasing and perfect.* (Romans 12:2, NLT)

> *Be sure that no one leads you away with false ideas and words that mean nothing. Those ideas come from men. They are the worthless ideas of this world. They are not from Christ.* (Colossians 2:8, ICB)

CARE FOR YOUR BODY AND USE IT IN THE RIGHT WAY

The apostle Paul wrote, "Do not let any part of your body become an instrument of evil to serve sin. Instead, give yourselves completely to God . . . use your whole body as an instrument to do what is right for the glory of God" (Romans 6:13, NLT). You can glorify God by taking proper care of your body—eat healthy, exercise each day, drink plenty of water, wash thoroughly, and brush properly. Avoid putting anything in your body that can harm it, and never use your body for any purpose that will break either man's law or God's law.

WORSHIP GOD FAITHFULLY AND JOYFULLY

A popular song sung in many churches declares, "You and I were made to worship." The Bible commands us:

> *Worship the LORD with gladness; come before him with joyful songs.* (Psalm 100:2)

> *Sing psalms, hymns and spiritual songs with gratitude in your hearts to God.* (Colossians 3:16)

We will look more closely at what worship means later in the book, but you should know that you can worship God anywhere at any time. Whether you're at church, at home, or riding in a car, you can lift your voice and heart to worship Him.

PRAY TO GOD ALWAYS

The Bible tells us to "pray continually" (1 Thessalonians 5:17). Elsewhere it says, "Don't worry about anything; instead, pray about everything. Tell God what you need, and thank him for all he has done" (Philippians 4:6). So how do you pray all the time? Pray about everything!

Pray for your friends, pray for your family, pray about anything that might worry or concern you. Pray to thank God for who He is and all He has done for you. Thank Him for your food, your clothes, your home, your family, and your friends. Thank Him for the sunshine and for the rain. Thank Him for the things that bring you joy and for the things that bug you (which He can use to give you patience).

Remember, prayer is a two-way conversation between two people who love each other. James 4:8 says, "Come close to God, and God will come close to you" (NLT). Many people talk to God but fail to listen for Him to talk back. Yet if we are to pray continually, and prayer is a conversation, then God must be speaking to us all the time! That doesn't mean He will send you an angel with a grand announcement, as He did with Mary, or speak to you from a burning bush, as He did with Moses. The most common ways God speaks to us are through His Word, through the Holy Spirit, through other people, and through our circumstances. We will look at these more closely throughout the series, but for now just remember two things:

1. God will never contradict Himself. If you think something you saw on TV is God's way of trying to tell you something, compare it to what you find in the Bible. You can always trust what you read in God's Word.
2. God wants you to know Him. He is not hiding from you. Talk to Him, then keep your eyes and ears and heart open. If you seek Him, you *will* find Him.

STAND AGAINST SATAN AND RESIST HIM

Temptation of Christ by Gustave Dore

Satan, also called the devil, is God's sworn enemy. He was created as a magnificent angel, "the model of perfection, full of wisdom and perfect in beauty" (Ezekiel 28:12). But he loved his beauty and status and decided he wanted to sit on a throne above that of God (Isaiah 14:13-14). Wickedness—pride—was found in him, and Satan was cast out of heaven. He became the ruler of this world (John 12:31) and made it his mission to destroy God's children. He accuses us before God (Revelation 12:10), he tempts us to sin (1 Thessalonians 3:5), and he deceives us (2 Corinthians 4:4). Jesus said of the devil, "There is no truth in him. When he lies, he speaks his native language, for he is a liar and the father of lies" (John 8:44).

Even though he was expelled from heaven, he still seeks to elevate his throne above God's. Satan will do anything and everything in his power to oppose those who follow God, to keep them from doing good. The very name Satan means "adversary, or one who opposes." And yet, because you are a child of God, you can overcome Satan simply by giving yourself completely to God and standing firm against the plans of the devil: "So humble yourselves before God. Resist the devil, and he will flee from you" (James 4:7). When you find you are tempted to do wrong, first pray and ask God to help you. Determine in your mind and heart not to do what the devil wants. Then do as Jesus did and quote scripture to Satan. He will have no choice but to run away. After all, Satan has already been defeated, and his ultimate fate is sealed: He will spend eternity in the lake of fire (Revelation 20:10). Until that time, he is determined to take as many people with him as he can.

PUT GOD FIRST, NOT THINGS OR MONEY

A few years ago there was a man who went hunting in the wilderness. He soon found himself all alone in a quiet, secluded area grown lush with plants and trees and little animals. As he looked around at his pristine surroundings, he wondered if he might be the very first human who ever walked in this place. Then, to his surprise, he stumbled over what appeared to be the remains of a very old car that had been rusted over, sunk into the ground, and hidden by trees and bushes. A family of birds was nesting inside. The hunter realized he wasn't the first to step foot here. His "pristine" area had simply been reclaimed by nature.

Only God knows what this car was doing here. Perhaps it once belonged to a very rich man. This car may have been his pride and joy. However, such things do not last. Our possessions in this life are fleeting; they can be easily stolen or destroyed or ravaged by time and decay. You might think a rich man could simply go out and buy another car, but in this day and age, an entire fortune can be made and lost in a matter of minutes. The Bible warns very specifically against putting our trust in money or possessions. Jesus said:

> *"Do not store up for yourselves treasures on earth, where moth and rust destroy, and where thieves break in and steal. But store up for yourselves treasures in heaven, where moth and rust do not destroy, and where thieves do not break in and steal. For where your treasure is, there your heart will be also."* (Matthew 6:19–21)

This does not mean that there's something evil about owning things or earning money. What is important is where your heart is, what your priorities are. How do you spend your time? Where do you spend your money? Do you put your own desires and wants first, or do you put God first? Do you spend your time mastering a video game that will be obsolete in six months, or do you pursue the things of God by studying His Word and by serving others? Are you building your life on the shifting sands of possessions, money, and popularity, or are you building on the Rock?

MAKE A NOTE OF IT

Title this entry in your notebook "Six Ways to Build the Foundation of Your Life on Sand." The Old Testament tells us that God's people often got into trouble when they did what was right in their own eyes. Refusing to obey God and relying on our own understanding are sure ways to build our lives on sand. Here are six things you will want to avoid doing if you want to build on the Rock. Write these in your notebook, then write out each of the Bible verses that warn us against these activities.

1. Deny the Existence of God — Psalm 53:1
2. Refuse to Obey God — Matthew 7:26; John 14:15
3. Trust in Myself Instead of God — Proverbs 28:26
4. Follow False Ideas — Colossians 2:8
5. Refuse to Thank God and Glorify Him— Romans 1:21
6. Put Money and Things Before God — 1 Timothy 6:9

A PRAYER

Dear God, thank you for being the Rock on whom I can build my life. Help me to build my life according to your blueprints, and help me to ignore what the world says about how I should live. Help me to love your Word and to learn it well. Help me to know the truth and follow the truth. Help me to keep my body clean and pure. Help me to remember to pray about all things and to worship you daily. Help me to resist the devil. And help me to put you first at all times and not put my trust in money or things. I ask these things in Jesus' name. Amen.

LOOKING AT THE WORLD

People often don't see or understand things the same way others do. Even when two people are looking at exactly the same thing, each one may see it differently. For example, look at Picture 1. What is the *first* thing you see?

Picture 1

Did you see a young girl first? Or did you see an old lady first? Can you now see both? What had to happen before you could see both a young girl and an old lady?

Repeat this activity by looking at Picture 2:

Picture 2

Did you see a goblet first? Or did you see two faces? As you can see from this activity, our eyes often play tricks on us. Pictures like the ones above are called *optical illusions*. We can see them in more than one way, depending on how our eyes focus on the picture. In the case of optical illusions, the object one person sees is just as right as the object another person sees.

A WORLD OF A DIFFERENT COLOR

Optical illusions are fun to look at. Even though some see one thing and others see something else, everyone can agree to disagree since what each person sees is right. However, truth is not an optical illusion. Yet many people look at the world in many different ways, and in these cases, how a person sees and describes something may be right, or it may be completely wrong.

Imagine, for example, people who always wear only green, yellow, or pink sunglasses. Do they see the world the same way you see it? If not, how do they describe it? Now think about people who wear clear eyeglasses or who have perfect vision and don't wear glasses at all. Do they see the world the same way you see it? If not, how do they describe it? Whose description of the real world is correct—the people wearing colored glasses or the people wearing clear glasses or no glasses? Why?

Even though the people wearing colored glasses are looking at the same world as the people wearing clear glasses or no glasses, they don't see the world with all of its true colors. They see the world and everything in it as green, yellow, or pink. Not until they take off their colored glasses will they see the truth about the real world—the truth that the world is filled with many beautiful colors.

MAKING SENSE OF LIFE AND THE WORLD

Have you ever had an eye exam? Were you able to read all the letters on the eye chart, or were some blurry or out of focus? Did your eye exam reveal that you needed glasses? If so, do your glasses now bring everything you see into focus? Until people who need glasses wear them, they don't realize they're seeing the world out of focus. Then after they get their first pair, they are likely to exclaim, "Wow! I didn't know everything in the world was so sharp and clear." They're now seeing the beautiful world as God created it.

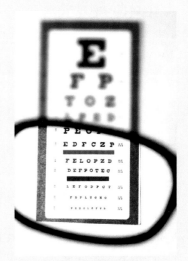

Most people see the physical world correctly. Without colored glasses and with good vision, they see and distinguish clearly between people and horses, mountains and prairies, trees and flowers, and rivers and lakes, and they can accurately describe the colors of a rainbow. However, making sense of life and the world we live in involves much more than being able to see and describe everything in the physical world correctly. Making sense of life and the world requires finding answers to questions much more difficult and important than "What color is a pine tree, and what does one look like?" To make sense of life and the world, people want and need to know answers to many questions like the ones below. As you read each question, think about what you believe is the true answer.

Questions About God
» Does God exist?
» If God exists, what is He like?
» Can I have a relationship with God?
» Do I have a responsibility to God?

Questions About the Universe
» Where did the universe come from?
» Has the universe always existed?
» Will the universe always exist?
» Where did our planet Earth come from?
» Why does the universe experience natural disasters?

Questions About People

» Where did we come from?
» Why are we here?
» Why do we have to die?
» What happens to us after we die?
» What is our responsibility and relationship to the earth?

Questions About Truth

» Is there such a thing as truth?
» How can I know if something is true or not?

Questions About Right and Wrong

» Are there such things as right and wrong?
» What is right? What is wrong?
» Why is there so much evil in the world?
» Are there solutions to all the problems in the world?

DIFFERENT WAYS OF VIEWING THE WORLD

Imagine that people's beliefs about the correct answers to questions about life and the world are like a pair of glasses. We could call these glasses "belief glasses." People look at their lives and the world through their belief glasses, trying to bring everything into focus to make sense of it. For example, suppose some people's belief glasses include the idea that God does not exist. How do you think they would answer the question *Where did the universe come from?* How might they answer the questions *Where did I come from?* and *Why am I here?* How would your answers to these questions differ from theirs?

All people wear a pair of "belief glasses" to help them make sense of their lives and the world. If their beliefs are true, then the glasses they wear are like clear ones that provide a focused or true view of life and the world. However, if their beliefs are not true, or only partly true, the glasses they wear are like colored or broken ones. Such belief glasses give a person a blurry or untrue view of life and the world.

What kind of belief glasses are you wearing? Are your lenses perfectly clear? Or are you wearing colored glasses or even broken ones? Are the beliefs you hold about life and the world true? Do you see the world in focus as it truly is?

EXPLORING THE WORLD OF BELIEFS

Throughout this book you will explore some of the beliefs that people hold about life and the world and particularly about God. You will study how people's beliefs and views differ. And you will find out why different beliefs lead people to behave and make choices about life in different ways. Most importantly, you will compare what people believe is true about life and the world with what God says is true. For it is God's truth as He reveals it to us in His Word, the Bible, that provides us with the perfect pair of belief glasses for rightly viewing, understanding, and living in the world.

HOW CAN I KNOW WHAT'S TRUE?

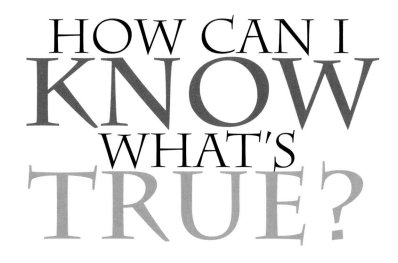

ISAIAH 45:19

THE BIG IDEA

When God created us, He gave us ways we can know if something is true or not. For example, if someone tells you that it's very cold outside, how would you know if that person were telling you the truth? You might look at a thermometer. Or to be absolutely certain, you might go outside. In just a few seconds you would know if what you had been told was true by the way the outside air feels. Using our senses—seeing, smelling, tasting, touching, and hearing—is one of the ways God created us to know if something is true. We can hear when the telephone is ringing. We can feel whether something is hot or cold, rough or smooth. And we can certainly smell when the baby needs changing! But we must be careful. Our senses may not always tell us the truth.

Another way we can know if something is true or not is by thinking or reasoning. If you're buying two pencils and the cashier tells you the total cost is $1.98, how can you know if he or she is telling you the truth? You would have to work a simple math problem to know if the cashier is asking for the correct amount. God gave us our minds, and we can reason with our minds to know what is true and what is false. But again, we must be careful. Reasoning and thinking do not always tell us the truth either.

Another way we can learn what is true is through reading and by listening to others who claim to know the truth. Parents, pastors, teachers, doctors, scientists, and others tell us things that are true. But again, we must be careful. Not everything we read or hear is true.

So is there any way that you can know if something is absolutely true? Is there anyone whose every word is true? Yes! God is our Rock, and everything He says is true:

All [His] words are true. (Psalm 119:160)

"He who is the Glory of Israel does not lie or change his mind; for he is not a man, that he should change his mind." (1 Samuel 15:29)

"Great and marvelous are your deeds, LORD God Almighty. Just and true are your ways, King of the ages." (Revelation 15:3)

When God says He created the heavens and earth, you can be certain it is true. In fact, the Bible tells us He speaks to us through His creation. He also speaks to us through the Bible and through His Son, Jesus. Unlike our senses, which can fool us, or even our best teachers, who can make mistakes, everything God tells us is the absolute truth. Therefore, what you feel, think, or learn from someone else must always be compared with what God says to us in the Bible.

WHAT YOU WILL DO

» You will define truth and identify four ways you can know what is true.
» You will explore three ways God speaks truth to you.
» You will lay the first stone of truth about God in your Foundation of Wisdom.
» You will examine the character trait of **obedience** and learn why it is an important response to the truth God speaks to you.

DARWIN'S TRAGIC LEGACY

Charles Darwin (1809–1882) was an English scientist who studied nature and believed that all species of life evolved over time from common ancestors through a process he called "natural selection." His five-year, around-the-world voyage on the HMS Beagle established him as an eminent naturalist, and publication of his journal of the voyage made him famous as an author. But it was his 1859 book *On the Origin of Species* that popularized his ideas concerning natural selection and gave rise to the controversial theory of evolution.

Sadly, 150 years later, modern evolutionary theory has become the basis for most biological studies and is taught as fact in our schools and universities, despite the truth that scientists are no closer to proving the theory after all this time. Meanwhile, the biblical account of God's creation of the universe is no longer taught in most schools due to legal challenges brought by those who do not believe in God or the authority of His Word.

In recognition of Darwin's work, upon his death he was honored with a state funeral and was buried in Westminster Abbey, close to Sir Isaac Newton.

HIKING UP BEAR CREEK TRAIL

"Now, remember, boys," Mr. Simmons said as Ben and Jeremy adjusted their backpacks, "always stay on the trail. And be sure you can see other adults at all times. Bear Creek Trail is very safe this time of year, with all the tourists and park rangers around. Don't go any farther than the one-mile marker by the waterfall. You can have your lunch there and then head back. It's ten o'clock now, so you should be back no later than two."

"Are there any bears on the trail?" Ben asked again for the fourth time.

"Probably not, especially this time of year with all the people around. Just stick with Jeremy. He knows the trail very well, and it's completely safe. Just enjoy God's beautiful creation," Mr. Simmons said with assurance.

"We'll ride our bikes to the trail head and lock them on the bike rack," said Jeremy. "Come on, Ben. I've got lots to show you."

In less than ten minutes, Ben and Jeremy had arrived at the trail and locked their bikes. The air was cool, but the sun warmed the hikers just enough to make it a perfect day for exploring Bear Creek Trail.

"Wow!" exclaimed Ben. "Look at all the wildflowers along the creek. And the fish in that pond. This is really cool. I bet you love living right here in the mountains, don't you?"

"I sure do," replied Jeremy. "But I miss all my friends back in Florida. And speaking of friends, how are Michael and Brent? Did you guys have a good year? What was your favorite subject?"

"Well, first, Michael and Brent are fine. They said to tell you 'hi.' As far as school goes, well, you know—school gets boring sometimes. But I did like my science class." Ben skipped a rock across the pond. "We learned really cool things about evolution and how the world really began—you know, not the way you hear about in Sunday school."

"So what did you learn about how the world began?" Jeremy asked as he drank from his water bottle.

"Well, everything began with like a big explosion. You know, it was really an accident. And then the Earth formed, then molecules started coming together on our planet in pools of water, and then little cells began, and then—"

"Wait a minute," interrupted Jeremy. "Don't you believe God created the world and everything in it?"

"Well, I'm not so sure," replied Ben. "God might have created it, but we can't really know for sure. And we can't really be sure He even exists. You can't see Him, and even if He does exist, He certainly doesn't talk to us. I guess if He did exist He would at least talk to us, wouldn't he?"

"But God does exist," said Jeremy as he climbed on a rock beside the trail to rest. "We know He exists because He *does* talk to us."

"I've never heard God talk," Ben said in challenge.

"Just look at everything around us—the trees, the flowers, the mountains, the trout, and . . . hey, look over there—three deer at the edge of the meadow. The Bible tells us that we can know God exists because His creation tells us so. Oh, I know flowers and stars don't speak with words. But just because they do exist tells us that someone created them. You know, something can't just make itself out of nothing."

"Well, I'm not so sure," said Ben. "My teacher said—"

"But God said that He *did* create everything. He not only speaks to us through what He made; He also told us in writing that He is the Creator. He actually speaks to us about creation through the Bible."

"Yeah, but just because something is in writing doesn't mean it's true."

"That's right," Jeremy said. "But everything God said about Himself and the creation, He actually showed us in person. That's why Jesus came to earth. Jesus is God's Son, and everything God said about Himself and creation, Jesus showed that it was true when He lived here. People actually saw Jesus. They saw His power and His love. And when He came back to life after dying on the cross, He proved that God is the Creator of all life."

"Well," said Ben after the boys had hiked farther up the trail, "I never thought about God speaking to us in so many ways. But I'm still not sure that God created everything."

Just as the boys turned a sharp curve in the trail, they saw a group of hikers and the forest ranger looking toward a stand of trees.

"Everyone stay calm," the ranger cautioned. "Look over at the grove of aspen trees straight ahead, and you'll see a small black bear climbing one of the trees. It's probably more afraid of us than we are of it, so don't be alarmed. Just stay on the trail and you'll be fine."

"I see it," whispered Ben as he stood behind Jeremy. "It's beautiful—and a little scary, too. I thought you said there weren't any bears up here."

"It's the first one I've ever seen," Jeremy said, squinting to see the bear as it disappeared up the tree. "Wait till I tell my folks! Come on. It's time to head back to the house. Will they ever be surprised!"

As the boys rushed into the kitchen, Ben exclaimed, "Wow! Look at that plate of brownies on the table. Did your mom make them?"

"My mom?" asked Jeremy. "Oh, I don't think so. I think they just baked themselves, came out of the oven, cut themselves into little squares, and hopped up on the plate, waiting for us to eat them."

"Yeah, right," laughed Ben. "You know brownies can't make themselves any more than . . ."

"Any more than the earth can make itself?" asked Jeremy with a smile.

"But who made them?" asked Ben again, as he reached for the biggest one on the plate.

"Hey, look. Here's a note. It's from my mom. It says, *Dad's in his office, and I'm at the store. I'll be back around 2:00. Help yourselves to the brownies. I took them out of the oven right before I left. Hope you like them. Love, Mom.*"

"You've got a great mom."

"But how can I be sure she's the one who made them?" said Jeremy. "And how do I know if she really loves me or not? Just because she said so in a note?"

"Jeremy," said Ben, a bit flustered, "you're strange. Here sits a plate of brownies that can't make themselves, and here is a note signed 'Love' from your mom who says she made them, and you're still not sure where they came from? Or if she loves you? I think you're stranger than strange!"

Just then Mrs. Simmons walked in, gave both boys a hug, and asked, "How was your hike? Did you see anything interesting on the trail? Oh, and by the way, did you find the brownies I left for you on the table?"

"See!" said Ben. "I told you she made the brownies, just like the note said. And now you know she did because she told you in person. And besides that, she gave us both a hug!"

"I know," laughed Jeremy, as Mrs. Simmons listened to the strange conversation without knowing what was going on. "Those brownies didn't make themselves any more than the earth made itself. And just like my mom wrote us a note telling us she made them for us, God wrote the Bible telling us for sure that He made the earth."

"Oh, I see," said Ben. "And just like your mom told us in person she made the brownies and loves us, God told us in person He made the earth and loves us when Jesus came to the earth."

"Ben, I think you've got it," Jeremy said. "God is always speaking to us and telling us how much He loves us. He speaks through silent words in His creation. We saw that He is the Creator on the trail today, especially when we got to see that amazing black bear. Then He gives us His written words in the Bible. But just in case anyone doubts whether God exists or speaks, He actually came to earth and spoke to us in person through Jesus."

"Did you say you saw a bear?" asked Mrs. Simmons apprehensively. "How close to the trail was it?"

"We did," said Ben excitedly. "And it was huge. I've never seen a real live bear except in the zoo. It was really cool!"

"Well, I'm glad God allowed you two to see a special part of His creation today. Not everyone gets to see a bear in the wild. Now, have another brownie. But only one more. I don't want you boys to spoil your supper."

"What are you making for supper, Mom?"

"Oh, I don't plan and cook the meals around here, you know," replied Mrs. Simmons with a teasing laugh. "They just cook themselves from nothing, and then we all sit down and eat whatever accidentally appears on the table."

Ben looked at Jeremy and then Mrs. Simmons. "Wow!" he said with a laugh. "I've gotta watch that. That's something I won't believe unless I see it happen."

"You'll be watching a long time," joked Mrs. Simmons. "In the meantime, I think I'd better start cooking supper. The last time I checked, tomato sauce, onions, meat, spices, and pasta still hadn't figured out how to get together and create a pot of spaghetti and meatballs by themselves!"

Photo: USFWS

THINK ABOUT IT

» What did Ben learn about creation in his science class?
» Why was Ben beginning to doubt whether God exists?
» Name three ways God speaks to us.

GOD ALWAYS TELLS US WHAT IS RIGHT AND TRUE

In "Hiking Up Bear Creek Trail," Ben told Jeremy that he believed his teacher was telling the truth when she explained how the earth began. But Jeremy did not think it was true. He believed that God was telling the truth when He explained how the earth began. So which boy was right? How do people know what is true and what is false?

As Jeremy explained to Ben on their hike up Bear Creek Trail, we can always trust what God says. When God says He created the heavens and earth, you can be certain it is true. In fact, everything God says is true, and He is always speaking His truth to us. He speaks to us through His creation, through the Bible, and through Jesus. What you feel, think, or learn from someone else must always be compared with what God says to us in the Bible.

WORDS YOU NEED TO KNOW

» **Truth:** Things, events, and facts that are real
» **Scripture:** The Bible, God's written truth
» **Obedience:** The act of doing what I am told with a willing and loving heart

HIDE IT IN YOUR HEART

"I, the LORD, speak the truth; I declare what is right." (Isaiah 45:19)

The law of the LORD is perfect, reviving the soul. The statutes of the LORD are trustworthy, making wise the simple. (Psalm 19:7)

PHENOMENAL BROWNIES

You could gather the following list of ingredients on your kitchen counter, then watch and wait for them to bake themselves into the world's greatest brownies. Or you could enlist a parent to help you follow this simple recipe:

» 8 1-ounce squares of unsweetened chocolate
» 1 cup butter
» 5 eggs
» 3 cups sugar
» 1 tablespoon vanilla
» 1½ cups flour
» 1 teaspoon salt
» 2½ cups chopped pecans or walnuts, toasted

Preparation:
Preheat your oven to 375 degrees F. Spray a 9x13 pan with pan spray. Melt the chocolate and butter in a saucepan over low heat, then set aside. With a mixer, beat eggs, sugar, and vanilla at high speed for 10 minutes, or beat for 20 minutes with a spoon. Blend in chocolate mixture, flour, and salt until just mixed. Stir in the nuts. Pour your mixture into the prepared pan. Bake for 35–40 minutes.

THREE WAYS TO KNOW SOME OF WHAT IS TRUE

Pontius Pilate famously asked, "What is truth?" Truth is defined as things, events, and facts that are real. Yet philosophers have been arguing for three thousand years over what is real. So how can we know what is real and what isn't? Let's look at three common ways we all go about finding the truth.

I CAN KNOW WHAT IS TRUE THROUGH MY SENSES

Your five senses—sight, hearing, touch, taste, and smell—can tell you something about what is real. Right now, as you're reading this, you're probably sitting on a piece of furniture, likely some sort of chair. Look at it. Feel it. Is it hard or soft? Large or small? What color is it? Try smelling it. Does it have a unique scent? By now, through observation, you've probably determined that this piece of furniture is "real."

By simply looking around you, you can know certain things. For example, is there a skunk in the room with you? Is there an American flag on the wall? How many people are currently in the room? (Don't forget to count yourself!) On the other hand, there are some things you may not know for certain. If your room had no windows or clock, and you had been asleep awhile, could you truly know whether it was day or night when you first awoke?

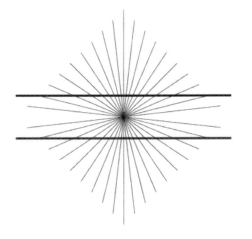

Now examine this pair of thick black lines: Do the two lines appear to be bent, or curved? Use a ruler to examine the lines more closely, and you will see that in fact the two black lines are straight and parallel to one another.

Which of the three lines in the figure to the right is the longest? Now use your ruler to measure each of the lines. Now you know that all three lines are the same length.

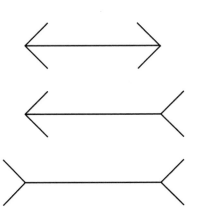

Get a tall clear glass and fill it with water. Now insert a pencil into the water and observe the pencil from the side. The pencil appears to be bent. But you know for a fact that the pencil was straight when you put it in the glass. And when you remove it from the glass, you can confirm that it is still straight.

You see, while your senses are a means of knowing truth, they do not always "tell" you the truth. Your senses can be fooled, sometimes deliberately. For example, rides called motion simulators have thrilled audiences all over the world, using a combination of video and hydraulic technology to create the sensation of riding a rollercoaster, hang-gliding over Yosemite, or even rocketing through outer space. Disney's long-running theme park attraction Star Tours makes use of modified flight simulators, which are more commonly employed by the military to train fighter pilots.

I CAN KNOW WHAT IS TRUE BY THINKING AND REASONING

Sherlock Holmes is a fictional character, the creation of Scottish-born author and physician Sir Arthur Conan Doyle. A brilliant, London-based "consulting detective," Holmes is famous for his intellectual prowess and is known for his skillful use of "deductive reasoning" to arrive at the truth and solve difficult cases. In the story "The Sign of the Four," he said to his close friend Dr. Watson, "How often have I said to you that when you have eliminated the impossible, whatever remains, however improbable, must be the truth?"

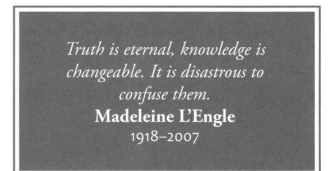

Truth is eternal, knowledge is changeable. It is disastrous to confuse them.
Madeleine L'Engle
1918–2007

One of the ways we can know what is true is by thinking through the evidence we've collected and using reason to arrive at the truth. If you look out the window tomorrow morning and see new snow blanketing the ground, you can reasonably deduce that the temperature outside is going to be what most people consider "cold." However, if you look outside and see the sun shining, can you assume that the temperature outside is "warm"? If you live in Minnesota, you've probably experienced many bright, sunny days when the mercury in the thermometer never reached ten degrees.

Read each of the following statements and determine whether each is true or false:

1. If my mom takes twenty coins out of a brown paper bag, and every one of the coins is a penny, the next coin she removes will definitely be a penny.

THE WORLD'S GREATEST LIBRARY

The Library of Alexandria in ancient Egypt was the largest and most renowned library in the ancient world. The library included colonnades for walking, gardens, a dining room, a reading room, lecture halls, and meeting rooms. Its exact layout is not known, but the design's influence may still be seen today in the layout of university campuses. The Library of Alexandria was considered the repository of all human knowledge collected to that time. Then in 48 B.C., Julius Caesar accidentally burned down the library during a visit to Alexandria, destroying many of its holdings.

Library of Alexandria by von Corbin

Carved into a wall of the library, above the shelves holding thousands of papyrus scrolls, was an inscription that read: *The place of the cure of the soul.* Indeed, reading is a peaceful, restful activity that strengthens the mind as exercise strengthens the body. Yet even the Ancient Greeks understood that knowledge is not sufficient to build a life on. The philosopher Heraclitus (540–480 BC) wrote, "Abundance of knowledge does not teach men to be wise."

The Bible tells us, "For the LORD gives wisdom, and from his mouth come knowledge and understanding" (Proverbs 2:6). God is the source of all wisdom, and a wise man builds his life on the Rock. Proverbs 9:10 says, "The fear of the LORD is the beginning of wisdom, and knowledge of the Holy One is understanding."

As for a cure for what ails the soul? As we will see, sin is the disease and Jesus Christ is the one and only cure.

2. If today is a warm and sunny day, tomorrow will certainly be warm and sunny.
3. If three books weigh three pounds, then four books will always weigh four pounds.
4. All my friends say that having the newest video game makes them very happy. Therefore, if I buy one, I know it will make me happy.
5. If someone does something kind for you, you can know for sure that person likes you.

If you answered "false" to each of these statements, congratulations! The next coin may in fact be a penny, or it may be a nickel. Tomorrow may be sunny, or it may rain cats and dogs. You simply cannot know based on the information you've been given. And, as we've already seen, sometimes our senses can provide us with information that is untrue. The fact is that thinking and reasoning may or may not lead you to the whole truth.

MAKE A NOTE OF IT

Write in your notebook about something that was presented to you as truth at one time in your life that you later discovered was not true. How did you feel when you learned the truth? Why do you suppose this person told you something that wasn't true?

I Can Know What Is True by Reading and Listening to What Others Tell Me

The New York Public Library at the corner of Fifth Avenue and 42nd Street in Manhattan—it's the building with the lion statues out front—is a wondrous place filled with more than 44 million catalogued books, magazines, maps, videos, and historical documents. The knowledge collected there is staggering to consider, but it's perhaps more important to know that not everything you see or read there is necessarily true.

Truth can be shared with you by those who know truth, such as your parents, teachers, pastors, and experts in various fields. And you should listen to what these people have to tell you. However, these people are human beings, and humans make mistakes. Also, many "experts" approach their field of study with a flawed worldview—one that ignores or even contradicts the wisdom of God. Then there are the many advertisements coming at us every day from television, radio, the Internet, and other media. Ads are not designed to disseminate information but, rather, to motivate us to buy something. Too often, what they're selling is a fantasy, not truth.

Make a Note of It

Read each of the following scenarios. Decipher the messages being communicated and determine whether they are true, partially true, or simply untrue (as in much advertising). Some scenarios may have elements of truth and untruth. Record your findings in your notebook.

1. A science program on TV tells you that human beings are only very intelligent animals who have evolved over millions of years from chemicals that came together in pools of water.

2. You read these words on a box of Tiger Wheat cereal: *Do you want to be as strong as a tiger? Eat Tiger Wheat every morning for a healthy breakfast. You'll become so strong that all your friends will want to eat Tiger Wheat too.*

3. Your pastor tells you that all people have a sinful heart and are separated from God because of sin. He tells you that the way back to fellowship with God is through repentance and faith in Jesus Christ, God's Son, who died on the cross for your sins.

4. The first scene of a television commercial shows an unhappy person driving an old brown car. The second scene shows the same person smiling while sitting in his brand-new red sports car. Many people are gathered around him, admiring the car and asking to go for a ride. The commercial ends with this slogan: "Bored with the plain life? Get a real life! Buy a new Sportaratti and start living today!"

5. A newspaper reporter asks 100 people in your town if they think the president of your country is doing a good job. Seventy people say no, and thirty people say

yes. The reporter then writes a news story based on his interviews. The headline reads: "President Not Doing a Good Job." The article says, "A survey of residents in Centerville reveals that the president is doing a poor job. It is time for us to elect a president whom the majority of people will like."

6. A friend tells you that Jesus died on the cross for your sins. He says that in order to have fellowship with God, you must not only repent of your sins and have faith in Jesus, you must also do good works every day in order to earn your way into heaven.

7. Your parents tell you that you should eat healthy foods, including fruits and vegetables, and avoid eating too much junk food. They also tell you that you should get plenty of exercise and sleep.

8. You read in a health book that it is important to develop a healthy mind and self-image. To do this, you must decide what you want to do and become, then put your mind to it and think positively. You have the strength within yourself to do and become anything you wish. Most importantly, you must never let other people tell you what is best for you.

GOD TELLS US THE WHOLE TRUTH AND NOTHING BUT THE TRUTH

While we can learn truth through our senses, by reasoning, and by listening to others, some truth can only be known by hearing what God says. We can always believe what God says, because He always tells us the truth:

> *"He who is the Glory of Israel does not lie."* (1 Samuel 15:29)

> *"I, the LORD, speak the truth; I declare what is right."* (Isaiah 45:19)

What's that you say? God hasn't spoken to you today? Listen closely.

GOD SPEAKS TRUTH TO ME THROUGH HIS CREATION

From the awesome power of distant stars to the cry of a newborn baby, from the magnificence of the Grand Canyon to the tiny seed that will grow into a mighty oak, God designed creation as a clear voice proclaiming His glory. Therefore, the Bible tells us, those who reject God's existence are without excuse for doing so:

> *They know the truth about God because he has made it obvious to them. For ever since the world was created, people have seen the earth and sky. Through everything God made, they can clearly see his invisible qualities—his eternal power and divine nature. So they have no excuse for not knowing God.* (Romans 1:19–20, NLT)

In the story "Hiking Up Bear Creek Trail," the brownies on the plate "spoke" to Ben and Jeremy, telling them that someone baked the brownies and that someone cared enough about the boys to leave them a tasty snack. In the same way, the sun, the moon, and the stars "speak" messages of truth to us:

The heavens declare the glory of God;
the skies proclaim the work of his hands.
Day after day they pour forth speech;
night after night they display knowledge.
There is no speech or language
where their voice is not heard.
Their voice goes out into all the earth,
their words to the ends of the world.
(Psalm 19:1–4)

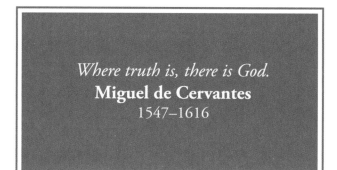

Where truth is, there is God.
Miguel de Cervantes
1547–1616

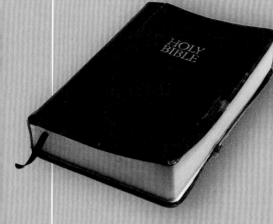

WHICH BIBLE TRANSLATION IS THE RIGHT ONE?

The Bible was originally written in three different languages—Hebrew, Greek, and Aramaic. For more than a thousand years, the only available Bible was written in Latin and could be read only by the Catholic clergy. Then in 1522, Martin Luther published a popular edition of the New Testament in the common German language. Three years later, William Tyndale translated the original text into English and began distributing copies.

In 1604, King James I of England authorized a new English translation, which was translated from the original manuscripts but was heavily influenced by the Luther and Tyndale translations. The 1611 translation, known as the *Authorized Version* or *King James Version*, was the standard English Bible for nearly four centuries.

Today, there are many fine translations available in modern English, including the New International Version (NIV), the New American Standard Bible (NASB), the English Standard Version (ESV), and the New Living Translation (NLT). Each of these was compiled by a team of Bible scholars and linguists trying to faithfully communicate Scripture in words and phrases that we use today, and each of these efforts has been subject to both praise and criticism. Some, like the NASB and the ESV, are considered literal word-for-word translations; others, like the NLT, are considered to be less formal, thought-for-thought versions that emphasize readability over accuracy. Others, like the NIV, try to balance these two approaches.

When it comes to reading and memorizing God's Word, your family may have a preferred translation. For study purposes, many Christian homes keep copies of multiple translations. A recent survey revealed that the average Christian home in America has nine copies of the Bible! It is important that you get yourself a good study Bible, with in-depth study helps, and read it daily.

As someone once observed, the universe is big. Really big. You just wouldn't believe how mind-bogglingly *huge* the universe is. You think it's a long drive to your grandma's, but compared to the universe, that's peanuts! Now imagine what the God who *created* the universe must be like. All of creation tells of God's goodness and His eternal power:

The heavens proclaim his righteousness; every nation sees his glory. (Psalm 97:6, NLT)

MAKE A NOTE OF IT

Have you ever lain on the ground on a summer night and looked at the stars? How did you feel? What did you think about? Write about the experience in your notebook. Or take a short nature walk and observe the birds or the plant life or the insects—something you particularly enjoy. Write about what this aspect of nature tells you about God. Now write your response to the following question: How does the whole of creation show us that God is good?

GOD SPEAKS TRUTH TO ME THROUGH THE BIBLE

In the story "Hiking Up Bear Creek Trail," the brownies the boys found on the table suggested to them the actions of a creator, as well as something of the intent of the person who baked them. Then they found a note left by Jeremy's mom that cleared up some of the mystery about where the brownies came from and why they were made. Likewise, God left us a "note" that reveals to us more truth than His creation alone can tell us.

Much of the New Testament was written in the Greek language. The first letter of the Greek alphabet is *alpha*. The second letter is *beta*. Put them together and you get the English word *alphabet*.

God's note to mankind is the Bible. In His Word, God tells us about Himself, His plan for creation, and the way we are to live in relationship with Him, with ourselves, with others, and with the earth. God's note is actually one big book made up of sixty-six smaller books. Each of these books has its own name, but each is still part of the one big book, the Bible.

How did God "write" His note? He used men of faith and guided them through the Holy Spirit. These men included Moses, Solomon, Jeremiah, and the apostles John and Paul. Over a period of 1500 years, God inspired forty different writers to record the essential truths about Himself and His plan for creation. The inspiration of the Holy Spirit ensured that what these men wrote down is without error and that it accurately tells us truths God wants us to know.

Paul's second letter to Timothy tells us that all Scripture is "God-breathed" and is useful for showing us what is wrong in our lives and teaching us how to live right (2 Timothy 3:16). Paul goes on to say that by reading and obeying what God tells us in the Bible, we will have everything we need to do good. In addition, if we will follow its teachings, the Bible will comfort us (2 Corinthians 1:3–4), guide us (John 16:12), encourage us (Joshua 1:1–9), and strengthen us (1 Corinthians 10:13).

GOD SPEAKS TRUTH TO ME THROUGH JESUS

You may have read many articles and stories about the current President of the United States. You may have seen or heard the president give a speech or answer questions from the media. And you've probably seen many photographs of the president participating in a variety of activities. But do you really *know* the president? Until you meet the president face to face and spend time with him (or her), you cannot truly know what the president is like as a person.

Supper at Emmaus by Caravaggio

Spending time with a person usually gives us a deeper understanding into that person's heart and personality than does written communication. Our time together with that person will tend to confirm or negate what we have heard or read about him or her.

The truth that God reveals to us through creation and through His Word was lived out fully and demonstrated for us in the earthly life of His Son, Jesus. In a prayer, Jesus said that an important part of why He came to live among us was to show us God the Father:

> *"Father, you are the One who is good. The world does not know you, but I know you. And these people know that you sent me. I showed them what you are like. And again I will show them what you are like. Then they will have the same love that you have for me."* (John 17:25–26, ICB)

God tells us many truths about Himself in the Bible, and He sent His Son to show us that everything He said about Himself is true:

> *In the past God spoke to our forefathers through the prophets at many times and in various ways, but in these last days he has spoken to us by his Son.* (Hebrews 1:1–2)

Here are just a few of the things Jesus did during His time on this earth:

Jesus went throughout Galilee, teaching in their synagogues, preaching the good news of the kingdom, and healing every disease and sickness among the people . . . and people brought to him all who were ill with various diseases, those suffering severe pain, the demon-possessed, those having seizures, and the paralyzed, and he healed them. (Matthew 4:23–24)

Because Jesus came to show us what God is like, through this passage we learn that God instructs us, that He wants us to know Him and to live in His kingdom, and that He heals all kinds of illnesses. Most importantly He shows that God loves us and cares for us.

The most wonderful way God spoke the truth of His love for us was by sacrificing Jesus' life to pay the penalty for our sins:

He was pierced for our transgressions, he was crushed for our iniquities; the punishment that brought us peace was upon him, and by his wounds we are healed. (Isaiah 53:5)

This is how we know what love is: Jesus Christ laid down his life for us. (1 John 3:16)

"For God so loved the world that he gave his one and only Son, that whoever believes in him shall not perish but have eternal life." (John 3:16)

MAKE A NOTE OF IT

Read a story from the Gospel of John that illustrates how Jesus revealed God's truth to us through His ministry and His response to people's needs (sickness, poverty, injustice, fears, doubts, etc.). Write in your notebook what this story tells you about who God is.

WHAT SHOULD I DO

We have learned so far that God is truth and that He reveals truth to us through His creation, through His Word, and through His Son. Now you have a choice. How will you respond to the truth that God shows you? Will you choose to build your life on the Rock and follow Him? Or will you choose to turn away from Him and disobey?

Think about what it means to obey your parents. Your mother and father have set certain rules for your home which you must then choose to obey or disobey. If you choose not to obey these rules, you know that there will be consequences—some form of discipline or loss of certain privileges. In much the same way, the Bible tells us that God "disciplines those he loves" (Hebrews 12:6) and that He "disciplines us for our good, that we may share in his holiness" (v. 10).

On the other hand, when you make a habit of cheerfully and willingly obeying the rules set down by your parents, there is peace in your home and you will enjoy the trust and blessings of your mother and father. Likewise, obedience to God and His Word is an important element of God's plan for your life and His design for creation. It is through your obedience to Him that He releases His blessings and fulfills His promises in your life. Jesus said:

> *"If you hold to my teaching, you are really my disciples. Then you will know the truth, and the truth will set you free."* (John 8:31–32)

What exactly does obedience look like? Here is a definition for you to remember:

> ### Obedience:
> The act of doing what I am told with a willing and loving heart.

Obedience is a choice. God has given you the ability to choose to obey or disobey. But it's not enough to just do what you're told. If you mumble and grumble all the while, then in your heart you are still arguing with God. You must obey with a willing and cheerful heart for your actions to be acceptable to Him. Likewise, He expects you to obey with a willing and cheerful heart those whom He has placed in authority over you. This is commonly called "having a good attitude."

Because we know that God is just and loving and that His commands are for our good, we should always be ready and willing to obey Him. In fact, obedience is a true test of our love for God and His truth. Jesus said, "If anyone loves me, he will obey my teaching" (John 14:23).

A PRAYER

Dear God, thank you for always telling me the truth. Whenever I'm feeling confused or hurt, I can trust you to tell me what is true. Thank you that you speak to me through your amazing, wonderful Creation. Thank you that you speak to me through your Word, the Bible. And thank you that you speak to me through your Son, Jesus, who lived and died and lives again for me. In His name I pray. Amen.

WHAT IN THE WORLD IS A WORLDVIEW?

As you learned in the previous lesson, all people have beliefs about God, the universe, people, truth, and right and wrong. Our beliefs are important because they guide us in doing two things.

First, our beliefs help us to interpret, explain, and define life and the world. In other words, we try to make sense of the world around us through what we believe about God, the universe, people, truth, and right and wrong.

Second, what we believe about life and the world influences our actions or behavior. We make choices and behave in certain ways because of what we believe. For example, suppose someone believes that all people are not created in God's image and do not have equal value or worth. He or she believes that some races or nationalities of people are better than others. How might that person choose to behave toward someone of another race or from another country? Now suppose someone else believes that all people are created having equal value or worth. How might that person choose to behave toward someone of another race or from another country?

Look at the picture on the left. What is happening? What beliefs about life and the world do you think the person pouring the water might have? Why might this person be pouring water into someone else's hands?

Now look at the picture on the right. What is happening? What beliefs about life and the world do you think the four children huddled in the group might have? Why might the group be rejecting the boy on the left?

As you can you see from these two examples, people's beliefs influence how they see the world and live their lives. Their beliefs will influence them to do good or to do wrong.

The set of beliefs through which you view and interpret life and the world and that guides your choices and behaviors is called a **worldview**. You will explore more fully the definition, characteristics, and main functions of a worldview at the end of each lesson in this book.

WHAT KINDS OF BELIEFS ARE INCLUDED IN A WORLDVIEW?

You know what it means to include or exclude someone from a group. If your group of friends is exclusive, that means it rejects or excludes certain people from being a part of it. However, if your group is *inclusive*, that means it *includes* everyone who would like to be a part of it. When we say that worldviews are inclusive, we mean that all worldviews include certain categories or types of beliefs. Whether people are Christians, atheists, Muslims, or Hindus, each of their worldviews includes five categories of beliefs about the world that affect their behaviors.

GOD

All people have beliefs about God. They may believe that there is only one true God or that there are many gods. Or they may not believe that God or any gods exist at all. If they believe that God or gods do exist, then they also have specific beliefs about what God or the gods are like. And if they believe in God or many gods, then they have beliefs about what kind of relationship they may or may not have with them.

PEOPLE

All people have beliefs about human beings. They have beliefs about where people come from and why they even exist at all. They have beliefs about how people should live their lives and whether all people are equal as individuals. And perhaps most importantly, people have beliefs about what happens to them after they die. If they believe in heaven or hell, their worldviews likely include beliefs about how to be saved.

THE UNIVERSE

All people have beliefs about the universe. They have beliefs about where the universe came from, how old it is, and how long it will exist. They have beliefs about why the earth often experiences natural disasters. And they have beliefs about their relationship with and responsibility to the earth.

TRUTH

All people have beliefs about truth. They have beliefs about what is true and what is not. They have beliefs about where truth can be found and how or if they can even know truth at all. Some people believe that what is true for one person may not be true for another and that people can create their own truth.

RIGHT AND WRONG

All people have beliefs about what is right and what is wrong. They have beliefs about what is good and what is evil. They hold beliefs about why evil exists in the world and what can be done to solve the problem of evil.

As you already know, all people do not have the same beliefs about God, the universe, people, truth, and right and wrong. For this reason, people do not behave or act in the same way.

THE HOUSE OF TRUTH: THE FIRST STONE

Throughout the four books that make up the What We Believe series, we will be building a House of Truth to help you remember what God says in the Bible about Himself, who you are, and how God expects you to live. When we are nearly finished, it will look something like this:

This is a special house, not one built from an architect's plans or with lumber, bricks, and other ordinary building materials. The plan for building our House of Truth is the Bible. Each part of this worldview model represents an essential truth from God's Word. Just as we build strong houses with good materials on strong foundations, so we must build our lives with the truths God gives us in the Bible. These truths will be displayed on the rock and in the foundation, walls, and roof of the House of Truth.

You know already that if you are wise, you will build your life on the Rock who is God. And we have learned that we must lay a foundation for life by pursuing wisdom, and wisdom is defined as "knowing, loving, and obeying God my Rock."

Wise people build a foundation of wisdom by first knowing and loving God and obeying all the truth He speaks to them. And in this lesson we laid the first stone of truth on the foundation of our House of Truth:

BIBLICAL TRUTH 1

God always tells me what is right and true.

Do you understand why this truth must be the very first stone in your foundation?

Biblical Truth 1
God always tells me what is right and true

FOUNDATION OF WISDOM
Knowing, loving, and obeying God my Rock

THE ROCK
God and His Word

WHAT IS GOD LIKE?
PART 1

1 TIMOTHY 1:17

THE BIG IDEA

Life is a classroom. From the moment you entered it at birth, you embarked on what Winnie-the-Pooh called an "expotition"—a journey to explore, discover, and understand the world around you. As an infant your first investigations were simple—touching, feeling, tasting, smelling, and listening to everything around you. When you were older you were able to understand more of the world by observing, thinking, and reasoning, and you grew in wisdom and knowledge.

Wisdom, however, is more than an accumulation of knowledge. A person can win a million dollars on a TV quiz show and yet be unwise in how he spends the money. The source of *true* wisdom is the One who *is* Truth, God the Creator. Only when we seek to know the Father and have a relationship with Him through His Son, Jesus, can we hope to find true wisdom and understanding:

The fear of the LORD is the beginning of wisdom, and knowledge of the Holy One is understanding. (Proverbs 9:10)

"Let him who boasts boast about this: that he understands and knows me, that I am the LORD, who exercises kindness, justice and righteousness on earth, for in these I delight." (Jeremiah 9:24)

According to these and many other Bible passages, God *wants* us to know Him. But how *can* we know God? And how can we describe God to someone who doesn't know Him?

We start by learning the **attributes** of our Creator—the unique characteristics and qualities that make Him God. Just as you know what your best friend is like—what he or she likes and doesn't like, what he or she looks like, and what it is about this person that makes you trust and like them—we must know and understand God's attributes if we are to have a close personal relationship with Him.

In the next two chapters, we will look at the essential attributes of God by looking at how the Bible answers some of the important questions people ask about Him.

WHAT YOU WILL DO

» You will explore the biblical answers to four basic questions about God: Does God exist? Is there more than one true God? What does God look like? Is God a person?

Photo: Éclusette

THE WHITE STONE

Dancing torch flames lit the ceiling of the blackened cave. Seated on his golden throne, King Rancor's evil eyes stared at his chained captives.

"At last, you wretched enemy," he said, "your death is sure. Now my kingdom will rule the universe forever."

Snarling cheers of victory filled the hall as King Rancor's evil ghouls danced in the firelight. "Death to King Veritas and his army!" they chanted. "Death to King Veritas! Long live King Rancor!"

The two captives sat bound in chains on the cold floor. "Father," whispered Prince Pax, "how could this have happened? Where is the white stone? It is our only hope."

"Peace, my son," said King Veritas softly. "There is a time for everything. Be patient. Soon King Rancor's kingdom will fall and all of his evil army with him."

"Have you anything to say, you filthy dog?" growled King Rancor as he rose from his throne and approached his prized victims.

"Only that I have a gift for you," replied King Veritas. "Free my hands that I might give it to you."

"A gift, you say," snarled King Rancor. "Loose his chains, but guard him carefully. He's no fool, you know."

"Father, what are you saying?" asked Prince Pax softly.

"Quiet, my son. Today will see the end of Rancor's kingdom. Trust me."

As the guards unlocked the chains, King Veritas rose to his feet. Slowly he reached his hand into his cloak and removed a small velvet bag tied with a silver cord.

"For you, King Rancor," said Veritas solemnly.

"A gift for your enemy? Why would *you* give *me* a gift?"

King Veritas did not reply as he placed the small sack in Rancor's hands.

With great anticipation, the evil king untied the silver cord and let it fall to the ground. Then he slipped his hand into the sack to retrieve its mysterious contents.

"Argggggghhhh!" screamed the king. "The white stone. No! No! Not the white stone! You have tricked me, Veritas, my old enemy!"

Suddenly, thousands of lightning bolts flashed from the stone as King Rancor threw it to the floor. Howls and screams from his army of ghouls pierced the smoking cave as the king and his army tried blindly to reach the entrance. But it was no use. One by one they fell until at last neither king nor ghoul could be heard.

King Veritas and Prince Pax stood silently.

"Pick up the stone, my son," commanded Veritas. "Today you have seen the power of truth defeat the forces of evil. Keep the stone with you, my son, for one day another evil king will arise when you are king. Always remember that with the white stone in your possession you will be victorious."

"Wow," exclaimed Ben as he and Jeremy left the movie theater. "That's the coolest movie I've ever seen. King Veritas was great. He knew just when to use his most powerful weapon to defeat Rancor."

"Yeah, it really was a neat movie," replied Jeremy. "What was your favorite part?"

Well," replied Ben, "I liked the ending, where Veritas gave Rancor the white stone. That was so cool when the lightning started coming out of the stone and killing the ghouls. Don't you think God might be like that? You know—like a powerful force of lightning that will one day destroy all the bad guys on earth."

"Well, God's not exactly like that," said Jeremy a bit perplexed. "Yes, He is good. And yes, He will destroy all evil one day when Jesus comes back. But God isn't just a force or power like the white stone."

"Well, if He's not a power like the white stone, how will He destroy all the bad guys?" asked Ben.

"First," said Jeremy, "God isn't a force. He's a real person. Yes, He's all powerful, and He will defeat evil one day, but you can't think of God as if He were just a white stone with magical powers."

"When you say God is a real person, do you mean a person like you and me?"

"Well, yes and no," said Jeremy as Mrs. Simmons drove up in front of the theater. "Hey, here's Mom. Hop in!"

"How was the movie, boys?" asked Jeremy's mom.

"It was great," Ben said. "It was all about this white stone and its magic power and King Veritas and King Rancor and how King Veritas used the stone to defeat Rancor and his army and—"

"Sounds pretty exciting to me," said Mrs. Simmons before Ben could take a breath.

"Mom," said Jeremy, "Ben and I were talking about how God is all powerful, but how He's not just a magic force like the white stone in the movie. He's a real person."

"That's right," she replied. "God thinks, He makes choices, He has feelings, and He's creative."

"Then what makes God different from us?" asked Ben.

"Well, first of all," replied Jeremy, "He's invisible. God is Spirit. No one has ever seen God except when He became a man through Jesus and lived on the earth."

"And God is all powerful," added Mrs. Simmons. "There's nothing He can't do."

"Just like the white stone was all powerful!"

"Not really," said Mrs. Simmons with a smile. "Remember, the power of the white stone was fiction. God's power is real, and His power is far greater than the power of a make-believe stone. He speaks and things happen—like when He spoke and the world was created."

"And besides that," said Jeremy, "there's nothing God doesn't know. There are no secrets hidden from Him. And He's everywhere at the same time. Even the white stone wasn't like that in the movie."

"But couldn't an evil force like Rancor defeat or capture God like he captured King Veritas? Isn't God sometimes weak?" asked Ben. "Wasn't Jesus captured and killed?"

"When Jesus came to earth, God allowed Himself to be killed on the cross," Jeremy replied. "But remember, Jesus rose from the dead. Not even death could destroy Him."

"So didn't Jesus die later when He got old?" Ben asked with a puzzled expression.

"Ben," said Jeremy, "let me try to explain. First of all, God was never born and He'll never die. He has always been alive and always will be. And God's Son, Jesus, was always alive with God the Father, before He was born as a baby on earth. And after He died on the cross and was raised from the dead, He went back to heaven to live with His Father. And He'll live forever too."

"Wow," said Ben. "That's confusing. You say Jesus was always alive with His Father in heaven *before* He was born?"

"That's right," said Jeremy.

"And then you say that Jesus was born as a human being on the earth and lived here until He died on the cross?"

"Right again."

"And then you say Jesus came back to life and returned to heaven and will live forever?" replied Ben.

"Yep." Jeremy smiled.

"How do you know if all of that is true?" asked Ben skeptically.

"Remember last week when we talked about how God speaks truth to us? You know, through His creation, the Bible, and through Jesus? Well, God's Word tells us these truths. And you know what's really exciting?"

"What's that?" asked Ben.

"One day we'll live with God the Father and His Son, Jesus, in heaven forever."

"Really?"

"We're home, boys," said Mrs. Simmons as she drove into the driveway. "I think the two of you have just had a very important conversation."

"I'll say," said Ben. "I didn't know that Jeremy knew so much about God. Where did you learn all that stuff? "

"From my parents, my teachers at Sunday school, and from reading the Bible," Jeremy said with a smile. "Hey, let's go upstairs. I wanna show you my rock collection. I've been collecting them along the mountain trails since we moved here."

"Supper will be ready in an hour," Mrs. Simmons said. "So stay close to the house."

"We will, Mom," said Jeremy as the boys raced each other up the stairs.

As Jeremy opened a large wooden box filled with various kinds of rocks, Ben's eyes fell on a large, smooth white stone.

"Cool!" he shouted as he lifted the rock out of the box. "That's just like the one in the movie. If we just carry it around with us and pull it out whenever any bullies give us trouble, we can zap 'em. We can conquer evil, we can be masters of the universe, we can—"

"Ben," said Jeremy, looking at him strangely. "That's just in the movies! It's all make-believe."

"I know," laughed Ben, falling down and rolling on the floor. "I just wanted to hear what you'd say. Don't worry, I learned a lot from you today. And one thing I learned for sure. God isn't a make-believe force. But I still have lots of questions about what He's really like."

"That's okay," replied Jeremy, relieved and laughing himself. "I do, too. But while you're here this summer, we can ask my mom and dad as many questions as we can think of, and for sure we can read the Bible."

"Boys," Mrs. Simmons called, "dinner's ready."

"What's for supper?" Jeremy asked as they headed down the stairs.

"White stone soup," Mrs. Simmons replied mischievously.

"White stone soup?" they both asked in unison. "What's that?"

"Look in the pot on the stove," answered Mrs. Simmons, trying not to laugh.

"Oh, Mom," exclaimed Jeremy," it's just potato soup!"

"Yes, and when we eat it, we'll have magic power over evil, and you can slay all the dragons and bad guys, and you can—"

"Oh no! Not again," cried Jeremy. "We've had enough stories for one day. Besides, I'm hungry. Let's eat!"

WHEN A STORY IS NOT JUST A STORY

The Chronicles of Narnia is a series of seven fantasy novels written by C. S. Lewis. The first and best known of these books is *The Lion, the Witch and the Wardrobe*, in which four children from our world are magically transported to the realm of Narnia, a place where animals talk, magic is common, and winter never ends. There the children are called upon by the lion Aslan to battle the White Witch and free Narnia from her tyranny.

At the heart of the novel is an **allegory** (pronounced AL-eh-GOR-ee), a story with a deeper meaning in which the characters and setting often represent real-life events. *The Lion, the Witch and the Wardrobe* is an allegory that tells the story of Jesus' death and resurrection. In the story, Aslan sacrifices himself to save Edmund, a traitor who deserved death, in the same way that Jesus sacrificed Himself to pay the penalty for our sins.

Aslan is a **symbol**, a character who represents Jesus in the story. Why did the author choose a lion to portray Jesus? In the Bible, Jesus is called "the Lion of the tribe of Judah" (Revelation 5:5). The lion is said to be king of the forest and is fearsome and intimidating and deserving great respect. Yet Aslan is also a big cat, full of joy, who romps and plays merrily with the children, just as Jesus loved to visit with young people.

In the third book of the Chronicles of Narnia, *Voyage of the Dawn Treader*, when Aslan sends the children back to our world, Edmund asks if Aslan is in our world too. "I am," says Aslan. "But there I have another name. You must learn to know me by that name. This was the very reason why you were brought to Narnia, that by knowing me here for a little, you may know me better there."

This is the purpose of C. S. Lewis's allegory—that by visiting Narnia and getting to know Aslan there, we will come to know Jesus even better in the real world.

59

YOU'VE GOT QUESTIONS, GOD HAS ANSWERS

As you read in "The White Stone," Ben asked several questions about God that Jeremy tried to answer. Ben also believed some things about God that were not true. Ben is not alone in having questions and wrong beliefs about God. In fact, everyone who has ever lived has thought about God and asked many questions about Him. Even people who do not believe in God have had to ask and answer the question "Does God exist?"

We've already learned that God speaks truth to us through His Word, the Bible. In the Bible we learn, for example, that God does exist and that He is the only true and living God. He is not, as Ben believed, a force or power like the white stone. Rather, He is a personal being who thinks, feels, and make choices. Although God is a person, He is different from you and me. We cannot see Him, yet He has always existed and will never die. Unlike us, God never sins. And God never changes, so we don't have to worry about God being kind one day and unkind the next or strong one day and weak the next.

If you think the fictional white stone was powerful, God is much more so. The Bible tells us that God is all powerful. Also, because He is God, He is all knowing, meaning He knows everything about everything, even before anything happens. And unlike the make-believe white stone, which could work its magic in only one place at one time, God is everywhere in creation at the same time. That is why God can hear and answer someone's prayer in China at the same time He hears and answers someone else's prayer in Australia.

Because people hold so many beliefs about God—some correct and some incorrect—it is important that you know the biblical answers to the questions people ask. Don't just accept what you see in a movie or what people tell you. Read God's Word, and He will speak to you through it. Remember, every word He speaks is true.

WORDS YOU NEED TO KNOW

> **Attributes:** a characteristic or quality belonging to a specific person
> **Atheist:** A person who does not believe that God exists
> **Faith:** A confident belief in God, His love for us, and His authority in our lives
> **Idol:** A false god that people make and worship
> **Person:** A living being who has mind, emotions, a will, a conscience, and a spirit

HIDE IT IN YOUR HEART

Now to the King eternal, immortal, invisible, the only God, be honor and glory for ever and ever. Amen. (1 Timothy 1:17)

QUESTION 1:
DOES GOD EXIST?

The first question people must ask themselves about God is "Does God exist?" The correct answer is yes. We already know that all of creation reveals the glory and existence of God. The great scientist Albert Einstein said that God "reveals himself in the harmony of all that exists." We know that God left us a note, the Bible, to tell us all about Him and His love for us. He even sent His Son, Jesus, to live among us and show us what God is like.

In fact, the Bible tells us it is foolish not to believe in God:

The fool says in his heart, "There is no God." (Psalm 14:1)

Yet many people choose to believe that God does not exist. A person who does not believe in the existence of God is called an **atheist**—the prefix *a-* means "without" or "not," and the root word *theist* means "one who believes in a god or God." Atheists do not believe that each and every one of us was created for a purpose and, therefore, must look elsewhere to find meaning in life, a search that will always fail.

A person who believes in God is said to have *faith*. Faith is a confident belief in God, His love for us, and His authority in our lives. Hebrews 11:6 tells us that "without faith it is impossible to please God, because anyone who comes to him must believe that he exists and that he rewards those who earnestly seek him."

> *"Could such a great symphony as the universe have no conductor?"*
> **Albert Einstein**
> 1879–1955

MAKE A NOTE OF IT
Write an entry in your notebook telling why it is important to believe in God. Then answer this question: What blessings (or rewards) does God give to those who believe in Him and who seek to know Him?

QUESTION 2:
HOW MANY GODS ARE THERE?

The Ancient Greeks worshiped twelve major gods, who were believed to reside at the top of Mount Olympus, as well as many lesser gods. Zeus was the god of thunder and the sky and was the king of the gods. Poseidon was the god of the sea and earthquakes. Athena was the goddess of wisdom and crafts. Apollo was the god of the sun, healing, the arts, and archery. The Ancient Greeks had a god for everything! Their religion also had a large mythology—stories they told of the gods and of how their actions affected humanity. Such a belief in more than one god is called **polytheism**—the prefix *poly-* means "many."

What does the Bible say about polytheism? It says clearly that there is only one true God:

> *There is no God but one. For even if there are so-called gods, whether in heaven or on earth (as indeed there are many "gods" and many "lords"), yet for us there is but one God, the Father, from whom all things came and for whom we live; and there is but one Lord, Jesus Christ, through whom all things came and through whom we live.* (1 Corinthians 8:4–6)

> *"There is no one like you, O LORD, and there is no God but you, as we have heard with our own ears."* (1 Chronicles 17:20)

> *"There is no other God besides me. I am the only good God. I am the Savior. There is no other God."* (Isaiah 45:21, ICB)

Like the Ancient Greeks, cultures that believe in many gods often create statues or objects—many in the forms of animals—that represent their gods so that they may see what they are worshiping. The Bible calls these man-made objects idols and warns us against worshiping them:

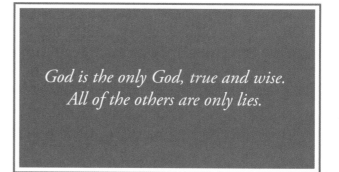

God is the only God, true and wise. All of the others are only lies.

> *"Do men make their own gods? Yes, but they are not gods!"* (Jeremiah 16:20)

> *We know that an idol is nothing at all in the world.* (1 Corinthians 8:4)

> *"Like a scarecrow in a melon patch, their idols cannot speak; they must be carried because they cannot walk. Do not fear them; they can do no harm nor can they do any good."* (Jeremiah 10:5)

MICHELANGELO'S *THE CREATION OF ADAM*

The Creation of Adam is one of the most famous images in the world. Painted by Michelangelo on the ceiling of the Sistine Chapel in Rome, it illustrates the biblical story in which God the Father breathes life into Adam, the first man. The chapel ceiling, painted between 1508 and 1512, is a breathtaking work of art illustrating nine scenes from the Book of Genesis, of which *The Creation of Adam* is the best known.

Michelangelo depicts God as an elderly bearded man, wrapped in a swirling cloak and surrounded by several angels called cherubim. God's right arm is outstretched to give the spark of life to Adam, whose left arm is extended in a pose that mirrors God's to show that God created man in His own image. Adam's finger and God's finger are separated by a slight distance.

The painting technique Michelangelo used was *fresco*, in which the paint is applied to damp plaster on a wall or ceiling. In order to reach the chapel's ceiling, the artist designed his own scaffold, a flat wooden platform upon which he then stood or lay to draw and paint the space above him.

The question of whether it is wrong to portray God in a work of art has been debated through the centuries. Being God, invisible and almighty, He is beyond the knowledge or ability of any artist to depict. But does God Himself prohibit the making of such images?

The Second Commandment expressly forbids us to worship "an image of anything in the heavens or on the earth or in the sea" (Exodus 20:4, NLT). In addition to many beautiful stained-glass depictions in churches around the world, pictures of Jesus have become commonplace in homes and churches and even in many Bibles. Yet it's important that we do not worship these pictures or pray to them because then we make idols of them. As Jesus told us, "God is Spirit, and those who worship Him must worship in spirit and truth" (John 4:24).

An idol can also be a person or thing that receives praise and "worship" and is given an unhealthy place in the life of another person. A popular music performer is sometimes called a "teen idol" and may even be referred to as a "god" by his or her fans. People make idols of star athletes, film and TV performers, politicians, sometimes even preachers of God's Word. Other people make idols of money or power or possessions—anything that is given too much importance in a person's life.

Only God is worthy of our worship and adoration: "For great is the LORD and most worthy of praise; he is to be feared above all gods" (1 Chronicles 16:25).

MAKE A NOTE OF IT

An idol is a false god that people "make" and worship. Write in your notebook your answers to these questions: What can an idol do for you? What can an idol not do? Why would someone refer to a particular musician or athlete as a "god"? Who or what are some of the things that could be a god to someone who does not believe in the one true God?

QUESTION 3:
WHAT DOES GOD LOOK LIKE?

Pentecost by El Greco

When asked by a new friend what your mother is like, you might begin by describing her physical attributes. You might say she is tall or short, pretty or plain, blond or brunette, and that her eyes are blue or green or brown. But how would you go about describing what God looks like?

You can't! Because, as the Bible tells us, "No one has ever seen God, or can see him" (1 Timothy 6:16, ICB). That is because God is invisible, or unable to be seen. John 4:24 tells us that "God is spirit," and as spirit, He has no physical form. And yet, "since the creation of the world God's invisible qualities—his eternal power and divine nature—have been clearly seen" (Romans 1:20) so that we know He is very real.

Although He cannot be seen, God has made His presence known to men and women throughout history. In Exodus 3:1–4, He spoke to Moses from a burning bush. Later, in Exodus 19:16–19, He revealed His presence to the people of Israel in the form of smoke and thunder, an earthquake, and a trumpet blast. At the baptism of Jesus, in Mark 1:9–11, God the Holy Spirit appeared as a dove descending from the heavens, and the Father spoke in a voice that sounded to many like thunder. On the Day of Pentecost, in Acts 2:1–4, the Holy Spirit appeared as a rushing wind and as tongues of fire visible above the heads of the new believers. Does this mean that God is fire or smoke? Or that He looks like a trumpet or a dove? Or even a shrub? No! These are simply pictures that God used to reveal something about Himself to us.

God the Father did reveal much about Himself, His character, and His nature in a visible way through Jesus Christ. Colossians 1:15 says that Jesus "is the image of the invisible God." Jesus Himself said that in seeing God the Son, we see God the Father (John 12:44–45). Of course, we can no longer see Jesus in person as He is in heaven, seated at the right hand of the Father (Ephesians 1:20). But He rewards those who believe anyway. After He had risen from the dead, Jesus told the apostle Thomas, "You believe because you have seen me. Blessed are those who believe without seeing me" (John 20:29).

MAKE A NOTE OF IT

Why do you think the invisible God would show His presence to Moses and the Israelites as thunder and lightning, an earthquake, a thick cloud of smoke, and a trumpet blast? What do each of these things—thunder and lightning, smoke and clouds, an earthquake, and a trumpet blast—tell us about what God is like?

QUESTION 4:
IS GOD A PERSON?

You are a person. Your parents are persons. Your pastor is a person. Even the old man down the street who hollers at you to keep off his grass is a person. What is a person? A person has a mind, emotions, a will, a conscience, and a spirit. As persons, we have the ability to think and know with our minds, feel with our hearts, make choices, know right from wrong, and enjoy fellowship with God through Christ with our spirits.

Although He is spirit and has no body, God too is a person. It is important that we understand this for the Bible tells us that you and I were created in God's image (Genesis 1:27). That doesn't mean that we physically resemble God, who is, after all, invisible and is not human. Instead it means that He created us to have those attributes that make God a personal being—a mind, emotions, a will, a conscience, and a spirit. Let's look more closely at each of these attributes of God.

GOD HAS THOUGHTS

God has thoughts, just as we do, but His thoughts are far greater than ours. "For my thoughts are not your thoughts, neither are your ways my ways," declares the Lord. "As the heavens are higher than the earth, so are my ways higher than your ways and my thoughts than your

Thinker by Rodin. Photo: Andreas Praefcke

thoughts" (Isaiah 55:8–9). For example, when you are feeling angry or bored or just mischievous, you might think of a neat trick you can play on another person. God does not think about evil things and is never tempted to do mischief. God's thoughts are always good, and He is always thinking:

God, your thoughts are precious to me. They are so many! If I could count them, they would be more than all the grains of sand. (Psalm 139:17–18, ICB)

MAKE A NOTE OF IT

Write out Isaiah 55:8–9 and Psalm 139:17–18 in your notebook. What do these scriptures tell us about God's thoughts? How are God's thoughts different from your thoughts? How many grains of sand do you think there are on a beach? How could God have more thoughts than the number of grains of sand? How does God make His thoughts known to us?

GOD HAS EMOTIONS

The Old Testament tells the story of the nation of Israel and the history of its turbulent relationship with God. Although they were God's chosen people, the people of Israel continually disobeyed His commands, turning away from Him and even worshiping idols. As a result they suffered the consequences of His anger. Yet after seventy years of captivity in Babylon, God, in His love and compassion, restored the people to their land. The range of God's emotions from anger to rejoicing is displayed in the biblical history of Israel:

They have refused to obey the teachings of the Lord of heaven's armies. They hated the Message from the Holy God of Israel. So the Lord has become very angry with his people. And he has raised his hand to punish them. (Isaiah 5:24–25, ICB)

"I will surely gather them from all the lands where I banish them in my furious anger and great wrath; I will bring them back to this place and let them live in safety . . . I will rejoice in doing them good and will assuredly plant them in this land with all my heart and soul." (Jeremiah 32:37, 41)

The LORD is gracious and compassionate, slow to anger and rich in love. (Psalm 145:8)

"The LORD your God is with you, he is mighty to save. He will take great delight in you, he will quiet you with his love, he will rejoice over you with singing." (Zephaniah 3:17)

Emotions are a gift from God and add "color" to our lives as people made in His image. Emotions are not sinful, but we often express our emotions sinfully. Only God expresses His emotions with complete righteousness.

MAKE A NOTE OF IT

Write out Isaiah 5:24–25 and Zephaniah 3:17 in your notebook. What made God angry with Israel? What makes God angry today? How does God show you His love?

Moses Smashing the Ten Commandments by Rembrandt

GOD MAKES CHOICES

One day, Moses called all the people of Israel together and said, "You are holy people. You belong to the Lord your God. He has chosen you from all the people on earth. You are his very own. The Lord did not care for you and choose you because there were many of you. You are the smallest nation of all. But the Lord chose you because he loved you" (Deuteronomy 7:6–8, ICB).

God has a will—that is, He makes choices. And because He is our Creator and Savior, He expects us to obey the choices He makes and the commands He gives:

For he chose us in him before the creation of the world to be holy and blameless in his sight. (Ephesians 1:4)

As a believer in Christ, you have been chosen by Him to live in a way that is pleasing to Him. Indeed, you have been chosen to live with Him for all eternity as His child. In a later chapter, we will look more closely at what it means to be a child of God.

GOD KNOWS RIGHT FROM WRONG

The prophet Jeremiah wrote, "Great and powerful God, whose name is the LORD Almighty, great are your purposes and mighty are your deeds. Your eyes are open to all the ways of men; you reward everyone according to his conduct and as his deeds deserve (Jeremiah 32:18–19). How does God know whether to reward us or punish us for our deeds? Because He knows right from wrong.

When God created Adam and Eve, He placed them in the Garden of Eden and told them that they may eat the fruit from any tree except the tree of knowledge of good and evil (Genesis 2:16–17). There was nothing essentially evil about the

tree or its fruit. However, when Adam and Eve ate the fruit, their act of disobedience brought sin and evil into the world and into their lives.

As we have seen, God wants all of us to do only what is right. So why did He put the tree of knowledge of good and evil in the garden in the first place? God placed the tree in the garden to give Adam and Eve a choice to obey Him or disobey Him. If God had not given Adam and Eve the choice, they would have essentially been robots, simply doing what they were programmed to do. God created Adam and Eve to be "free" beings—persons—able to make decisions, able to choose between good and evil. In order for Adam and Eve to truly be made in the image of God, they had to be free to choose.

Each of us also has this freedom. Every day, every hour, every minute, we must choose to do what is right or to do what is wrong. Which will you choose today?

GOD IS A SPIRITUAL BEING

We also know that God is a person because He is a spiritual being. Every person is a spiritual being—we each have a spirit, and this spirit will live on for all eternity. Of course, God does not *have* a spirit because He *is* spirit. And when we believe that Jesus is our Lord and Savior, God sends His Spirit to live inside of us:

> And the Spirit [of God] himself joins with our spirits to say that we are God's children. (Romans 8:16, ICB)

MAKE A NOTE OF IT

Write down the five characteristics that make God a person, then answer these questions: If you are a person and God is a person, are you God too? Why not? How are you as a personal being different from God as a personal being?

A PRAYER

Dear God, thank you for loving me and caring for me. I'm glad you're a real person and not a make-believe force or useless idol. I want to talk with you and learn from you, and I want to know you better. I'm sorry for the times when I have made an idol out of something or someone by spending more time talking about them than about you. You are the one true God, and you are my Rock. In Jesus' name I pray. Amen.

DO I HAVE A WORLDVIEW AND WHERE DID IT COME FROM?

If someone were to say to you, "Tell me, when did you develop your worldview? You do have one, don't you?" how would you respond? If you are like most people, you might stammer and stutter a bit, not quite sure what to say. Most people have never had a "worldview lesson" while sitting on their father's or grandfather's lap. Your mother has probably never said, "Now sit down and listen. Today, I'm going to teach you your first worldview lesson." So just how do people acquire or develop a worldview—their beliefs about God, the universe, people, truth, and right and wrong? Let's look at four different ways.

OBSERVATION

Infants don't ask questions, but they're still very interesting in learning about their new world. They are very observant, taking in colors, sounds, shapes, smells, and textures. They hear language being spoken. They see laughter, anger, joy, and fear in those around them. They begin to learn that some things are good or right to do when they are praised. And, of course, they begin to learn that some things are wrong or harmful because they experience discipline or painful consequences for doing them.

As you grew older, you were (and still are) like a sponge. You absorbed many things about your world just by living in it. And this happened without daily worldview lessons. You may have seen your parents pray or listened to them read the Bible. Slowly, you began to understand and form beliefs about God. You may have seen arguments and fights and came to understand that these behaviors are harmful to everyone, even without anyone telling you they are. In today's technological world, you observe and learn the worldviews of others by watching television and movies, by listening to music, and by surfing the Internet on a computer—even though you may never hear anyone say the word "worldview."

TEACHING

Although you acquire much of your worldview just by living and observing life and the world, you also learn it through teaching. Your parents, pastor, and Sunday school teachers have taught you many things about understanding life and the world. They have taught you that some things are always right and that some things are always wrong. And although they may never have spoken the word "worldview," much of what they have taught you has become part of your worldview. Can you think of some of the things you have been taught that are now a part of your worldview?

PERSONAL STUDY

You have developed or acquired many of your worldview beliefs simply by reading and studying on your own. Of course, it's important to know whether the things you read are true or not. This is why it's important to compare what you read and hear with what God's Word says and to ask trusted authorities if what you have read or heard is really true. Can you think of a book you have read that has influenced your view of life and the world?

REASONING AND IMAGINATION

When God created you in His image, He gave you a mind capable of thinking, reasoning, and creating. When you look up at the stars on a very dark night, what thoughts go through your mind? President Teddy Roosevelt once said that when he got feeling too big for his britches, he would go outside and look up at the stars until he remembered just how small he really was and how great our God is. Does witnessing the majesty of the universe prompt you to ask difficult questions? If so, what do you think and ask? Can this experience shape your beliefs about the creation or God or even yourself?

Everyone acquires worldview beliefs through reasoning and imagining, but like beliefs acquired through all other means, they need to be compared to the truth of God's Word. Sometimes our imaginations lead us to beliefs that are only fantasy or completely wrong.

WHAT IS GOD LIKE?
PART 2

"AS FOR GOD, HIS WAY IS PERFECT; THE WORD OF THE LORD IS FLAWLESS. HE IS A SHIELD FOR ALL WHO TAKE REFUGE IN HIM."

2 SAMUEL 22:31

THE BIG IDEA

In May 1977, a farm boy and a knight, a smuggler and a princess, a pair of droids, and a Wookiee landed in theaters and the American movie industry would never be the same. The original *Star Wars* quickly became a cultural phenomenon, earning more money than any film ever made to that time and launching a galaxy of *Star Wars* merchandise, including action figures, games, breakfast cereals, books, music, and TV shows. In this and five more live-action films, *Star Wars* creator George Lucas also popularized the concept of the Force, a mystical power that enables our hero to perform spectacular feats of derring-do and defeat the evil Empire.

What is this powerful Force? Obi-Wan Kenobi, a Jedi Knight who lives like a hermit and dresses like a monk, tells young Luke Skywalker that in order to save the princess he must learn "the ways" of the Force. Another character refers to the Jedi's devotion to the Force as "their religion." Darth Vader, the villain and a former Jedi, declares, "The ability to destroy a planet is insignificant next to the power of the Force." Whoa. So is the Force just another name for God? Or is it like God? Or is it something else altogether?

Obi-Wan describes the Force as "an energy field created by all living things" that "surrounds us and penetrates us and binds the galaxy together." He also reveals that the Force has a "dark side" which can be used for evil purposes. Let's stop right there. First of all, the one true God is not an impersonal energy field; He is a personal being who loves you and cares for you and whose mighty hand first formed energy. He created all things, whereas in *Star Wars* all things created the Force. And as we will see in this lesson, God has no dark side. The Bible tells us He is always good and "does not change like shifting shadows" (James 1:17). His glory is too vast to be captured on film and too dazzling to be seen on any high-definition screen. He cannot be manipulated, for good or evil, for He alone is all present, all knowing, and all powerful.

WHAT YOU WILL DO

» You will explore the biblical answers to six more common questions about God: Does God ever sin? How old is God? Does God ever change? Where is God? How strong is God? How much does God know?

» You will define the word *reverence* and learn why it is an important response to your understanding of God's character.

» You will lay the second stone of truth about God in the foundation of your House of Truth: *God is the only true and almighty God.*

WORDS YOU NEED TO KNOW

» **Sin**: To do what is wrong, or not do what is right, according to God's rules

» **Holy**: Spiritually perfect, without sin

» **Eternal**: Without beginning or end

» **Immortal**: Deathless, or free from ever dying

» **Immutable**: Without change

» **Omnipresent**: All present—being everywhere at once

» **Omnipotent**: All powerful

» **Omniscient**: All knowing

» **Reverence**: An attitude of respect and honor for God

HIDE IT IN YOUR HEART

He who forms the mountains, creates the wind, and reveals his thoughts to man, he who turns dawn to darkness, and treads the high places of the earth—the LORD God Almighty is his name. (Amos 4:13)

It is the LORD your God you must follow, and him you must revere. (Deuteronomy 13:4)

QUESTION 5:
DOES GOD EVER SIN?

Sin is doing what is wrong, or not doing what is right, according to God's rules. If God says "Do not lie" and you tell a lie, then you have sinned. If God says "Do not steal" and you steal, no matter how small the item, then you have sinned. But does God ever sin? We have learned that God knows the difference between right and wrong. He gave us the Bible so that we too would know what is right and what is wrong. Nevertheless, we sometimes fail to do the right thing, but God never sins:

He is the Rock, his works are perfect, and all his ways are just. A faithful God who does no wrong, upright and just is he. (Deuteronomy 32:4)

"It is unthinkable that God would do wrong, that the Almighty would pervert justice." (Job 34:12)

"As for God, his way is perfect; the word of the LORD is flawless." (2 Samuel 22:31)

"Who will not fear you, O Lord, and bring glory to your name? For you alone are holy." (Revelation 15:4)

Your Bible may have the words "Holy Bible" printed on its cover. And you've probably heard many songs in church in which God is called "Holy Father" or "Holy God." The word holy means "without sin." You see, God is perfect. His thoughts, His emotions, and His choices are always holy. He will never cheat or lie to you. He will never break His own rules. He will always be fair, and He will always keep His promises. You can trust in Him completely.

> *What is impossible to God? Not that which is difficult to his power, but that which is contrary to his nature.*
> **Ambrose**
> 340–397

QUESTION 6:
HOW OLD IS GOD?

Sarah's great-grandmother celebrated her 100th birthday last week. What do we mean when we say that Sarah's great-grandmother is 100 years old? We are saying that her great-grandmother was born at a specific time on a specific day and has lived for 100 years since that moment. She may even have her birth certificate, an official document issued by the hospital where she was born that states the time and date of her birth. Therefore we can measure in

HOW TO MAKE A SAMURAI SWORD

The samurai were a class of Japanese warriors who flourished from about the eighth century to the nineteenth century. Samurai led their lives according to the code of *bushido*, or "the way of the warrior," which stressed loyalty to one's master, self-discipline, and respectful behavior. They were skilled with weapons such as bows and arrows, spears, and guns, but their most famous weapon and their symbol was the sword.

The curved samurai sword, called a *katana* (pronounced kah-TAH-nah), is a marvel of aesthetic beauty and skillful engineering. It is said that the katana could cut even a hair

in the air. Making a samurai sword is a complex and tedious art that may require as many as fifteen men and nearly six months to create a single sword by hand. Samurai swords are so difficult to make because they require flexibility—to prevent breakage from high impacts in battle—as well as strength, or hardness, to keep their sharp edge.

To make a katana, the swordsmith heats the metal until it is red-hot to get rid of anything that might weaken the sword. Then he hammers and folds the hot metal again and again, like kneading bread. If the metal has any tiny impurities, such as dirt, that the fire didn't burn away, it is thrown out and the swordsmith must start over. Weaknesses or flaws, such as pockets of air, could cause the sword to break or crack.

The Bible says that it is like a sword: "Sharper than any double-edged sword, it penetrates even to dividing soul and spirit, joints and marrow; it judges the thoughts and attitudes of the heart" (Hebrews 4:12). Because God is holy and perfect, His Word, the Bible, is also perfect, having no impurities or flaws. In fact, the Bible is a Christian's best protection against false ideas: "Put on the full armor of God so that you can take your stand against the devil's schemes. . . . Take the helmet of salvation and the sword of the Spirit, which is the word of God" (Ephesians 6:11, 17).

units of time how old she is.

On July 4, 1976, the United States of America celebrated its Bicentennial, or 200th birthday. The country was created on July 4, 1776, when the Continental Congress approved the final wording of a document declaring this new nation's independence from Great Britain and the rule of King George III. The nation's "birth certificate," the Declaration of Independence, prominently displays the exact date on which the United States of America was created, so we know how old the country is today.

In order to know how old something is, we must first know when it was created. But God was not created. He has always existed. He had no beginning. We cannot know how old God is because He existed before time. In fact, God *created* time. As the creator of time, God exists outside of time, so He will never grow old and He will never die:

> *Surely you know. Surely you have heard. The Lord is the God who lives forever. He created all the world. He does not become tired or need to rest. No one can understand how great his wisdom is.* (Isaiah 40:28, ICB)

> *Before the mountains were brought forth,*
> *or ever you had formed the earth and the world,*
> *from everlasting to everlasting you are God.* (Psalm 90:2, ESV)

> *Trust in the LORD forever, for the LORD, the LORD, is the Rock eternal.* (Isaiah 26:4)

From these scriptures and many others, we learn that God is **eternal**, meaning He has no beginning and no end. God is ageless and **immortal**, which means He will never die. He

THE MÖBIUS STRIP

Photo: David Benbennick

A Möbius strip is a geometric shape discovered in 1858 by two German mathematicians, August Möbius and Johann Listing. This unique shape has only one side and one edge! Sound complicated? Yet you can make a Möbius strip for yourself by following these simple directions. Here's what you will need: a sheet of paper, a pair of scissors, a pen or pencil, and tape.

First, cut a rectangular strip of paper about an inch wide. Don't worry—it doesn't have to be perfectly straight. Holding one end of the strip in each hand, bend the ends together to form a circle. Now flip one end upside down, so there is a twist in the strip, and tape the ends together on both sides. You've just made a Möbius strip!

Now try this experiment to prove that it has just one side. Take a pen or pencil and draw a line along the strip, making sure the point of your pen doesn't leave the paper. You should end up right back where you started! Another test is to make a dot on one of the edges, to mark your starting point. Then pinch the strip between two fingers and gently follow the edge. (Watch out for paper cuts!) Without letting go of the paper, you will touch the entire outside edge and still end up back at your dot!

Just like your Möbius strip, God has only one side: He is always good, always holy, and will never do anything evil. And like the Möbius strip, God doesn't have a beginning or an end. He has always existed and will continue to exist eternally.

existed before anything that now exists, and He will exist forever.

Why is it important that we know God is eternal? Because He lives outside of time, He can see the beginning and the end of everything—our lives, the church, and the earth. So when God tells us what will happen in the future, as in Matthew 24, we can rest assured that those events will happen just as He described. And we can live now in peace knowing that when we die we will live with Him forever.

> ## MAKE A NOTE OF IT
>
> Draw a straight line in your notebook. Now draw a wavy line. These lines symbolize life that is created—no matter how many twists and turns life takes, it has a definite beginning and ending. Now use a compass or glass to help you neatly draw a perfect circle in your notebook. You should not be able to tell where your circle begins and ends. Now write briefly about how the circle can be a symbol of the eternal nature of God. Like a circle, what can a ring symbolize about God?

QUESTION 7:
DOES GOD EVER CHANGE?

For you and me, change can be a good thing. Eleanor Roosevelt once said, "People grow through experience if they meet life honestly and courageously. This is how character is built." The courageous young woman Anne Frank wrote, "[If] you try to improve yourself at the start of each new day . . . you achieve quite a lot in the course of time. Anyone can do this, it costs nothing and is certainly very helpful."

In any case, certain changes are unavoidable. Take a look at this sequence of photos depicting a person at different points in her life:

As you can see, the most obvious changes we experience in life are physical changes. As we age, we first grow taller, then later we grow shorter. Starting at about age forty, people typically shrink about a half inch in height every ten years. Likewise, we first learn more as we grow, then later we begin to forget more. People may also change their beliefs and behaviors depending on their experiences in life. Can you think of other ways people can change?

God, however, never changes. His attributes are **immutable**, meaning they never change. God is always God. He will never sin, He will never grow old, He will always keep His promises, and He will always remain the same:

In the beginning you laid the foundations of the earth,
and the heavens are the work of your hands.
They will perish, but you remain;
they will all wear out like a garment.
Like clothing you will change them
and they will be discarded.
But you remain the same,
and your years will never end.
(Psalm 102:25–27)

Whatever is good and perfect comes down to us from God our Father, who created all the lights in the heavens. He never changes or casts a shifting shadow. (James 1:17, NLT)

"I the LORD do not change." (Malachi 3:6)

Jesus Christ is the same yesterday and today and forever. (Hebrews 13:8)

If we are to dedicate our lives to serving God, as He wants us to, it's important that we know that God is immutable. If we are to tell the world about Him and about what Jesus Christ has done for us, as He has commanded, we must be sure that He is who the Bible says He is. We must be confident that He will never change His mind about us or take away from us our position as children of the Most High God. You can always count on Him to be faithful:

"Be strong and courageous. Do not be afraid or terrified because of them, for the LORD your God goes with you; he will never leave you nor forsake you." (Deuteronomy 31:6)

> ### MAKE A NOTE OF IT
> Write about a time when you did something wrong even though you knew it was wrong. Now answer this question: As a person grows older as a Christian, how should his or her behavior and actions change? Try to find one or more Bible verses to support your answer.

QUESTION 8:
WHERE IS GOD?

Have you ever wished you could be in two places at once? At two different birthday parties scheduled for the same day? Or exploring the jungles of Africa while you sail the South China Sea? God is the only one who can be in two places at once. As a matter of fact, He is in *all* places at *all* times. That means He can hear and answer a prayer in Great Falls, Montana, while attending a Bible study in Mumbai, India. He can protect your family as you drive home through a storm even as He oversees the birth of a new star in a distant galaxy. The word that describes this attribute of God is **omnipresent**—the prefix *omni-* means "all."

God is everywhere. There is never a time or place where God is not present. He fills all of time and space, yet He is not limited by the laws of time and space. He is omnipresent throughout creation, yet He exists apart from creation. He is unique—there is nothing and no one like Him anywhere:

"Am I a God who is only close at hand?" says the LORD. "No, I am far away at the same time. Can anyone hide from me in a secret place? Am I not everywhere in all the heavens and earth?" (Jeremiah 23:23–24, NLT)

Where can I go from your Spirit?
Where can I flee from your presence?
If I go up to the heavens, you are there;
if I make my bed in the depths, you are there.
If I rise on the wings of the dawn,
if I settle on the far side of the sea,
even there your hand will guide me,
your right hand will hold me fast.
(Psalm 139:7–10)

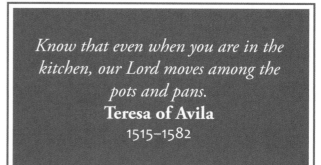

Know that even when you are in the kitchen, our Lord moves among the pots and pans.
Teresa of Avila
1515–1582

Take comfort in the knowledge that God is with you wherever you go. He will be there when you fly in a plane. He will be with you whether you're in a submarine deep underwater or climbing a mountain. If you move to another town, another state, or even another country, God will be there to protect you and watch over you:

The eyes of the LORD are everywhere, keeping watch on the wicked and the good.
(Proverbs 15:3)

MAKE A NOTE OF IT
Write out Proverbs 15:3 and Job 34:21–22 in your notebook. Now write your response to these questions: Does God have eyes like we do? Why not? What does the proverb mean when it says that "the eyes of the Lord are everywhere"? How does it make you feel knowing that God sees everything you do—both the good and the bad? What would life be like if God were not omnipresent?

Christ in the Storm on the Lake by Rembrandt

QUESTION 9: HOW STRONG IS GOD?

The story is told in Mark 4:35–41 that after a long day of teaching by the Sea of Galilee, Jesus was tired and needed a break from the crowds. He said to his disciples, "Let's cross over to the other side of the lake." So they hoisted the sail in their fishing boat and set off for the other side, a little more than four miles away. A cool breeze and the gentle rocking of the boat quickly lulled Jesus to sleep as He lay His head on a cushion.

He continued sleeping even as a furious squall blew in, sending huge waves crashing over the side of the small boat. A number of the disciples were experienced fisherman who knew this lake well, and even they began to panic as the storm grew more intense. The men dropped sail and began bailing water from the bottom of the boat. Things were looking pretty grim when one of the disciples shook Jesus awake and cried, "Lord, save us! We're going to drown!" Another called to Him, "Don't you care that we're about to die?"

Jesus stood up, holding onto the mast for balance. He then held up a hand and spoke to the wind and the waves, His voice barely audible above the storm: "Quiet! Be still!" Immediately the wind died away and the water became calm. The flapping ropes fell limp against the mast, and wet clothes clung to the amazed disciples. Jesus turned to His friends and asked, "Why were you so afraid? Do you still have no faith?"

Why were the disciples terrified of the storm? Didn't they know they were in the presence of God? Had they never heard the scriptures that declare:

You made the mountains by your strength.
You have great power.
You stopped the roaring seas,
the roaring waves
and the uproar of the nations.
(Psalm 65:6–7, ICB)

*Mightier than the thunder of the great waters,
mightier than the breakers of the sea—
the LORD on high is mighty.* (Psalm 93:4)

Jesus showed Himself to be God when He calmed the sea. He would later tell His disciples, "With God all things are possible" (Matthew 19:26). You see, God is not just strong; He is all powerful. We say that God is **omnipotent** (om-NI-po-tent), from the prefix *omni-*, meaning "all," and the root word *potent*, meaning "powerful." We sometimes call Him the Almighty or Almighty God. God created all things, and He sustains all things, from providing food for the smallest creature to keeping the galaxies in motion. Likewise, God is able to renew all things through the power of His Word.

THE SEA OF GALILEE

The Sea of Galilee is actually a lake set along the Plain of Gennesaret in northern Israel. The lake is thirteen miles long and seven miles wide and is only 150 feet deep at its deepest point. It is a place of rare beauty, and Jesus did much of His teaching near its shores, especially in the harbor village of Capernaum. In the Jewish book called the Talmud, the rabbis wrote of the Sea of Galilee, "Although God has created seven seas, yet He has chosen this one as His special delight."

The lake is surrounded on four sides by hills and actually sits several hundred feet below sea level. As warm winds rush in off the surrounding plateaus, they tend to mix with cool air over the water, creating sudden, violent thunderstorms like the one described in Mark 4:35–41.

The apostles Peter, Andrew, John, and James were all fishermen who worked the Sea of Galilee. In 1986, a wooden fishing vessel from the time of Christ was discovered on the lake's northwestern shore. The boat was approximately twenty-six feet long and seven feet wide—big enough for fifteen men. Pictured here are the remains of that ancient boat.

QUESTION 10:
HOW MUCH DOES GOD KNOW?

A newspaper cartoon from Gary Larsen's 1980s comic-strip "The Far Side" depicts God as a contestant on a *Jeopardy!*–like game show. He is shown as a robed older man, three times the size of his opponent, with light streaming from Him in all directions. His score is impressive, while the other contestant, who is glaring at Him, has a big, fat zero. The host is saying, "Yes! That's right! The answer is Wisconsin. Another 50 points for God, and . . . uh-oh, looks like Norman, our current champion, hasn't even scored yet." The cartoon is silly and absurd (as are pretty much all of the "Far Side" cartoons—that's why so many people love them) but it makes a couple of important points: 1) God knows everything, and 2) if you go up against God, you're not going to win. Let's consider the first of these for a moment.

As we know, God is eternal. He existed before time, and as the creator of time, He exists outside of time. Therefore, God can observe all events throughout the course of our history as if they were all happening at the same time. We also know that God is omnipresent, mean-

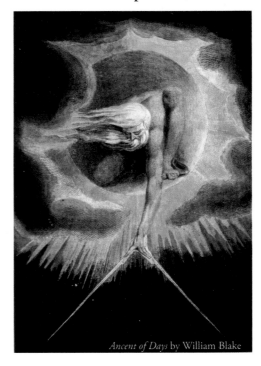

ing He is in all places all of the time. We know His eyes are everywhere, so it's not too hard to imagine that God also *knows* everything too. He knows everything that has happened or will happen in the past, present, and future. But more than just observing what we do, He can also see everything that goes on *inside* of us. He even knows our thoughts before we think them:

> O LORD, you have searched me
> and you know me.
> You know when I sit and when I rise;
> you perceive my thoughts from afar.
> You discern my going out and my lying down;
> you are familiar with all my ways.
> Before a word is on my tongue
> you know it completely, O LORD.
> (Psalm 139:1-4)

Ancent of Days by William Blake

For God is greater than our hearts, and he knows everything. (1 John 3:20)

Great is our Lord and mighty in power; his understanding has no limit. (Psalm 147:5)

We call this attribute of God **omniscience** (om-NISH-ence), from the prefix *omni-*, meaning "all," and the root word *science* which means "possession of knowledge." When we say that God is omniscient, we mean that there is nothing that He does not know or understand. There is nothing we can hide from Him:

Nothing in all the world can be hidden from God. Everything is clear and lies open before him. And to him we must explain the way we have lived. (Hebrews 4:13, ICB)

God sees everything we say and do. He knows everything we think. And the Bible tells us that when Jesus returns each and every one of us will stand before His "judgment seat" to answer for the way we have lived (2 Corinthians 5:10). On that day, those people who deny that God exists, and those who refuse to do what is right according to His Word, will have to face the consequences of the choices they have made.

Since God knows everything, how then should you live? Should you be frightened all the time, scared that God will zap you for even *thinking* of taking an Oreo from the cookie jar between meals? No, God does not keep a lightning bolt with your name on it, just waiting for you to mess up and do something wrong. Instead of living in fear of what will happen if we do something bad, we should always *want* to do what is good to show God how much we love Him. The Bible says we should "make it our goal to please him" (2 Corinthians 5:9). If you will make it your goal to do good and to honor God in every part of your life, then He will strengthen you to do good:

The eyes of the LORD search the whole earth in order to strengthen those whose hearts are fully committed to him. (2 Chronicles 16:9)

Someone once said about prayer that it's difficult to have a conversation with someone who already knows what you're going to say before you say it. But God *wants* you to talk with Him! And if you will pray and ask Him to strengthen you to do good, He won't let you down.

MAKE A NOTE OF IT

Write in your notebook the following statements, all of which describe God. The scriptures listed below are about God. Read each of the verses, then match the scriptures about God with the statements about God. Two scriptures match each statement. Write the matching scripture references next to the attribute of God it describes.

- » God exists.
- » God is the one true God.
- » God is invisible.
- » God is a personal being.
- » God is eternal.
- » God is immutable.
- » God is holy.
- » God is omniscient.
- » God is omnipotent.
- » God is omnipresent.

Isaiah 40:28, 1 John 3:20, Psalm 139:7–10, Jeremiah 16:17, 1 Corinthians 8:4–6, Job 34:10, Psalm 65:6–7, Psalm 90:2, 1 Chronicles 17:20, Luke 1:37, Exodus 3:14, John 4:24, 1 John 4:9, James 1:17, Psalm 102:24–27, Psalm 145:17, Deuteronomy 4:39, Isaiah 55:8–9, 1 Timothy 6:16

WHAT SHOULD I DO?

You have learned that God is all knowing, all powerful, and always present throughout creation. You have learned that He has always existed and always will and is the one and only God. You have also learned that He is holy, completely without sin, and that He will never change. Now you have a choice. How will you respond to the entirely wondrous nature of

God? Will you choose to know Him, love Him, and obey Him? Or will you choose to make your own god out of earthly things like money, popularity, or talent? Will you worship the eternal God and glorify Him because of who He is, or will you spend your time and money glorifying an athlete or actor or musician whose career will last several years at best?

When confronted by the awesome grandeur of God, if we truly understand how amazing He is and the incredible depth of His love for us, the only way our hearts can respond is by showing **reverence** for Him. Reverence is respect for God. While people may be worthy of respect and honor, reverence is for God alone. "It is the LORD your God you must follow, and him you must revere" (Deuteronomy 13:4). We demonstrate reverence by knowing, loving, and obeying Him and by telling others about the only true, almighty, and eternal God. Revering God includes worshiping Him through prayer and praise, adoring His perfection, and giving our lives to serve Him. It means having a healthy respect for His power and acknowledging Him as King over all creation and ruler over every part of our lives.

A PRAYER

Father God, thank you for showing me who you are. You are Almighty God who knows all things and sees all things. You have always been alive and always will be. You are with me wherever I go. There is nowhere I can hide from your love. You are holy, Lord, without sin, and you will never change. I can always trust you completely, and I know you will always love me. Help me to know you better. And help me to live every day in a way that pleases you. Amen.

HOW A WORLDVIEW IS LIKE A CAKE

All people have a worldview—a set of beliefs that helps them to understand life and the world—and this worldview influences how they act or behave. However, if you were to ask someone, "Do you have a worldview?" or "Can you tell me about your worldview?" he or she would probably just stare at you with a puzzled look. But why?

As you learned earlier, you don't deliberately set out to develop a worldview. You absorb your basic beliefs about life and the world by observing your family, your community, and the world around you. You develop your worldview from the teaching of others and through your own studying, reasoning, and imagining. But as your worldview is being shaped, you never stop and think, *Now, let's see. This belief goes with my beliefs about God. And this belief goes with my beliefs about people. And this new belief goes with my beliefs about the universe. And all of these beliefs are part of my worldview!* In other words, although you have a worldview, you don't consciously think about it as you go about your daily activities. Just as people who wear glasses or contacts don't think or say, "I'm looking at the sunset through my glasses," people don't think or say, "I'm looking at the world through my worldview, and I'm making choices each day because of my beliefs about God, the universe, people, truth, and right and wrong."

Let's compare a worldview with a cake. People all over the world bake cakes. Most cakes contain at least five basic ingredients—milk, eggs, flour, sugar, and butter. After you gather the ingredients together, do you know how to make a cake? First you measure each ingredient according to a recipe. Then you mix the ingredients together to make a batter. Next you pour the batter into a baking pan and put it in the oven to bake. When the cake is done, you let it cool, slice it, and enjoy!

Now suppose you give slices of your freshly baked cake to some friends. As they take their first bite, would you expect them to say, "Wow! This is delicious. I just love the flour. And the eggs, well, they're just fantastic. I really like the taste of the milk. And what kind of butter and sugar did you use? I've never tasted anything like them!"? Of course not. No one ever responds this way when eating a piece of cake. But why not? It's because they don't taste each ingredient by itself. All the ingredients have been blended together into a batter that, when baked, produces a cake with its own unique taste and texture.

Now if your friends want to bake a cake like yours for themselves, what would they need? They would need the recipe that would tell them how much of each ingredient to use, how to mix the batter, and at what temperature and for how long the cake needs to bake.

Can you see how a worldview is somewhat like a cake? All the beliefs of a worldview blend together to produce a particular view of the world. People don't think about the categories of their beliefs every time they look at the world or before they act in a certain way any more than they think about the ingredients that make up the cake they are eating. But if you take time to analyze what goes into your worldview, you'll find that it's also made up of ingredients—ingredients of beliefs. And like cakes that people around the world make with flour, sugar, butter, milk, and eggs, your worldview includes the ingredients of beliefs about God, the universe, people, truth, and right and wrong.

DOES OUR WORLDVIEW EVER CHANGE?

Think about some of the changes you've seen in the world during the last several years of your life. Technology has advanced. Televisions have become larger while our phones have gotten smaller. Clothing and hair styles have changed. New names and faces have appeared on our magazine covers. Even our nation's leaders have changed.

Now think about the changes in your own life over the past several years. The books you're reading are longer, and the topics of the books have changed to reflect your changing interests. Your circle of friends has probably changed. You may even live in a different city or state. You know much more than you did when you were younger, and you understand better how the world works.

We learn new things throughout our lives. Through observing, teaching, studying, reasoning, and imagining, our worldview changes over time. *This does not mean that truth changes.* It means that our understanding of what is true and what is not true changes over time. All Christians grow in their understanding of God's truth, and as they grow, their Christian worldview changes. As you study the subject of worldviews, you will find your own worldview changing—perhaps a little or perhaps a lot.

We do not change our worldviews easily. We hold them deep within our hearts, even if we don't think about them very often, if at all. For example, how easy would it be for you to change your beliefs about the existence of God or the truth that all people are equally created in God's image? How easy would it be for you to change your mind about the need to love and care for others? Would you ever accept as part of your worldview the belief that stealing and cheating are good behaviors?

For people to change their worldview, they have to realize that what they have believed about life and the world is not true. For example, if a young boy from one race or nationality is taught that another race or nationality is inferior, he may treat people from the other race or nationality with little respect or even ignore them altogether. But suppose one day the prejudiced boy meets a boy of the race or nationality he's learned to disrespect. Day after day, he observes this other person. He discovers that this boy is intelligent. He has feelings and laughs and cries just like all people do. This person is friendly and does his work well. This person is part of a loving family, with parents who love him and strive to teach him and provide for him. What do you think may begin to happen to the prejudiced boy's worldview? How might it begin to change?

When we realize that what we believe about life and the world does not really line up or agree with what we observe or know, we have to make one of two choices. In the example of prejudice against others, one choice we can make is to hold on to our prejudiced beliefs. We can choose to do this even though our worldview beliefs don't agree with the truth we have come to know about people of other races. Another choice we can make is to admit that what we believe is wrong and therefore change our beliefs. This is not an easy choice. It requires humility and a willingness to change. A change in our worldview should lead to changes in our actions and behaviors.

People want and need a worldview that agrees with the truth they see in people and the world around them. Of course, some people choose not to accept the truth even when they see and understand it. This choice usually leads to an unhappy conflict in their minds and hearts.

MAKE A NOTE OF IT
Pretend your friend is having a difficult time trying to make sense of the world. She believes many things, but she's having trouble sorting out all her beliefs. You decide to use the illustration of a cake to help her think more clearly about what she believes. Write out what you would say to your friend.

THE HOUSE OF TRUTH: THE SECOND STONE

Remember our House of Truth? When fully completed, the House of Truth will help you remember what God says in the Bible about Himself, who you are, and how God expects you to live.

Wise people build foundations of wisdom by first knowing God and His truth. Then they continue to build foundations of wisdom by loving God and by obeying the truth He speaks to them. In lessons 3 and 4 we laid the second stone of truth in the foundation of our House of Truth:

BIBLICAL TRUTH 2

God is the only true and almighty God.

Biblical Truth 2
God is the only true and almighty God

FOUNDATION OF WISDOM
Knowing, loving, and obeying God my Rock

THE ROCK
God and His Word

WHO ARE THE FATHER THE SON, AND THE HOLY SPIRIT?

> MAY THE GRACE OF THE LORD JESUS CHRIST, AND THE LOVE OF GOD, AND THE FELLOWSHIP OF THE HOLY SPIRIT BE WITH YOU ALL.

2 CORINTHIANS 13:14

THE BIG IDEA

You have learned many things about what God is like. You've learned that He is the one true God, who is a personal being yet is invisible. You've learned that God is eternal, holy, and unchanging. And you have learned that God is omnipotent, omnipresent, and omniscient. In this lesson you will study a truth about God that is difficult to explain, but is an important truth that Christians believe by faith through study of the Bible.

Many people believe there is a God who created the heavens and earth. And many people believe in Jesus and what He taught. What many people don't believe is that Jesus is God's Son and that He is also God. They think that Jesus was just a good teacher who lived on earth many years ago. However, the Bible tells us that Jesus is truly God. It also tells us that the Holy Spirit is God. Some people accuse Christians of believing in three different Gods. They say that God the Father is one god, Jesus the Son is another god, and the Holy Spirit is a third god. You'll remember from Lesson 3 that a polytheist is a person who believes in more than one god.

The Bible tells us, however, that God is not three gods. He is one God in three Persons—Father, Son, and Holy Spirit. This is called the **Trinity**. It means that God is one God in three Persons. He is God the Father, God the Son, and God the Holy Spirit. This may seem difficult to fully understand, and indeed it is. But God is greater than our understanding. This great truth of the Trinity is one that the Bible reveals to us and we believe to be true by faith.

People like to find word pictures or diagrams to help us understand the Trinity. For example, the book *3 in 1: A Picture of God* by Joanne Marxhausen uses an apple to help us "see" the meaning of the Trinity. The apple has three parts—peel, flesh, and core—but it is still one apple. An equilateral triangle has three equal sides and angles, but it is still one triangle. Legend has it that Patrick, the patron saint of Ireland, taught the Irish people about the Trinity by using a three-leaf clover, or shamrock. As helpful as these diagrams and word pictures are, there is really no perfect way to illustrate the Trinity. For this reason, it is important to know what the Bible tells us about it.

WHAT YOU WILL DO

» You will learn why the word *Trinity* describes the one true God in three Persons.
» You will explore scriptures that tell us God the Father is God, His Son Jesus is God, and the Holy Spirit is God.
» You will identify the special responsibilities that each Person of the Trinity fulfills.
» You will lay the third foundational stone in your House of Truth: *God is God the Father, God the Son, and God the Holy Spirit.*

ANGEL FALLS

Deep in the jungles of Venezuela is the world's highest waterfall, Angel Falls. At 979 meters, or 3,212 feet, this wonder of nature is fifteen times higher than Niagara Falls in North America. The height of the falls is so great that before getting anywhere near the ground, the water is vaporized by strong winds and turned into mist. In the indigenous Pemon language, Angel Falls is called *Kerepakupai merú*, meaning "waterfall of the deepest place."

Photo: Yosemite

Despite their magnificence, the falls were not known to the outside world until an American bush pilot from Missouri, Jimmie Angel, flew over them on November 16, 1933, while searching for a legendary deposit of gold ore. He returned four years later with his wife, Marie, and two other companions. Jimmie tried to land his Flamingo monoplane atop the plateau above the falls, but the plane was damaged when the wheels sunk into the marshy ground, and the expedition was forced to descend the *tepui*, or table-top mountain, on foot. It took them eleven days to make their way back to civilization, but news of their adventure spread, and the waterfall was later named Angel Falls in Jimmie's honor.

Today, Angel Falls is one of Venezuela's top tourist attractions, but a trip to the falls is not a simple affair. Because of the dense jungle surrounding the falls, this gift from God to mankind is still best seen from the air.

ONE + ONE + ONE = ONE

"Okay, boys, up to bed. Tomorrow's Sunday," said Mr. Simmons. "You can read for thirty minutes, but then it's lights out."

"What are we gonna do tomorrow?" asked Ben, always ready for another adventure in the mountains.

"We'll go to church, rest a bit, and then probably drive up to Three Falls lookout for a picnic. There's a spectacular waterfall I think you'd like to see. And we can do some hiking if you're up for it," answered Mr. Simmons.

"That sounds super," Ben said as he and Jeremy headed up the stairs.

"I'm gonna sleep on the floor in my bedroll," Jeremy said as he grabbed a book off the shelf and rolled out his sleeping bag.

"Whatcha gonna read?"

"I'm on the last chapter of *Prince Caspian*," said Jeremy as he wriggled down into the bedroll. "I think I can finish it tonight. It's my favorite book in the Chronicles of Narnia."

"I've never heard of the Chronicles of Narnia, and besides, I don't read much," said Ben. "I'd rather watch TV or play video games."

"I bet you'd like these books," said Jeremy as he tried to continue reading.

"Hey, what's this book about?" Ben pulled a thin book off the shelf and looked at its cover. "It says *3 in 1: A Picture of God*, and it's got a picture of an apple on the front. I thought you said God was invisible. I bet if we could see Him he wouldn't look like an apple!" he joked.

"Of course not," laughed Jeremy, although he was growing annoyed at Ben for interrupting his reading. "It's a book about the Trinity. You know, God the Father, God the Son, and God the Holy Spirit."

"I thought you said there was only one God," said Ben with a perplexed frown. "Now I really am confused."

"Oh, Ben," said Jeremy as he marked his place in his book, "I know it may sound confusing, but the Bible tells us that the one true God exists as three Persons— the Father, the Son, and the Holy Spirit. Read the book. I think it'll help you picture what God is like. But remember, it's not a real picture of God. We can't really explain the Trinity with any pictures or examples on earth. It's like a great mystery about God that we believe by faith."

"But I don't even know what the word 'trinity' means," said Ben, still confused.

"It's not a word in the Bible," answered Jeremy, closing his book with a sigh. "But it's a word that means 'three in unity.' You take the letters 'tri,' meaning 'three,' and put them together with the last four letters of the word *unity*, and you get 'Trinity.' It means God the Father, God the Son, and God the Holy Spirit living together in unity as one God."

"Sorry to ask so many questions," said Ben, as he began to read. "It's just that I don't know much about God like you do."

"It's okay, Ben," replied Jeremy. "I have lots of questions about God too. And so do most people. That's why we need to study the Bible, and even then we won't have every answer to every question we ask. There are some things about God we'll never know because He's so great. But don't worry—the most important things about God that He wants us to know are in the Bible."

"Lights out, boys," called Mr. Simmons up the stairs. "Sleep well. See you in the morning. And don't forget to say your prayers."

"Wow, your family sure prays a lot," sighed Ben as he pulled the covers up. "Do you think God really listens to you and answers?"

"I know He does," said Jeremy.

"But I don't know how to pray," replied Ben with a yawn.

"Just talk to God like you'd talk to a friend. You can thank Him for things, ask Him to help other people, and of course you can ask Him to help you. And you can pray out loud or silently."

"I'll just pray silently," said Ben, gazing up at the dark ceiling.

"I will too," said Jeremy. "See you in the morning."

As the early morning sun began to creep into Jeremy's bedroom, Mr. Simmons opened the door. Ben had kicked off his covers and was sleeping with his head at the foot of his bed. Jeremy had disappeared deep into his bedroll. The books they had been reading still lay open on the floor.

"Rise and shine, boys," said Mr. Simmons, noticing the blankets, bedroll, and books. "You must have been fighting tigers in your sleep, Ben," he laughed. "And Jeremy, you look like a bear in hibernation."

Jeremy's head emerged from the bedroll. Both boys opened their sleepy eyes, looked around, and began to laugh.

"Breakfast will be ready in about thirty minutes," said Mr. Simmons.

"That was a great breakfast, Mrs. Simmons," said Ben on the way to church. "I love pancakes."

"You're quite welcome," she replied. "I'm glad you liked them."

As Mr. Simmons pulled into the church parking lot, Jeremy explained to Ben, "We'll go to the worship service first with my parents and then to my Sunday school class."

As they entered the church, Ben looked around with curiosity at the beautiful windows, the altar with the cross, and the pulpit. "Wow," he whispered loudly. "This is beautiful. I've never been to a church before. I don't know what to do."

"Don't worry," Jeremy whispered back. "I'll explain the parts of the service as we go along."

As the service began, the congregation stood and sang:

"Holy, Holy, Holy,
Lord God Almighty,
Early in the morning
Our song shall rise to Thee.
Holy, Holy, Holy, merciful and mighty,
God in Three Persons, Blessed Trinity."

"There's that word 'Trinity' again," whispered Ben.

"Yeah. And did you notice the other words—'God in Three Persons'?" Jeremy asked softly.

As Pastor Williams began his sermon, Ben tried to listen attentively.

"God the Father loved each of us so much that He sent His Son to die on the cross for our sins," said the pastor. "And when we turn from our sins and receive Jesus, who is God the Son, as our Lord and Savior, God the Holy Spirit comes to live in our hearts."

Ben nudged Jeremy quietly as he held up three fingers close to his lap. Jeremy nodded and smiled.

After the sermon, Pastor Williams announced, "Today we are very happy because Emma Grace Roberts has received Jesus as her Savior and is going to be baptized."

As Ben watched and listened with great curiosity, he heard Pastor Williams say, "Emma Grace Roberts, I baptize you in the name of the Father, and of the Son, and of the Holy Spirit."

Ben nudged Jeremy again softly. He didn't say anything, but Jeremy knew what he meant.

On the way home, Ben said to Jeremy's parents, "I really liked going to your church. And you know something really interesting? Last night I read Jeremy's book *3 in 1*. It was about the Trinity. Then we sang about the Trinity, and the pastor talked about the Father, Son, and Holy Spirit in his sermon and then again during the baptism. It seems like the words 'Father,' 'Son,' 'Holy Spirit,' and 'Trinity' are everywhere."

"Actually, Ben," replied Mrs. Simmons, "it's not just that the words seem to be everywhere—the Trinity actually *is* everywhere. Each Person of the Trinity is everywhere all the time. The Father, Son, and Holy Spirit are equally God and equally present everywhere at the same time."

Photo: www.flickr.com, jasonb42882

"O-kaaay," said Ben, trying to understand everything he had read and heard in such a short time. Then he remembered the plans for the afternoon. "Are we still going to the Three Falls lookout, Mr. Simmons?" he asked.

"We sure are, and remember to wear shoes you can do some hiking in," replied Mr. Simmons.

After changing clothes, everyone piled back into the car and headed for the falls. The road snaked into Black Rock Canyon and followed the roaring Cougar River. As the road began to twist and climb deeper into the canyon, the river seemed to play hide-and-seek. Sometimes it was visible, but at other times it disappeared behind huge boulders and trees.

"Get ready, Ben," said Mr. Simmons with excitement in his voice. "Just around this next turn in the road you're going to see something really beautiful."

"Wow!" exclaimed Ben as he caught his first view of Three Falls. "That's so cool! Three waterfalls in one place."

"We'll eat lunch at the lookout and then hike closer," said Mr. Simmons.

"Are there three rivers flowing over the rocks from above?" asked Ben as he stuffed another bite of cheese sandwich into his mouth.

"No," said Mr. Simmons. "All three waterfalls come from the Cougar River. Just at the top of that cliff, the rock formations force the river into three separate channels. Each channel flows over the cliff as a separate waterfall. Then at the bottom of the falls there's a small pool where the water from each of the falls comes back together. From there, the Cougar River flows on down the canyon as one river again."

"Is that kind of like the Trinity?" asked Ben. "You know—one river with three waterfalls but still one river?"

"Well, you might think of the Trinity like that," Mr. Simmons replied. "There is one God, like the one Cougar River. And there are the three Persons of the Trinity, like the three waterfalls. Although each fall is unique, each one is still part of the one Cougar River. And just as God the Father, Son, and Holy Spirit are unique Persons, they are still the one true God. But you must remember something very important, Ben: There is really no perfect illustration of the Trinity. For example, the three waterfalls are separate from each other. The Father, Son, and Holy Spirit are always in unity. Any physical illustration or picture we make to help us understand the Trinity is incomplete and can't really show the absolute unity of the three but distinct Persons. We believe in the Trinity because the Bible tells us that the Father, Son, and Holy Spirit are equally God. It's one of the mysteries of our Christian faith, but it's very important. Maybe you can remember it this way: One plus One plus One equals One," Mr. Simmons suggested. "Now come on. Here's the trail to the top of the falls. You'll see up there that each waterfall is part of the same Cougar River."

As everyone began the steep hike up the trail, Ben's eyes were on the trail, but his mind was on everything he had heard, read, and seen since Saturday night. He prayed quietly, "God, please help me to know you. Help me to know what you're like. And thank you for making it possible for me to come and visit Jeremy and his family this summer."

THINK ABOUT IT

» On the outing to Three Falls lookout, Ben was searching for a "picture" that would help him understand the biblical truth about the Trinity. How did Mr. Simmons wisely answer Ben when he compared Three Falls with the Trinity?

» Why do you suppose there is no perfect example or picture that explains the Trinity?

» What do you see happening to Ben during his visit with Jeremy's family?

HOLY, HOLY, HOLY

A hymn is a traditional song of praise or worship written to God. Today, many churches sing fewer traditional hymns and instead sing more contemporary songs of worship. Yet traditional hymns continue to move us with profound words and beautiful music that engage our minds and lift our hearts to heaven.

One of the most famous Christian hymns is "Holy, Holy, Holy." The words were written by an English bishop, Reginald Heber, who was born in 1783. He wanted a special song to help teach the truth of the Trinity—that God is made up of three Persons in one God. He wrote it especially to be sung on Trinity Sunday, which was celebrated eight Sundays after Easter. Listen to the words of the first verse:

> Holy, holy, holy! Lord God Almighty!
> Early in the morning our song shall rise to Thee.
> Holy, holy, holy, merciful and mighty!
> God in Three Persons, blessèd Trinity!

Over the past two centuries this hymn has become so popular that it is now sung throughout the year. Why? Because it expresses many wonderful truths about who God is and why He is worthy of our love and praise, as in the third verse:

> Holy, holy, holy! though the darkness hide Thee,
> Though the eye of sinful man Thy glory may not see.
> Only Thou art holy; there is none beside Thee,
> Perfect in power, in love, and purity.

If your family does not own a hymnal, or book of hymns, borrow one from your local library. Many of the songs can even be heard on the Internet. The great hymns of the past can help you to understand and remember the teachings of the Bible so that you can become more like Christ each day.

WORDS YOU NEED TO KNOW

» **Mystery:** Anything that cannot be understood without the revelation of the Holy Spirit
» **Trinity:** One God in three Persons—the Father, the Son, and the Holy Spirit
» **Lord:** A name for God meaning He is the master, owner, and ruler of all things
» **Sovereign:** Having supreme authority
» **Immanuel:** A name for Jesus meaning "God with us"
» **Loyalty:** Continuing faithfulness in loving and serving God and others

HIDE IT IN YOUR HEART

May the grace of the Lord Jesus Christ, and the love of God, and the fellowship of the Holy Spirit be with you all. (2 Corinthians 13:14)

He who pursues righteousness and loyalty finds life, righteousness and honor. (Proverbs 21:21, NASB)

GOD IS THE LORD

You have seen the word **Lord** already used many times in this book. So who are we talking about when we refer to the Lord? The word *Lord* is used in the Bible to refer to each member of the Trinity—God the Father, God the Son, and God the Holy Spirit—though the Bible also makes it perfectly clear that there is only one God:

So remember this and keep it firmly in mind: The LORD is God both in heaven and on earth, and there is no other (Deuteronomy 4:39, NLT).

"There is no one like you, O LORD, and there is no God but you, as we have heard with our own ears" (1 Chronicles 17:20).

One name for God, the Hebrew word *Adonai*, means "lord, master, or owner." When we call God "Lord," we are calling Him the master, owner, and ruler of all things. We are saying that He is **sovereign** (SOV-uh-ren), meaning that He has supreme authority over all things. We are declaring His rightful place as King of the universe and that He has the authority to tell us how to live our lives. Can you think of anyone better qualified for the job?

"Do any of the worthless idols of the nations bring rain? Do the skies themselves send down showers? No, it is you, O LORD our God. Therefore our hope is in you, for you are the one who does all this." (Jeremiah 14:22)

Scripture tells us that those who call God their Lord are blessed indeed:

Yes, joyful are those who live like this! Joyful indeed are those whose God is the LORD. (Psalm 144:15)

So who is the Lord? The Lord is God.
Who is our God? The Lord is our God.
Who is God? God is the Lord.

GOD IS GOD THE FATHER

You were born to a mother and a father, a woman and a man. It is your parents' job, assigned by God, to protect you and provide for your needs and to raise you, under their authority, according to God's laws and His design for your life. You are their child. But you are also a child of God. Before He formed you in your mother's womb, He knew you. He created you and nurtures you and provides for you, and so He is your Father in heaven, or your *heavenly Father*. He is God the Father, the first Person of the Trinity:

The Creation of the Sun and Moon (detail), by Michelangelo

Yet, O LORD, you are our Father. We are the clay, you are the potter; we are all the work of your hand. (Isaiah 64:8)

Have we not all one Father? Did not one God create us? (Malachi 2:10)

Your heavenly Father has been raising sons and daughters for thousands of years. He knows and understands your needs and struggles. You can be thankful that He created you for a purpose, that He placed you in a particular nation, race, and culture. He does not make mistakes, and He has a long-term plan for your well-being. He specially selected the unique set of parents He gave you; therefore you should thank God for your parents and always honor them, as commanded in Ephesians 6:2.

God is a special Father to those who no longer have an earthly father. The Bible calls Him the "Father of the fatherless" (Psalm 68:5). King David wrote, "When my father and my mother forsake me, then the LORD will take me up" (Psalm 27:10). God the Father is ready and willing to care for those whose fathers have died or are no longer with the family. In fact, He invites each of us to have such a close and special relationship with Him that, through our faith in Jesus, we may call God "Abba," just as Jesus does. (*Abba* is an intimate Hebrew word meaning "daddy.") How does one be-

come a child of God? A person becomes His child by placing his or her trust in Jesus Christ as Lord so that their sins can be forgiven. They are then adopted into His family. Each one of us can make a choice to belong to Him.

But God does not merely adopt us then disappear from the scene! He wants to be *with* us, talking with us and walking with us every day of our lives, whether we begin to know Him at age six or sixty. When we begin the Christian life, we all start out as "little children" in the family of God (Matthew 18:3). He sends His Holy Spirit to live in our hearts, to guide us, and we soon begin to grow by feeding on the Word of God. And yes, like all children, we will make some mistakes along the way. But like a good earthly father, our heavenly Father will discipline and correct us because He loves us:

My child, don't reject the LORD's discipline, and don't be upset when he corrects you. For the LORD corrects those he loves, just as a father corrects a child in whom he delights. (Proverbs 3:11–12)

If we listen to our Father and obey Him, we will grow to become mature men and women of faith "encouraged in heart and united in love, so that [we] may have the full riches of complete understanding in order that [we] may know the mystery of God, namely, Christ, in whom are hidden all the treasures of wisdom and knowledge" (Colossians 2:2).

MAKE A NOTE OF IT

Write this verse in your notebook: "See how very much our Father loves us, for he calls us his children, and that is what we are! But the people who belong to this world don't recognize that we are God's children because they don't know him" (1 John 3:1, NLT). Now think of two ways some people show that they do not recognize Christians as children of God and write these down.

GOD IS GOD THE SON

You and I are adopted children of God, but the Bible calls Jesus the "only begotten Son" of God (John 3:16, 1 John 4:9, NKJV). The phrase "only begotten" is translated from a Greek compound word that comes from the words *monos*, meaning "only," and *gennesis*, meaning "birth." Jesus was born as a human child made from the very essence of God, so that He is the only Son of God by nature. As the one and only Son of God, during His time on earth He was able to reveal the Father to us like no other person before or since.

Jesus Saying Farewell to His Mother by Strigel

Jesus is God the Son, the second Person of the Trinity. Unlike you and me, Jesus was not created. Like God the Father, He is eternal, having no beginning and no end. The Bible calls Him the living Word who has always existed:

In the beginning was the Word, and the Word was with God, and the Word was God. He was with God in the beginning. Through him all things were made; without him nothing was made that has been made. (John 1:1–3)

Another name for Jesus in the Bible is **Immanuel**, which means "God with us" (Matthew 1:23). That's because Jesus is God. He shares all the same attributes of God the Father, including being omniscient, omnipotent, and omnipresent. The Bible tells us that, from the beginning, Jesus "was like God in everything. He was equal with God. But he did not think that being equal with God was something to be held on to. He gave up his place with God in heaven and made himself nothing" (Philippians 2:6–7, ICB). He allowed Himself to be born as a human baby to a lowly family with no wealth or social status. As a child in the village of Nazareth, Jesus learned to work and study, and He played and laughed and helped His parents as you do. He was also faced with all the same temptations that challenge you and me, and yet He never sinned (Hebrews 4:15).

As a man of about thirty, Jesus began traveling the countryside teaching about the Father and His kingdom. He only taught what the Father told Him to say. He was called Messiah and the Christ, literally the "anointed one." Jesus attracted a great many followers, but He called twelve of them to be apostles, or "sent ones," whom He trained and taught and

THE JESUS FILM PROJECT

The life of Jesus has inspired artists, composers, and writers for nearly two thousand years. Almost from the time the cinema was invented, movie-makers have attempted to portray the events of Christ's life on film. Of the many black-and-white silent movies made about Jesus, perhaps the most famous is the 1927 film *The King of Kings*, directed by Cecil B. DeMille and starring H. B. Warner as Jesus. Warner went on to appear in several beloved films including *Lost Horizon* and *It's a Wonderful Life*.

The JESUS Film Project

Since that time, more than 250 movies have been made in which Jesus is portrayed by one or more actors. Yet many of these have been criticized by people in the church for inaccurate or incomplete depictions of the Gospels. Then in 1979, the ministry Campus Crusade for Christ made a movie simply called *Jesus* in an attempt to show people how Jesus lived and died for everyone. They based their script on the Gospel of Luke, because it provides the most complete record of what happened while Christ was on earth.

They tried to make the movie as accurate as possible, asking Bible scholars to check all the details. When they found that several scenes showed eucalyptus trees, which didn't grow in the region in Jesus' time, they chose to go back and shoot those scenes again to get everything just right. The movie was filmed in the Middle East, where Jesus lived, and actor Brian Deacon was selected to play Jesus because he looked like someone who might have lived in Jesus' time.

Although the movie was largely unsuccessful on its initial release in the United States, Campus Crusade decided to translate it into many different languages, so that people who didn't speak English could learn about Jesus too. Two years later, they started shipping the movie to countries around the world. Today, the *Jesus* film has been translated into more than a thousand languages, from Arabic to Zulu, and more than 1,800 teams of people are working in countries around the world to show the movie. Sometimes the teams must transport generators, lights, and projection equipment a long way to reach places where people have never seen a film or heard about Jesus.

The movie is now all but forgotten in Hollywood, but it has been shown in so many big cities and tiny villages in so many countries that the *Jesus* film is sometimes described as the most-watched movie of all time. It's estimated that between 175 million and 225 million people have come to believe in Jesus after seeing the film. It's amazing how God has used one movie to change the lives of so many people!

sent into the world to make followers of everyone who believed their message. Some of His followers wanted Jesus to make Himself an earthly king, to destroy the Roman armies who then occupied Jerusalem. However, Jesus told them that He did not come to be served but "to serve others" and to give His life to pay for the sins of many (Mark 10:45).

He was and is the ultimate expression of God's love for us. In everything, Jesus obeyed His Father, even when obedience meant allowing Himself to be killed on a cross, a form of death reserved for only the worst criminals. He died on a Friday. He was wrapped in strips of linen, and His body was anointed with special oils and fragrances. He was laid in a garden tomb, then a large stone was rolled into place to seal the entrance. On Sunday morning He appeared to Mary Magdalene, who stood outside the tomb crying because she found the stone rolled away and thought that the Lord's body had been stolen. He later spoke to many hundreds of His followers so that they would know that He lived and was returning to His Father's side in heaven:

> *So God raised Christ to the highest place. God made the name of Christ greater than every other name. God wants every knee to bow to Jesus—everyone in heaven, on earth, and under the earth. Everyone will say, "Jesus Christ is Lord" and bring glory to God the Father.* (Philippians 2:9–11, ICB)

> *Now Christ has gone to heaven. He is seated in the place of honor next to God, and all the angels and authorities and powers accept his authority.* (1 Peter 3:22, NLT)

One day, when He returns to the earth, if we believe that Jesus is the only begotten Son of God, you and I will live with Him and the Father in heaven forever (John 3:16). When we realize that the one and only Son of God gave His life to save you and me, we cannot help but be overcome with awe, thankfulness, and a deep sense of wonder and reverence.

MAKE A NOTE OF IT
Write this verse in your notebook: "He came to the world that was his own. But his own people did not accept him. But some people did accept him. They believed in him. To them he gave the right to become children of God" (John 1:11–12, ICB). Now write about why you think that many people who met Jesus did not recognize Him for who He is. Why do many people today still fail to recognize Him as God the Son?

GOD IS GOD THE HOLY SPIRIT

The third Person of the Trinity is God the Holy Spirit. For centuries He was called the Holy Ghost, and an air of mystery, if not spookiness, surrounded His Person. In the Old Testament, which was written in Hebrew, the word used to talk about the Spirit literally means "wind." In the New Testament, which was written mostly in Greek, the word used to talk about the Spirit means "breath." Sometimes the Holy Spirit is called the Breath of God.

There has been much confusion over who or what the Holy Spirit is. Many people throughout the ages have thought of the Spirit more as a thing than a Person. Nothing could be further from the truth! He is God—a "He," not an "it." There's nothing spooky about Him at all. He is an expression of the God who created you, loves you, redeemed you, and longs for you to know Him better. In fact, as you begin to know the Person of the Holy Spirit, you will want to have a closer relationship with Him.

Photo: www.flickr.com, IdeacreamanuelaPps

So who is the Holy Spirit? The Bible tells us "the Lord is the Spirit" (2 Corinthians 3:17). We know that the Lord is God and that there is only one God. Therefore, the Spirit must be God. He was with the Father and the Son in the beginning and participated in the creation of all things (Genesis 1:2). He shares all the same attributes of God the Father and God the Son, including being omniscient, omnipotent, and omnipresent. Just like the Father and the Son, God the Holy Spirit is a personal being who has thoughts and emotions and makes choices:

For his Spirit searches out everything and shows us God's deep secrets. . . . . No one can know God's thoughts except God's own Spirit. (1 Corinthians 2:10–11, NLT)

And do not bring sorrow to God's Holy Spirit by the way you live. (Ephesians 4:30, NLT)

While they were worshiping the Lord and fasting, the Holy Spirit said, "Set apart for me Barnabas and Saul for the work to which I have called them." (Acts 13:2)

As you can see from these Bible passages, the Holy Spirit has a mind—He thinks and knows all that the Father and the Son know. He has emotions and can feel sorrow (and joy). He also has a will—He can make decisions and give commands. He knows right from wrong, and obviously, He is a spiritual being. This is how we know that He is a person.

But the most amazing truth about the Holy Spirit is that He lives inside you! The Bible calls your body "the temple of God" because the Spirit lives there (1 Corinthians 3:16). When you chose to become a follower of Jesus, when you first believed that He is the one and only Son of God, God sent His Spirit to live in your heart to be with you and to help you. So just what is He doing in there? Here's a short list:

1. He teaches you (John 14:26).
2. He guides you (John 16:13–15).
3. He prays for you (Romans 8:26–27).

4. He helps you to remember and understand the Word of God (John 14:26).
5. He gives you gifts that help you to help others (1 Corinthians 12).
6. He helps you to act more like Jesus (Galatians 5:16–26).

In fact, the Spirit helps us to grow as Christians so that we will have the same character-istics that Jesus displayed during His time on earth. These characteristics are called "the fruit of the Spirit," and they include "love, joy, peace, patience, kindness, goodness, faithfulness, gentleness and self-control" (Galatians 5:22–23). When you add it all up, the main job of the Holy Spirit is to reveal Jesus to us, just as Jesus revealed the Father to us. Jesus said:

Holy Trinity, a fresco by Luca Rossetti da Orta at the St. Gaudenzio Church in Turin, Italy. The Holy Spirit is often portrayed in art as a dove, as He appeared in this form at the baptism of Jesus.

> *"When the Spirit of truth comes, he will guide you into all truth. He will not speak on his own but will tell you what he has heard. . . . He will bring me glory by telling you what-ever he receives from me."* (John 16:13–14, NLT)

The Holy Spirit also speaks to people who don't believe in God, drawing them to Him by helping them to understand their need for His forgiveness and revealing to them the truth about Jesus (John 16:8–9).

THE FATHER, SON, AND HOLY SPIRIT WORK TOGETHER

As you have read, there is only one God, but He exists in three Persons. These Persons are equal and eternal and are unified in purpose. Although each of these Persons has special re-sponsibilities, not one of them does anything apart from the other two. The three Persons of the Trinity always work in harmony as one God. For example, although the Father is called the Creator, the Bible shows us that the Son and the Spirit also take part in the act of creation:

In the beginning God created the heavens and the earth . . . and the Spirit of God was hovering over the waters. (Genesis 1:1–2)

For the Spirit of God has made me, and the breath of the Almighty gives me life. (Job 33:4)

Through his power all things were made— things in heaven and on earth, things seen and unseen, all powers, authorities, lords and rulers. All things were made through Christ and for Christ. (Colossians 1:16, ICB)

According to legend, Saint Patrick used the three-leaf old white clover, or shamrock, to illustrate the three-in-one Trinity for the people of Ireland. Today, the shamrock is a registered trademark of the Irish government.

Likewise, Jesus called the Holy Spirit our Helper: "I will ask the Father, and He will give you another Helper, that He may be with you forever; that is the Spirit of truth" (John 14:16–17). However, the Bible clearly shows that the Father and the Son are also our Helper:

"So do not fear, for I am with you; do not be dismayed, for I am your God. I will strengthen you and help you." (Isaiah 41:10)

Because [Christ] himself suffered when he was tempted, he is able to help those who are being tempted. (Hebrews 2:18)

So you see, the one true God—who is God the Father, God the Son, and God the Holy Spirit—is our Helper, He is our Creator, He is our Savior, and He is our Lord. And when we are baptized, we are baptized in the name of the Father, of the Son, and of the Holy Spirit, as Jesus Himself taught us:

Jesus came and told his disciples, "I have been given all authority in heaven and on earth. Therefore, go and make disciples of all the nations, baptizing them in the name of the Father and the Son and the Holy Spirit. Teach these new disciples to obey all the commands I have given you. And be sure of this: I am with you always, even to the end of the age." (Matthew 28:18–20, NLT)

MAKE A NOTE OF IT

Write down your response to these questions: Why did Jesus tell us to baptize people in the name of the Father and the Son *and* the Holy Spirit? Why not just in Jesus' name? Did Jesus make a mistake when He told His disciples to go and baptize people in the *name* (singular) of the Father, Son, and Holy Spirit instead of in their *names* (plural)? Why not?

WHAT SHOULD I DO?

What is **loyalty**? If I tell you that you are a loyal friend, what do I mean? Loyalty is a character trait that you show by being absolutely faithful to another person with whom you have a relationship. Loyalty is a commitment you make to love, honor, and support one another even in tough times—even when one of you fails the other.

The three Persons of the Trinity exhibit perfect loyalty. Their eternal love for one another and the oneness of their fellowship show us the kind of relationship God wants us to experience with Him, with our families, and with our fellow Christians. He expects us to be loyal, to stick together "through thick and thin," to remain faithful in loving and serving Him and others:

> *He who pursues righteousness and loyalty finds life, righteousness and honor.* (Proverbs 21:21, NASB)

We demonstrate faithfulness and loyalty in our relationship with God by obeying Him, by showing reverence toward Him, and through acts of loving kindness toward others (1 John 4:20–21). We show patriotic loyalty to our city, state, and country by obeying the law (Matthew 22:21), participating in civic duties such as voting or serving on a town council, and by showing respect for the authorities which God has placed over us (1 Peter 2:17).

Loyalty remains steadfast, never changing, as modeled by the faithfulness of God toward us. The apostle Paul wrote, "For I am convinced that neither death nor life, neither angels nor demons, neither the present nor the future, nor any powers, neither height nor depth, nor anything else in all creation, will be able to separate us from the love of God that is in Christ Jesus our Lord" (Romans 8:38–39). If Almighty God is loyal to us, how can we be anything but loyal to Him?

A PRAYER

God the Father sent God the Son to die for our sins. He sent the Holy Spirit to teach us and fill our lives with love, joy, and peace. If you have never received Jesus as your Lord and Savior, you may wish to do so now. Read and pray the prayer below, asking God to save you and make you a new person.

Dear Father, I believe that Jesus is your Son. I believe that you sent Him to earth to die on the cross to take the punishment I deserve for my sins. I ask you to forgive my sins. I ask you to make me new through your Holy Spirit. Please change me to become more and more like you. Thank you for hearing my prayer. In Jesus' name. Amen.

MAKE A NOTE OF IT

Loyalty is a mark of any true friendship and of a committed relationship with God. Write down your responses to each of the following:

» What are some ways you can you show loyalty to your friends, to your church, and to your family?

» What are some ways you can you show loyalty to God?

» How would you respond to a friend who has been disloyal? How *should* you respond?

» Write about a time when you were disloyal to a friend. Think of ways you could make amends.

» Think of something that would test your loyalty to God or to a friend. How would you be able to remain loyal and pass the test? Where could you find help?

» How do you show loyalty to your country? What kinds of actions or behaviors would be considered disloyal to your country?

DOES OUR WORLDVIEW REALLY MATTER?

Read the conversation below between Joshua and Amanda. Or grab a partner and act it out between you:

Joshua: "I believe it's important to think about and know what you believe about life and the world."

Amanda: "Oh, I just sort of accept the way the world is. I don't really think about it all that much."

Joshua: "Really? Don't you think it's important to know what you believe about God? Or about what's right and wrong?"

Amanda: "What difference does it make what you believe? You can believe what you want to, and I can believe what I want to. Besides, who knows what's really right?"

Joshua: "I think what you believe makes a big difference. What you believe affects the choices you make—you know, the way you live your life."

Amanda: "It's boring to think about life and the world and all that kind of stuff. I just do what I like to do. Hey, are you going to the party at Roger's house tonight? All the cool kids will be there—cool music, great food—just lots of fun. Lots more fun than thinking about the world! And I'm wearing my new jeans. They're really *in*. Julie will be so jealous!"

Joshua: "Matt and I and some others said we'd help the coaches with the Special Olympics this afternoon. Then there's the awards ceremony and picnic afterwards. It's lots of fun and you get to meet some really neat kids."

Amanda: "Whatever! See ya later!"

As you can see from this conversation, both Joshua and Amanda have a worldview, even though Amanda seems never to have considered that her view of life and the world affects her behavior. After thinking about Joshua's and Amanda's worldviews and choices, ask yourself these questions:

1. Does it matter what worldview I have?
2. If it matters, why does it matter?

NOT ALL WORLDVIEWS EXPLAIN THE MEANING OF LIFE TRUTHFULLY

All people try to explain the meaning of life and the world by looking through their worldview (or belief) glasses. However, as you have already learned, all worldview glasses do not provide a truthful or focused view. For example, what does death mean to someone who does not believe in God? An atheist would say that death means the end of life forever. No closing credits. Finito. Over and out. Period.

Now, what does death mean to someone whose worldview includes a belief in God and the Bible? This person would say that death means the beginning of a wondrous eternal life with God for all Christians. But it also means the beginning of eternal life separated from God for all who do not believe that Jesus is God's Son and reject Him as their Savior.

If we don't have a correct or truthful worldview, the meaning we give to events such as death will be false. And an untruthful understanding of death, life, and the world leads not only to separation from God, but it will also lead to problems in our present life on earth.

Does your worldview matter? Absolutely!

As you saw in the conversation between Joshua and Amanda, worldviews influence a person's choices and actions. If we don't understand the true meaning of life and the world, we will not make right choices. And wrong choices and behaviors always lead to painful consequences. People who don't accept or believe they have to obey the law will inevitably suffer the consequences of arrest and imprisonment. And those who don't believe in God or eternal life make the choice to reject Jesus as their Savior. This choice results in the painful consequence of eternal separation from God.

Does your worldview matter? Absolutely!

THE HOUSE OF TRUTH: THE THIRD STONE

In this lesson, you took another step toward developing a worldview that is true and has eternal value. You have already chosen to construct a House of Truth by first building on the Rock who is God. You prepared the ground to build by knowing and loving God and by obeying the truth He speaks to you. Then you began laying the foundation for your house.

The first stone of truth you used to lay the foundation is that God is truth and always tells us what is right and true. The second stone of truth is that God is the only true and almighty God.

Now it's time to lay the third stone in our foundation:

BIBLICAL TRUTH 3

God is God the Father, God the Son, and God the Holy Spirit.

Biblical Truth 3
God is God the Father, Son, and Holy Spirit

FOUNDATION OF WISDOM
Knowing, loving, and obeying God my Rock

THE ROCK
God and His Word

IF GOD CREATED THE WORLD, WHY ISN'T IT PERFECT?

THE BIG IDEA

So far, you have laid down three stones of biblical truth to form your Foundation of Wisdom. These stones are truths about God that He reveals to us in the Bible. The first truth is perhaps the most important because it tells us that God exists and speaks truth to us. We can trust that every one of God's words in the Bible is absolutely true. The second truth tells us that God is the only true and almighty God. He is a personal being, not simply a force like the white stone, as Ben thought. God has a mind, a will, and emotions, and He is absolutely holy, eternal, and unchanging. In lesson 5, you added the biblical truth about the Trinity to your Foundation of Wisdom. This very important truth tells us that God is one God in three Persons—Father, Son, and Holy Spirit. Each Person of the Trinity is equally God, and each works in harmony with the other two. You learned that together They created us and saved us and continue to teach us and help us.

In this lesson, you will add the fourth stone of biblical truth to your Foundation of Wisdom. It tells us that the one true and almighty God is the Creator of everything in heaven and on earth. He created the universe, the earth, the plants, and all the animals just by speaking! He didn't need special materials or blueprints to create things. Remember—God is omnipotent! Just by the command of His voice, everything came into existence. And it was all perfect. There was peace and harmony throughout the world. Wolves lay down beside lambs without thoughts of having the lambs for dinner. Every day was perfect for a picnic. And God Himself came and walked and talked with Adam and Eve in the Garden of Eden.

So what happened that changed everything? Why do we now have tornados, floods, and earthquakes? Why is the news dominated by reports of crime, suicide, scandal, and rumors of war? Why can't we all just get along with one another? It's all because of sin. Sin entered the world and disrupted the harmony of all of creation, and we are still suffering from sin's effects and its consequences.

But have no fear. God has a plan. In fact, He had a plan from the very beginning to restore all things. And if we will trust in Him, we will one day get to see creation as God intended it to be.

WHAT YOU WILL DO

» You will identify the four relationships of creation as revealed in the Bible.
» You will contrast these relationships before and after the Fall.
» You will describe God's eternal plan for restoring harmony to His creation.
» You will lay the fourth stone of truth in your Foundation of Wisdom: *God is the Creator.*

THE HUBBLE SPACE TELESCOPE

On a clear, moonless night, far from the lights of the city, you can look up and see so many stars that it would take years to count them all. But God knows exactly how many stars He made. He even knows each star by name (Isaiah 40:26)! For thousands of years, people have looked to the sky and wondered about the stars. Many created stories to explain their presence and placement in the heavens.

Then in the seventeenth century, the Italian astronomer and mathematician Galileo Galilei, improving greatly on a Dutch design, brought the heavens closer with his development of the telescope. A telescope uses lenses and mirrors to magnify our view of things that are very far away. The bigger the telescope is, the farther you can see. The problem is that no matter how dark it is where you're standing, Earth's atmosphere limits our ability to see into the far reaches of the vastness of space.

However, one very special telescope, the Hubble Space Telescope, is actually in space, circling our planet. The telescope takes pictures of what scientists wish to see, then sends those pictures to a nearby satellite. The satellite then transmits the pictures to earth, where scientists study them carefully to learn all they can about the universe. Because the space telescope can capture images of stars too dim to see from earth, scientists are discovering many distant galaxies they didn't know existed.

The Hubble Space Telescope was launched into space in 1990. Soon after it became operational, scientists discovered the telescope had a problem: Its main mirror had been made incorrectly, and so the telescope couldn't "see" clearly. So astronauts, working from the space shuttle, were sent to repair the telescope. Since then, the Hubble Space Telescope has sent us numerous never-before-seen images of God's creation. The space telescope has helped scientists measure how fast the universe is expanding and discover other planets orbiting other suns. It even took pictures of a comet crashing into the planet Jupiter!

CAMPOUT ON COUGAR RIVER

"How did you like Three Falls lookout?" Mr. Simmons asked on the way back into town after their Sunday picnic.

"It was really cool," replied Ben. "I'd love to go exploring up the Cougar River before I go back home next Saturday."

"Well, actually," said Mr. Simmons with a twinkle in his eye, "I was going to ask you and Jeremy if you'd like to go camping on the river sometime this week. The weather forecast looks great, and a campout might be the perfect ending to your visit."

"Yeah! Let's go tomorrow, Dad," Jeremy said excitedly.

"Yeah! Let's!" echoed Ben. "I've never even been on a camping trip."

"It'll have to be Tuesday and Wednesday, boys. I have meetings Monday morning, and we'll need Monday afternoon to get things organized and packed."

At breakfast Monday morning, Mr. Simmons gave Jeremy a list of supplies to gather for the campout. "You know where the camping gear is down in the basement. Bring up the tent, the backpacks, and the cooking gear. Your mom will help you and Ben get your clothes together and pack the food. When I get back from my meeting this afternoon, we'll load up the car for an early start tomorrow morning."

By Monday evening, the car was packed.

"Off to bed, boys," Mr. Simmons said. "We have an early start in the morning and then a long hike up the river to our campsite."

"I can't wait," said Ben as he headed up the stairs. "This is gonna be the best adventure ever."

The next morning Mr. Simmons roused Ben and Jeremy out of bed before sunrise. "Rise and shine, sleepy heads. Breakfast is ready, and we need to be on the road by six o'clock."

"It's still dark," Ben yawned. "I never get up this early."

"When you go camping with my dad, every day begins early. Just wait until you try his pre-sunrise campfire breakfast," teased Jeremy, trying to wake up.

As the sleepy but eager campers piled into the car, Mr. Simmons prayed for a safe and enjoyable adventure. Then he backed out of the garage and headed toward Black Rock Canyon and the Cougar River. Jeremy and Ben tucked pillows under their heads and quickly fell back asleep.

"Hey, boys," said Mr. Simmons as they neared the Three Falls lookout. "Wake up. You're missing all the beauty of God's creation."

"Are we there yet?" asked Ben as he rubbed his eyes.

"We'll be at the lookout in about thirty minutes. We'll park there, then hike up to our campsite."

After parking at the lookout, Mr. Simmons helped the boys with their backpacks. He adjusted his own pack then announced the rules of the trail. "Stay on the trail. Don't go near the edge of the river, even when it looks safe. The rocks are slippery, and the current is pretty swift. I don't want anyone falling in. At the campground, there are some calm beaver pools where you can explore the water more closely."

The trail climbed gently at first as the sunlight darted through the aspen trees and glistened on the river. Then it made a sharp turn and became much steeper. Mr. Simmons kept a steady pace as Jeremy and Ben struggled to keep up.

"I'm tired and hot," mumbled Ben. "And this pack's too heavy. I need to stop and rest."

"We'll take a ten-minute break," Mr. Simmons said. "You boys stay here while I scout the trail up ahead."

The boys slipped off their backpacks and collapsed on the ground. Ben looked longingly at the river. "I'm gonna just splash some water on my face to cool off," he said as he got up and headed for the bank.

"Be careful," Jeremy said. "Remember what Dad said about slippery rocks."

"Don't worry," Ben said confidently. "I won't fall in."

As Ben looked for a way to reach the water safely, he spied a large, flat rock. "This will be perfect," he said to himself as he placed both feet on the rock. Then he knelt down and cupped his hands to scoop up some water. Much to his surprise, he lost his balance, and his feet slid out from under him. With a scream, Ben fell face first into the cold, rushing waters of the Cougar River.

"Grab that tree branch on your left," hollered Jeremy as he quickly worked his way toward the edge of the river.

Ben grabbed the branch and began to pull himself toward the bank. Jeremy held tightly to another branch while reaching out his hand toward Ben. After what seemed a very long time, Ben's left foot found a solid rock near the bank, and Jeremy pulled him from the icy water.

"Are you okay?" Jeremy asked with a quivering voice.

"Yeah, I think so," said Ben as he stood shivering. "But it's your fault I fell in!"

"My fault?"

"Yeah! It was your idea to come on this dumb camping trip in the first place. If we hadn't come, I wouldn't have fallen in the river."

"Wait a minute!" snapped Jeremy. "You're the one who asked my dad if we could go exploring and camping. Remember? Grow up, Ben. You're acting like a big baby—a big, wet baby."

"I'm bigger than you are. You're the one who needs to grow up," snarled Ben.

"Oh, yeah?" said Jeremy as he gave Ben a shove.

Just then Mr. Simmons came down the trail. "Hey, boys," he shouted angrily. "Knock it off! What's the matter with you two? I could hear the commotion clear up the trail. You're both acting like two-year-olds. If you don't straighten up, we're heading back to the car and home. As for you, Ben, I told you not to leave the trail in the first place. Now both of you apologize to each other right now."

"Sorry," Jeremy said in a muffled voice, without meaning it or looking at Ben.

"Sorry," Ben mumbled, hugging himself trying to get warm.

"All right, fellas, I know neither of you meant what you said. I think all three of us need to cool off a bit," Mr. Simmons said. "On second thought, Ben needs to cool off *and* warm up!"

Both boys snickered at the joke.

"Here, Ben. Change into these dry clothes," Mr. Simmons said as he reached into Ben's backpack. "We'll dry your wet ones by the campfire tonight."

While Ben was changing his clothes, Mr. Simmons said, "Boys, I'm sorry I lost my temper. I really apologize. I know you aren't two-year-olds. I was upset at seeing you two fighting and knowing that Ben had disobeyed and fallen into the river. Still, that's no excuse for saying the things I did. Will you forgive me?"

"I do, Dad," said Jeremy.

"I do, too," said Ben as he pulled on his socks. "And I apologize for the things I said to you, Jeremy. Will you forgive me?"

"Of course," said Jeremy. "I'm just glad you're safe. Do you forgive me?"

"Sure," Ben said with a shivering smile.

"All right," said Mr. Simmons. "I think we'd better get going or we won't make camp before dark. Besides, I want you two to keep your eyes open. You may see a herd of elk in the valley. For sure you'll see lots of beautiful wildflowers, and in the river you'll see rainbow trout."

"It's beautiful here, Mr. Simmons," Ben said as he looked at the valley below. "But what's that black area on the other side of the valley?"

"That's a burn area," answered Mr. Simmons. "Last year there was a large forest fire over the next ridge, and some of it spread down into this valley before the fire-fighters were able to stop it. It may have been started by lightning or maybe by careless campers."

"Wow! That's awful," Ben said. "And what's the matter with the pine trees on this part of the trail? They look yellow, and some are dead."

"Well, some of the pine trees in this part of the forest have been attacked by the pine bark beetle. They destroy the bark of the trees, and that causes the trees to die. It's a very serious problem."

"I thought everything was always beautiful in the forest and the mountains," said Ben, saddened to see the destruction. "But now I see it really isn't after all."

"You're right, Ben. We don't live in a perfect world, as beautiful as it is," answered Mr. Simmons, picking up the pace of the hike.

Soon Jeremy's and Ben's legs began to ache. Their backpacks began to feel heavier and heavier.

"How much farther, Dad?" asked Jeremy. "I think Ben and I have had it for one day."

"About a mile," replied Mr. Simmons without slowing the pace. "Just around the next turn in the trail, then downhill a bit to the river. There's a flat place there good for pitching the tent."

"Are we gonna camp right next to the river?" asked Ben. "I've had enough river water for one day."

"Where we're going to camp, the Cougar River is fairly shallow. And there are no storms forecast for tonight that could cause the river to overflow its banks. So yes, we'll be right on the river."

Just as the sun dropped behind the mountain peak, the three hikers arrived at the campsite. They pitched their tent, lit a fire, and relaxed while a campfire stew simmered slowly in a pot over the coals. After supper, Mr. Simmons brought out the marshmallows and made s'mores.

"Yum," said Jeremy. "This is my favorite part of camping."

As darkness slowly filled the sky, the valley, and surrounding forest, millions of stars seemed to come out of hiding. They filled the night sky with dancing galaxies. Some even chose to entertain the three campers by streaking through the sky like flaming arrows.

"There *has* to be a God," sighed Ben as he lay back on the ground staring up at the sky.

"You're right," said Mr. Simmons quietly. "Listen to the night sounds of the forest. Look at the stars. Listen to the river. It's an awesome God who created it all.   So beautiful. So peaceful."

As Ben continued to stare into the sky in deep thought, Jeremy asked quietly, "What are you thinking, Ben?"

"Oh, just about a lot of things. Sometimes everything is so beautiful and perfect, like now. But sometimes everything seems not so perfect. You know, like today when we got into a fight and your dad lost his temper. And the ugly burned-out forest, and the pine trees killed by the pine bark beetle. I wish everything could always be perfect. I wish my parents got along like your parents. I wish I had good friends at home like you, Jeremy. And I wish . . ."

"Wish what?" asked Jeremy.

"Sometimes I wish I weren't me. I wish I were like other kids I know. They seem cool and happy, but I don't always like the way I am."

Jeremy gave his dad a puzzled look. Mr. Simmons sat staring into the fire, listening quietly to Ben's words. The only sounds were the crackling of the fire and the gurgling of the river over the rocks.

After a while, Mr. Simmons stoked the fire. Without looking at Ben, he said, "Ben, you're a very observant young man. The world is beautiful, but the world is also filled with ugliness. And the things you wish for . . . well, they're things that many people have wished for throughout all of human history."

"Yeah," said Ben, still looking up at the stars. "But why is the world like that? It's like everything has two sides—a good side and a bad side, a beautiful side and an ugly side."

"Well, Ben," replied Mr. Simmons, "the way the world is today is different than it was when God created it long ago. In the beginning, everything was in perfect harmony. Adam and Eve had a perfect, loving relationship with God. They knew they were God's most special creation on earth. There was perfect peace in their hearts—no anger, fear, jealousy, or shame. They loved themselves in the right way, knowing that they were made in the image of God, with a mind for knowing God, a heart for loving Him, and a will for obeying Him."

"Yeah, and I bet they never fought or argued," said Ben, thinking about his own parents.

"That's true," said Mr. Simmons quietly. "They loved each other perfectly. They knew nothing about arguments and fights. They served each other, helped each other, and lived together in harmony with God."

"And," said Jeremy, pulling another marshmallow off the stick, "the world Adam and Eve lived in was perfect. No forest fires, no pine bark beetles, floods, earthquakes, or anything bad or ugly. Even the animals got along."

"So what happened?"

"The Bible tells us that God's enemy, Satan, tempted Adam and Eve to disobey one of God's commands," Mr. Simmons said, taking a sip of coffee.

"What command was that?" asked Ben.

"The command not to eat from the tree of the knowledge of good and evil that God had planted in the Garden of Eden. He warned Adam and Eve that if they ever ate from that tree, they would die."

"So what happened?" asked Ben, now very curious.

"Satan lied and told Eve that the fruit would make her wise like God," answered Mr. Simmons. "He also said that she and Adam would not die. Sadly, Eve believed Satan's lie and ate the fruit. Then she gave some to Adam, and he ate it. They disobeyed God, and at that very moment, sin entered the world. And sin caused the harmony between God and Adam and Eve to be broken."

"That's also when disharmony entered the earth," said Jeremy.

"You mean like forest fires and pine bark beetles?" asked Ben, scooting a little closer to the fire.

"Not only that," said Jeremy, "Adam and Eve began to die. Oh, they didn't die immediately. But they began to grow older and older until the day they did die."

"It's all pretty depressing," said Ben, staring into the fire. "I thought you told me God was all powerful and that He loved us. How could He let something like that happen? It seems to me that Satan must be stronger than God."

"Sometimes it might look that way," replied Mr. Simmons. "But God is all powerful. After Adam and Eve sinned and disharmony came into creation, God announced a plan to restore harmony to His creation. It wasn't just a plan God thought up after Satan deceived Adam and Eve. God had His plan worked out even before He created the earth."

"So what plan was that?" asked Ben, growing more curious and interested.

"To send Jesus, His Son, to earth," said Jeremy. "God the Father sent God the Son to pay the penalty we deserve for our sins and rebellion against God. That's why Jesus died on the cross—so we don't have to die and live separated from God forever."

"That's what Pastor Williams said Sunday in church," said Ben.

"Glad you heard that, Ben," said Mr. Simmons. "And it's true. Jesus died for us so that we can live forever in harmony with God in the new heavens and earth He will one day create. Not everyone believes that message from God, but for those who do believe, God makes them His children—part of His family."

"But why doesn't God just make everything perfect right now?" asked Ben.

"God has His own time for everything," said Mr. Simmons, taking his last sip of coffee. "For now, when we trust in Jesus as our Savior, we become God's children and He makes us new. And He makes all of his children one big family."

"But what about the earth?" asked Ben, still thinking about the parts of the forest destroyed by fires and beetles.

"It'll be made brand new when Jesus returns to the earth. And when that happens, nothing will ever again destroy the harmony of God's new creation," Mr. Simmons said confidently.

Ben sat quietly for a long time. So many thoughts were racing through his mind. He looked at the stars again. He listened to the river. He thought about what God is like, and He thought about who Jesus is.

Finally, Ben broke the silence. "Mr. Simmons, I have so many questions about everything. But I think I know something for sure after my vacation here: God must exist. Only God could create such a beautiful world. And if He created such a beautiful world, He must love it enough to make it all right again. And if God loves the world enough to want to make it right, He must love me enough to make me right, just like Adam and Eve were in the beginning."

Photo: www.flickr.com, Eric Dufresne

"You're exactly right, Ben," said Mr. Simmons, putting his hand on Ben's shoulder.

Jeremy stood up quietly and went into the tent. He reached into his backpack and took out his Bible and flashlight. "Ben, I want to read you something from the Bible," he said, sitting down next to his friend. "'For God so loved the world that he gave his one and only Son, that whoever believes in him shall not perish but have eternal life. For God did not send his son into the world to condemn the world, but to save the world through him.'"

Jeremy closed his Bible. No one said a word. All three campers sat quietly, staring at the last red coals of the dying campfire. The only sounds were the occasional popping of a coal, the rushing of the river, and the silent words of millions of stars that loudly proclaimed God's glory and presence.

After a long silence, Ben said softly, "I do believe in Him. I really do."

S'MORES CLUSTERS

S'mores are such a camping tradition that if you've set up a tent and started a campfire, making s'mores is practically required by law. Everyone has memorized the traditional s'mores recipe by the age of six: You poke a stick through a marshmallow, hold it over fire, and hope it doesn't burst into flames. Insert the warm marshmallow between chocolate and graham crackers and eat.

Now you can bring this tasty treat home, whether you're sleeping under the stars in the backyard, having a pajama party, or just taking a break from school.

Photo: Peggy Webb

Ingredients:
- » 6 milk-chocolate candy bars (1.55 ounces each), broken into pieces
- » 1½ teaspoons olive oil
- » 2 cups miniature marshmallows
- » 8 whole graham crackers, broken into bite-size pieces

Directions:
In a large microwave-safe bowl, toss chocolate and oil. Microwave the mixture, uncovered, at medium power for 1½ to 2 minutes, or until the chocolate is melted, stirring once while cooking. Stir in the marshmallows and graham cracker pieces until well coated. Spoon into a paper-lined muffin tin (about one third of a cup each). Cover and refrigerate for about one hour, or until the mixture is firm. Recipe makes one dozen s'more-velous snacks!

THINK ABOUT IT
- » What parts of this story illustrate disharmony between people? In the earth? With one's self?
- » How did Jeremy and Mr. Simmons explain the presence of disharmony in God's creation? What solution for disharmony did they share with Ben?
- » Would you say the campout on Cougar River was a perfect ending or an imperfect ending to Ben's visit? Why?

WORDS YOU NEED TO KNOW

- » **Harmony:** To be at peace or in agreement with one another
- » **Temptation:** A lie of Satan that promises something good if you will disobey God
- » **The Fall:** The moment when sin entered God's creation through Satan's temptation and Adam and Eve's disobedience
- » **Prophecy:** A declaration from God that reveals future events
- » **Redeem:** To pay something in order to free a person from a debt, punishment, or captivity
- » **God's plan for redemption:** God's plan to redeem each relationship of creation from the consequences of the Fall through the payment of Jesus' death on the cross
- » **Gratitude:** Thankfulness that we express to God and others for the blessings we receive from them

HIDE IT IN YOUR HEART

For in six days the LORD made the heavens and the earth, the sea, and all that is in them, but he rested on the seventh day. (Exodus 20:11)

In everything give thanks; for this is God's will for you in Christ Jesus. (1 Thessalonians 5:18, NASB)

THE FOUR RELATIONSHIPS OF CREATION

The English word **harmony** comes from the Greek noun *harmonía*, meaning "agreement," and from the verb *harmozo*, meaning "to fit together, to join." Today, it means to be at peace or in agreement with one another. The Father, Son, and Holy Spirit live eternally in a relationship of harmony, and so the world they created in the beginning was filled with harmonious relationships. In this lesson, we will be looking at four special relationships created by God, what happened to destroy the harmony of these relationships, and God's miraculous plan to restore all things.

The first relationship of creation was the relationship God created for people to have with Him. The first humans, Adam and Eve, enjoyed a wonderful relationship of fellowship with God. They walked with Him and talked with Him in the cool of the garden, and together with Him began to carry out God's plan for creation.

In harmony with God, Adam and Eve enjoyed the second relationship of creation—

a relationship of harmony with themselves. Unlike Ben, who told Jeremy and Mr. Simmons that he didn't like himself very much, the first man and woman loved themselves in the right way. They knew who they were and why they were created, and they knew nothing about fear or shame.

As you probably know, when two people are at peace with themselves, they usually get along quite well together. In the Garden of Eden, where Adam and Eve lived, that is exactly how it was. In this third relationship of creation, Adam and Eve lived in perfect harmony with each other. There were no fights like the one Jeremy and Ben got into on their campout. Adam and Eve loved and served each other perfectly, just as each member of the Trinity loves and serves the others.

Do you remember when Ben noticed the parts of the forest burned by fire? And the trees that had been destroyed by the pine bark beetles? Up to that time, Ben thought everything in the forest and the mountains was supposed to be beautiful and perfect. Actually, at the very beginning of creation, everything in the earth *was* perfect. The world God gave Adam and Eve to be their home was in perfect harmony. And the fourth relationship of creation—the one mankind has with the earth—was also perfect. The earth provided for Adam and Eve's needs, and they ruled over and cared for God's creation (Genesis 1:26). There was no killing of animal life—God gave plants to Adam and Eve and to the animals for them to eat (Genesis 1:29). This relationship is one we find hard to imagine, just as it is hard to imagine a perfect relationship with God, with ourselves, or with others.

Eden by Bruegel

So what happened? As Mr. Simmons explained to Ben that night around the fire, God's enemy, Satan, deceived Adam and Eve and persuaded them to disobey their Creator. The moment they disobeyed, the harmony of each relationship of creation was destroyed. Adam and Eve no longer had a perfect relationship with God, and they certainly didn't have harmony with themselves or each other. As a consequence of their disobedience,

God allowed death, decay, and disharmony to enter the earth. This tragic event in human history is called the Fall.

If this were the end of the story, life would be pretty depressing, just as Ben said that night at the campfire. But God, whose good plan for creation has never changed, already had an eternal plan for restoring harmony to every relationship of the world He created. His plan was to send God the Son to earth to pay the penalty for Adam and Eve's disobedience and for the disobedience of every person who has ever lived on earth. This wonderful truth is God's plan for redemption. God's plan for redemption—for restoring us in harmony with Him, with ourselves, with others, and with the earth—is a plan for all people who believe that Jesus Christ is God's Son and ask Him to be their Savior.

Do you remember the scripture Jeremy read to Ben at the campfire? "For God so loved the world that he gave his one and only Son, that whoever believes in him shall not perish but have eternal life. For God did not send his son into the world to condemn the world, but to save the world through him" (John 3:16–17). Think about what this says. Do you believe it? Do you *really* believe it? If you do, you too can be restored in relationships of harmony with God, yourself, and others now. And when Jesus returns to the earth, you will enjoy a perfect relationship of harmony forever on the new earth that God promised to create for His children.

MAKE A NOTE OF IT

Think about the Fall and consider that we wouldn't need such things as door locks, eyeglasses, or hospitals if it weren't for the Fall. List as many modern products you can think of that could be said to be a result of the Fall.

Creation by Schnorr von Carolsfeld

SOMETHING OUT OF NOTHING

What do people mean when they say, "Look at what I've created"? They're saying, "I made this, I think it's good, and I want to share it with you." We create all sorts of things—art, books, music, clothes, machines, medicines, and much more. Yet no matter how clever we are, human beings cannot make something out of nothing. We must work with raw materials and specialized tools to create the things we dream up. The book you hold in your hands was made using ink, paper, cardboard, and glue. But what about the content, the words themselves? Even these were written based on the established rules and structure of language—vocabulary, spelling, grammar, and syntax—and the thoughts behind the words are based on a great deal of research and study of the teachings of God.

Yet when God created the heavens and the earth, there were no raw materials available. Only He existed. Instead, He simply *spoke* the universe into existence. On the first day, He said, "Let there be light," and there was light (Genesis 1:3). On the fifth day, He said, "Let the water teem with living creatures, and let birds fly above the earth across the expanse of the sky," and suddenly there were fish and birds on the earth (verse 20). God did not need raw materials. He created all things that exist, and He created it all out of nothing by the mere power of His words.

Many scientists believe that the universe exploded into existence from an infinitesimally small, infinitely hot, infinitely dense concentration of energy. This view of events is called the Big Bang theory and is a popular way to explain the origin of the universe and the beginning of time as we know it. However, this theory has its problems, the most glaring of which are these: Where did this infinitesimally small, infinitely hot, infinitely dense concentration of energy come from? And

Pillars of Creation. Photo: NASA

Creation stained glass window by Troyes

what caused it to explode in the first place? The idea that the building blocks of the universe existed eternally and the notion that they exploded without being acted upon by some outside force violate every law of nature known to science.

The fact is that you cannot explain the presence of Creation without acknowledging the existence of a Creator. Whether we're talking about a book on the shelf, a dress in the store window, the meal you ate last night for dinner, or the whole of the universe, the very presence of these things tells us that someone created them. And as we know, only God can create something out of nothing.

The Bible tells us that God created the earth in six days. On the first three days of creation, God gave form to the earth. He separated the light from the darkness, the sea from the clouds, and the dry land from the sea. He also created plants. On the fourth, fifth, and sixth days of creation, He filled His creation with heavenly bodies, flying and swimming creatures, and land animals. He completed day six by creating Adam and Eve, the only members of creation who were made in His image. Each day, God reviewed His work and called it "good." Indeed, it was all perfect.

On day seven, God rested. This does not mean that God was tired or that He needed a day off. When the Bible says God rested, it means that He had completed His work. In doing so, He set an example for us to follow. We call this day of rest the Sabbath, from a Hebrew word meaning "to cease." We are to set apart one day each week for worship and prayer, enjoying His creation, and spending time with our heavenly Father.

DISHARMONY ENTERS THE CREATION

Quinces are a luscious, bright yellow fruit related to apples and pears. Many people have speculated that the forbidden fruit of the Garden of Eden was a quince. Photo: Mbdortmund

What does it mean when a person says, "I'm tempted to do something I shouldn't do"? He is saying that he knows the difference between right and wrong and yet is considering doing what is wrong because he thinks he'll get something good out of it. All temptation is a trick of Satan that promises us something good if we will do something wrong. It's an old trick, but the devil never gets tired of using it—after all, people keep falling for it again and again. In fact, he told this very same lie to Eve in the garden.

As discussed in the previous lesson, Satan was created as an angel of light, and the Bible tells us in 2 Corinthians 11:14 that he can still disguise himself in this form (so always be careful whom you accept advice from). For some reason the devil chose to appear to Eve in the form of a serpent, or snake, the craftiest of all the animals in the garden. You probably know the story, but read it again in light of what you have learned so far in this study:

> One day [the serpent] asked the woman, "Did God really say you must not eat the fruit from any of the trees in the garden?"
>
> "Of course we may eat fruit from the trees in the garden," the woman replied. "It's only the fruit from the tree in the middle of the garden that we are not allowed to eat. God said, 'You must not eat it or even touch it; if you do, you will die.'"
>
> "You won't die!" the serpent replied to the woman. "God knows that your eyes will be opened as soon as you eat it, and you will be like God, knowing both good and evil."
>
> The woman was convinced. She saw that the tree was beautiful and its fruit looked deli-

cious, and she wanted the wisdom it would give her. So she took some of the fruit and ate it. Then she gave some to her husband, who was with her, and he ate it, too. (Genesis 3:1–5, NLT)

First, Satan created doubt in Eve's mind by questioning whether God "really" said what she thought He had said. Then he lied to her by contradicting God's words. Then he promised her that something good would happen if she would disobey God. This is pretty much the strategy that Satan has used ever since. This is why it's important that you learn and know God's Word. Always compare everything you see, read, and hear to what God says—if it doesn't agree with the Bible, turn around and walk away from it.

Sadly, Adam and Eve did not turn away. They chose to disobey God and gave in to temptation. And at the moment they ate the forbidden fruit, death and disharmony entered creation. We call this event the fall of mankind, or simply the Fall. The consequences of Adam

Expulsion from Eden (detail) by Masaccio

and Eve's sin quickly began showing. Although the man and woman did not immediately drop dead, their once-perfect bodies began at once to age and decay, and disease and death became inevitable. Their eyes were opened, they realized they were naked, and for the first time they felt shame. They heard God walking in the garden, so they hid, and for the first time they felt fear.

And so the harmony of the four relationships of creation was destroyed, and these became broken relationships. Let's take a closer look at how the Fall affected each of these relationships.

DISHARMONY BETWEEN PEOPLE AND GOD

You are probably very much like your mother and father. You not only share physical characteristics with your parents, but you also learn certain behaviors from them as you grow. You walk and talk with your parents, and as long as you are obedient, you want them to talk to you. You would feel very bad if someone took you far away from your parents and you could no longer see them or talk with them.

Before Adam and Eve sinned, they enjoyed perfect fellowship with their Creator. As the only creatures made in God's image, they had a very special relationship with Him. They walked and talked with God in the garden, and God talked to them. He provided for their every need. He taught them and gave them important responsibilities within the home He provided. Theirs was a perfect love relationship.

A necessary part of any such relationship is free will. Unless we are given the ability to

WHERE WAS THE GARDEN OF EDEN?

Mouth of the Tigris River in Iraq

Have you ever wondered where the Garden of Eden was? If so, you're not alone. People have been searching for the location of the garden for thousands of years. Genesis 2:10–14 says that the garden was near four rivers, so that's a good place to start.

Modern maps show two rivers with the same names as two of the rivers in Eden. One is called the Tigris (pronounced TIE-griss). The other is the Euphrates (yu-FRAY-tees). Today, these rivers flow through the modern country of Iraq into the Persian Gulf. Find Iraq on a map. It's in the Middle East, situated between Turkey and Saudi Arabia. Once you find it, trace your finger south to the thin bit of ocean that touches Iraq. This is the Persian Gulf. Your map should show a blue line, representing a river, flowing into the gulf. Trace your finger up this line until it splits into two lines. The river on the right is the Tigris. The river on the left is the Euphrates.

But was the Garden of Eden really somewhere near these modern rivers? The truth is that we can't know for certain. Remember that many years after Adam and Eve left the garden, God sent a great flood to destroy the world. Because the landscape changed so much during the flood, we can only guess at where these rivers once flowed. It may even be that these are two different rivers that were given the same names as those in the Bible.

Today, archeologists and scholars are using contemporary science to figure out where the Garden of Eden might have been. Some believe the garden was in what is now the country of Armenia. Others say it was in Africa. Others say the garden was located on the current site of the city of Jerusalem. Wherever the garden was, people will continue to search for paradise as long as their hunger for God remains unfulfilled.

choose, we cannot truly love someone. Many people think that love is an emotion or a desire, but it isn't. Love is a *decision*. Love is a decision to put another's desires ahead of your own. So God gave us the ability to choose—to choose to love God or to put ourselves first. Adam and Eve made the wrong choice and brought sin into the world, and every man and woman since have been "lovers of pleasure rather than lovers of God" (2 Timothy 3:4).

When Adam and Eve sinned, and they heard God walking in the garden, they hid themselves. They were ashamed of their nakedness and their sin, and they became afraid of God and what He might do or say. Of course, God is holy and can have no part of sin, and so from this time forward people would no longer be able to see God or talk with Him face to face. And because they no longer spent time with Him, they grew apart from Him and did what they thought was right and not what God said was right. Mankind was now separated from God, and they could no longer have a perfect relationship.

DISHARMONY WITH ONE'S SELF

Before the Fall, Adam and Eve were both at ease with themselves and with their bodies. Adam knew he was a child of God, and he was happy in his work naming the animals and cultivating the garden. Eve was comfortable in her role as a woman and was happy to be helping Adam in his work. Adam didn't worry about what kind of car he drove or whether he was bigger or stronger or made more money than his neighbor. Eve didn't worry about whether she was gaining weight or if Adam still found her attractive. Neither of them was ever anxious or nervous or scared about anything.

However, once they chose to disobey God, all that changed. Immediately, Adam and Eve became unhappy with their appearance and began making rash decisions out of fear and shame. Shame is an emotion caused when a person is painfully aware of his flaws or his failures or his guilt over having done something wrong. Since the disobedience of Adam and Eve in the garden, everyone has sinned and fallen short of the glory of God (Romans 3:23). And Satan, the accuser, has used our sins to fuel our fear and shame and lead us ever deeper into sin.

DISHARMONY WITH OTHERS

Before the Fall, Adam and Eve were perfectly at ease with one another. They worked hand in hand tending the garden, helping one another as needed. They never argued or fought or misunderstood one another. Neither was jealous of the other's position or power or physical attributes. Eve never told Adam, "Dad made you first. He likes you better." Adam never complained about how much time Eve spent in the bathroom putting on her makeup.

However, when God confronted them about their sin, Adam immediately pointed a finger at Eve: "The woman you put here with me—she gave me some fruit from the tree, and I ate it" (Genesis 3:12). Adam blamed Eve—and God—for his own disobedience: *It's all her fault! I would never have touched the stuff if she hadn't given it to me. Come to think of it, who put that woman here in the first place?* Of course, Eve tried to shift the blame elsewhere. "The serpent deceived me," she said. "That's why I ate it" (v. 13, NLT).

Because we are ashamed or because we're afraid of punishment, as Ben was after falling into the river, we often try to avoid taking responsibility for our own wrongdoing by shifting the blame to someone else. "It was his idea." "She talked me into it." "The devil made me do it." People have been pointing fingers at one another ever since the Fall, and so our relationships are marred by fear, hatred, misunderstanding, and distrust, and our history is marked by war, slavery, and murder. Indeed, it is natural for us to want to blame Adam and Eve for our problems, but we have all sinned and none of us would have done any differently in their position.

DISHARMONY WITH THE EARTH

Before the Fall, Adam and Eve existed peacefully alongside all the creatures of the earth. Adam walked among them, naming each one in turn (Genesis 2:19–20). Adam was also given a job. Yes, a job. Man and woman were not put in the garden to just kick back and enjoy the scenery. Adam didn't put up a hammock and a satellite dish and ask Eve to fetch him lemonade. It was Adam's job to tend and watch over the garden (v. 15). You see, work has always been a part of God's perfect plan, even before the Fall. God did it. Adam and Eve did it. Work is a very good thing.

But after Adam sinned, everything changed. God said to him:

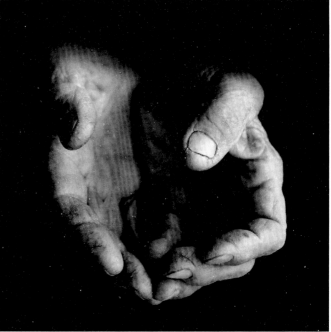

"Since you listened to your wife and ate from the tree whose fruit I commanded you not to eat, the ground is cursed because of you. All your life you will struggle to scratch a living from it. It will grow thorns and thistles for you, though you will eat of its grains. By the sweat of your brow will you have food to eat until you return to the ground from which you were made." (Genesis 3:17–19, NLT*)*

Suddenly, Adam's work became a struggle. The earth would no longer respond easily to his efforts. He had to work much harder just to grow enough food for his family to live. Eve would also labor greatly in childbirth. God told her, "I will greatly increase your pains in childbearing; with pain you will give birth to children" (v. 16).

More than an increase in hard labor, the Fall meant that the earth itself was cursed. Disease and decay entered creation, and the land became inhospitable. God killed an animal and clothed Adam and Eve in its skin to cover their nakedness and protect them from the

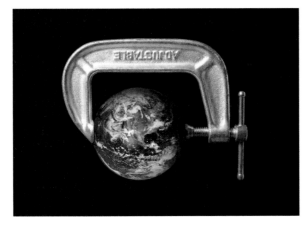

elements, and they were forced to build shelters for themselves and their family. Death became part of the natural order of things, an inevitability in the seasons of nature and in the seasons of life.

Then God banished Adam and Eve from the Garden of Eden and stationed an angel with a flaming sword to guard the entrance. Mankind would henceforth live apart from God's presence and the perfection of His creation.

Make a Note of It

Write about some "good things" Satan promises to get us to do the wrong thing and disobey our parents or God. What "good" does the temptation to lie promise you? What "good" does the temptation to steal promise you? What "good" does the temptation to cheat promise you?

Harmony Restored to Creation

Redemption is the act of buying something back. The word *redeem* is often used to describe the act of freeing someone from distress or harm, as in paying a ransom for a person who's been kidnapped. Or it may refer to paying a person's debt in order to release him from the threat of stiff penalties for not being able to make his payments.

When we sin against God, we suddenly find ourselves in very serious debt, a debt we cannot pay. For disobeying a holy and perfect God, there can be only one penalty—death and eternal separation from God. Satan knows this all too well, and he is tireless in making accusations against God's people and demanding that we be forced to pay the ultimate price.

Things were looking pretty bleak for Adam and Eve after the fall. Satan surely thought he had won. He had never understood God's love for these frail humans whom He had made in His own image. God had favored them above even the angels, giving humans dominion over all the earth. So Satan, in a jealous rage, had tricked the man and woman into bringing death and decay to all of creation. He probably expected God to strike them down on the spot and pulverize them into dust once more. But no matter. From now on, the devil would have control over this world that God had made (1 John 5:19).

But God had a plan. He had always had a plan. In Genesis 3, we find the first promise from God that He would send a Savior to redeem men and women—that is, pay the price for their sins—and restore the harmony that had been lost in the Fall. In this passage, God speaks to the serpent:

"Because you have done this, you are cursed more than all animals, domestic and wild. You will crawl on your belly, groveling in the dust as long as you live." (Genesis 3:14, NLT)

Many scholars speculate that prior to the Fall the snake moved about on four legs like most other reptiles. By cursing the serpent to crawl on the ground, God gave us a vivid and constant reminder of Satan's humiliating punishment for his rebellion against God. The Lord then went on to say to the serpent:

"I will make you and the woman enemies to each other. Your descendants and her descendants will be enemies. Her child will crush your head. And you will bite his heel." (Genesis 3:15, ICB)

This was the first prophecy that Jesus would come to set things right once more. Prophecy is a word from God that reveals to us future events. Jesus is the child mentioned here who would one day "crush" Satan by defeating and destroying his kingdom of darkness. The Bible says, "The Son of God came for this purpose: to destroy the devil's work" (1 John 3:8, ICB). He came into the world as a child, born to the virgin Mary, a descendant of Eve. God knew that Satan would try to defeat Jesus, but Christ's death on the cross was no more than a bite on the heel. Having lived a sinless life, Christ paid the debt we owe for our sin. Christ was raised from the dead, Satan's power was broken, and harmony in our relationships once again became a very real possibility.

Today, God still allows Satan to rule over the kingdoms of this world. However, believers in Christ have power over him through the Holy Spirit who lives within us. And when Christ returns, Satan and his demons will be assigned to eternal punishment in hell.

Let's look once more at the four relationships of creation and how they are affected by God's plan for redemption.

THE RESTORATION OF HARMONY WITH GOD

Romans 4:25 tell us, "Jesus was given to die for our sins. And he was raised from death to make us right with God" (ICB). Because Jesus died to pay the price for our sins and was raised again, those who believe in Him can once again have fellowship with God. Not only can we talk with Him and hear what He has to say, but we also have the Holy Spirit living within us to teach us the truth about all things.

Does that mean we now live in perfect harmony with God? No. On the cross Christ indeed finished the work necessary to restore us to full fellowship with God, but we experience this restoration as a process. Because God is holy—without sin—we must become holy if we are to enjoy perfect harmony with Him. This means we must become like Christ. The Bible tells us that He will be faithful to help us grow to be like Him and that He will complete this work in us (Philippians 1:6). When will this work be completed? On the day Jesus returns

Photo: www.flickr.com, BrokenWing739

and we are taken to see the Father face to face. Then we will live with Him forever in perfect harmony.

In the meantime, if you should happen to sin—and you will sometimes—you need to seek God's forgiveness. Confess your sin to Him and repent. To repent means to turn around, away from sin, and walk in the other direction. Stand firm against the strategies of Satan. Read God's Word faithfully and spend time in prayer with Him. Ask the Holy Spirit to help you become more and more like Christ.

THE RESTORATION OF HARMONY WITH OURSELVES

The Bible says that the moment you first believed that Jesus is the one true Son of God and that He paid the price for your sins, you became a "new creation":

Therefore, if anyone is in Christ, he is a new creation; the old has gone, the new has come! (2 Corinthians 5:17)

You have begun to live the new life. In your new life you are being made new. You are becoming like the One who made you. (Colossians 3:10, ICB)

Because you are a new creation, you must begin thinking differently about yourself.

Although your body is still subject to the effects of aging and decay, God's Word says that, as a believer, you "show the Lord's glory" and you're "being changed to be like him" (2 Corinthians 3, ICB). Your body is a temple of the Holy Spirit, so take good care of it. But don't listen to what the world says about you. Satan wants you to believe that you must be tall and thin and tan, that you must drive a nice sports car, and that you must aspire to be super talented and super rich. He will use the messages in advertising, movies, TV shows, and songs to tell you that you are somehow worth less if you don't meet the world's expectations. It's not true! Here's what the Bible says:

> That isn't what you were taught about Jesus Christ. He is the truth, and you heard about him and learned about him. . . . You must give up your old way of life with all its bad habits. Let the Spirit change your way of thinking and make you into a new person. You were created to be like God, and so you must please him and be truly holy. (Ephesians 4:21–24, CEV)

You no longer have to be afraid. You don't have to make choices out of fear or shame. "It is for freedom that Christ has set us free" (Galatians 5:1), and "if the Son sets you free, you will be free indeed" (John 8:36). You have been set free from the chains of sin that Satan would use to hold you captive. The world thinks the way Satan tells it to; as a new creation, you must dare to think differently. Spend time every day reading God's Word and learning the truth, and one day, when Christ returns, you will live in perfect harmony with yourself forever.

THE RESTORATION OF HARMONY WITH OTHERS

Ever since the Fall, people have been unable to get along for any length of time. Someone wants something that someone else has and tries to grab it. Someone makes a mistake and blames someone else. Someone becomes angry at something someone else says, grabs the nearest blunt object, and hits the other person over the head with it. However, because we are new creations in Christ, we no longer have to live this way.

The apostle Paul wrote to God's people, "Get rid of anger, rage, malicious behavior, slander, and dirty language. Don't lie to each other, for you have stripped off your old sinful nature and all its wicked deeds. Put on your new nature, and be renewed as you learn to know your Creator and become like him" (Colossians 3:8–10, NLT). God especially wants us to live in harmony with other believers. He even calls us a family:

> You are all sons of God through faith in Christ Jesus, for all of you who were baptized into Christ have clothed yourselves with Christ. There is neither Jew nor Greek, slave nor free,

male nor female, for you are all one in Christ Jesus. (Galatians 3:26–28)

Both the one who makes men holy and those who are made holy are of the same family. So Jesus is not ashamed to call them brothers. (Hebrews 2:11)

Jesus warned us that the world will hate us because we have chosen to follow Him instead of living the way the world wants us to (John 15:18–20). But by living in harmony with other believers, we show the world what life would be like if they, too, followed Jesus. In fact, the unity of our fellowship tells the world that Jesus was sent by God to save the world, thus helping the world to believe. In His prayer following the Last Supper, Jesus said to the Father:

"I am praying not only for these disciples but also for all who will ever believe in me through their message. . . . May they experience such perfect unity that the world will know that you sent me and that you love them as much as you love me." (John 17:20, 23, NLT)

Does the family of God live in perfect harmony? No. The existence of many denominations within the church makes it plain that we have a long way to go to achieve perfect unity. Although we are all new creations, we have not yet been perfected in Christ, and so we will have occasional disagreements, and sometimes we will even fight. But keep in mind that Jesus' prayer for unity is one that you can help answer. Then one day, when Christ returns, we will indeed live together forever in perfect unity.

THE RESTORATION OF HARMONY WITH THE EARTH

Ever since the Fall, men and women have struggled to make a living from the earth. Even with modern technology at their disposal, farmers must still work hard to prepare the land to produce food. Then they must pray for rain to water their crops—but not so much rain that it washes away the harvest. Even those of us who don't work the land sometimes find ourselves at the mercy of the elements. We build sturdy homes to protect us from rain and snow and the extremes of heat and cold. Yet our homes may vanish in an instant in an earthquake, hurricane, fire, tornado, or flood.

The truth is that harmony between people and the earth and harmony within the earth will not be restored until Jesus returns. Romans 8:21–22 (NLT) says, "Against its will, all creation was subjected to God's curse. But with eager hope, the creation looks forward to the day when it will join God's children in glorious freedom from death and decay." The New King James Version says that all of creation "groans and labors with birth pangs" in anticipation of this day.

So how will God restore our relationship with creation? He will create for us a new heaven and a new earth!

Photo: NASA/JPL

God made a promise to us. And we are waiting for what he promised—a new heaven and a new earth where goodness lives. (2 Peter 3:13, ICB)

Then I saw a new heaven and a new earth. . . . And I heard a loud voice from the throne saying, "He will wipe away every tear from their eyes. There will be no more death or mourning or crying or pain, for the old order of things has passed away." (Revelation 21:1–4)

On the new earth, there will be no more death and decay, no more sadness or crying or pain. Until that time, we must still obey God's command to care for the earth and rule over it (Genesis 1:26–28). It is God's creation, and He declared it good.

MAKE A NOTE OF IT

Suppose a friend owed a lot of money and couldn't pay his or her bills. Would you be willing to pay the bills and set the friend free from debt? Suppose this friend had committed a crime and was under arrest. Would you be willing to go to jail in this friend's place so he or she could be set free? In order to make this sacrifice, you couldn't have any debt yourself, nor could you be guilty of a crime yourself. Otherwise, you would deserve to suffer the same penalties. How is this like what Christ did to pay our debt?

WHAT SHOULD I DO?

When you think of what God the Son has done—stepping down from His throne to be born as a baby, to live among us and teach us, then allow Himself to be killed in the most humiliating way possible to pay the penalty for our sins—how can your heartfelt response be anything but gratitude? Simply defined, **gratitude** is the thankfulness in your heart that you express to God and to others for the blessings you receive from them. We must show our gratitude to God each day for who He is, for everything He created, and for His goodness toward us. In fact, the Bible says, "In everything give thanks; for this is God's will for you in Christ" (1 Thessalonians 5:18, NASB).

A PRAYER

Dear God, thank you for your wonderful creation. Thank you for your amazing plan to save your creation. Thank you for making a way for me to know you and to spend eternity with you. Thank you for loving me so much that you sent your Son to die on the cross and pay the price for my sins. Help me to be thankful every day for all the ways you bless me and my family. In Jesus' name. Amen.

How We Can Be Influenced by Other Worldviews

As we have seen, people hold all kinds of beliefs about God, the universe, people, truth, and right and wrong. So how can we know which of these beliefs are the truth? Most people believe that the worldview glasses they are wearing give them the true view of the world around them. They believe in their worldview and may consciously or unconsciously influence others to accept or believe it as they do. But how can this happen? Can we be influenced to believe in another person's worldview even if it is not true?

You can learn a lot about a person's worldview just by watching his or her behavior. Not only that, but your own worldview can be greatly influenced by the worldviews and actions of those you observe. You may like and even envy how this person lives, especially if his or her life seems to be filled with fun and excitement. Then, deliberately or even without thinking, you may begin to adopt that person's attitudes and behaviors. All or part of their worldview now becomes a part of yours.

You've already learned that your worldview is influenced by what you study and read. Whether you're reading a textbook, a magazine, a novel, or a newspaper, you're reading words written by someone who has a worldview. What people write always reflects their worldview. The pages they write are filled with events or comments that reflect their own personal beliefs about God, the universe, people, truth, and right and wrong. Unfortunately, some people believe that everything they see in writing must be true!

TV shows, movies, music, and Internet sites are all produced by people with worldviews. Each of these is a very powerful tool that can shape what you believe to be true about life and the world. Without even thinking about it, you can begin to absorb the values and beliefs that you see and hear portrayed in the media day after day. People sometimes say, "Oh, it doesn't matter what I watch. It's only a movie!" But whether you realize it or not, your worldview is being influenced and developed by the sights and sounds you absorb into your mind and heart.

Do you believe everything you see or hear in advertisements and commercials? Can you identify the hidden messages in advertisements that try to persuade you to buy the product? Ads are created by people with worldviews, and their ads often contain images and words that reveal what they believe to be true about life and the world. You can unconsciously begin to absorb these worldview messages into your mind and heart, and soon these messages become part of your own worldview.

Does your worldview matter? Absolutely!

WHAT DOES GOD SAY ABOUT WORLDVIEWS?

With so many worldview messages bombarding your heart and mind and influencing your actions every second of every day, it's important that you understand which messages are true and which are false. Unless you do, you will not be wearing truthful worldview glasses that focus your view of the world. You must be careful not to allow false worldview beliefs to keep you from seeing the world in focus. Remember, what you believe is true will determine your choices and actions. And all choices and all actions have consequences, either for good or for evil.

God warns us about the powerful influence that others' worldviews can have on us. He warns us that beliefs that are not true can capture our hearts and minds. The apostle Paul wrote about this to an early Christian church in the city of Colossae. His words were true then, and they're still true today. Memorize them and hide them in your heart. Let them guide you as you begin to study and think about worldviews:

See to it that no one takes you captive through hollow and deceptive philosophy, which depends on human tradition and the basic principles of this world rather than on Christ. (Colossians 2:8)

MAKE A NOTE OF IT
List four powerful things from your everyday life that can influence your worldview and take your thoughts captive. Give an example of how one of these has influenced what you believe.

THE HOUSE OF TRUTH: THE FOURTH STONE

Throughout this book, you have begun building a House of Truth that will help you to define and share your Christian worldview. In this lesson, you set down the fourth and final stone in your foundation of wisdom:

BIBLICAL TRUTH 4:

God is the Creator.

Biblical Truth 4
God is the Creator

FOUNDATION OF WISDOM
Knowing, loving, and obeying God my Rock

THE ROCK
God and His Word

WHY DID GOD CREATE ME?

HE WILL TAKE GREAT DELIGHT IN YOU,
HE WILL QUIET YOU WITH HIS LOVE,
HE WILL REJOICE OVER YOU WITH SINGING.

ZEPHANIAH 3:17

THE BIG IDEA

After builders lay the foundation of a house, they begin to erect the walls. These walls must be built of sturdy materials so that the house can protect the people who live in it from heat and cold and storms. When it comes to building your life, a wise builder knows to build his or her walls with truth from God's Word. God's Word is strong and true and cannot be broken. There is no finer building material.

In the next four lessons, you will build the first wall of truth for your life. This wall represents the relationship God created you to have with Him. It is called the Fellowship Wall, and you will construct it using four pillars of biblical truth. The first two truths will explain what God intended your relationship of fellowship with Him to be like. The third truth will explore what the Fall did to your relationship with God. The fourth truth will explain God's plan for redemption that opens the way for your relationship of fellowship with God to be restored.

In this lesson, you will construct the first pillar of truth in the Fellowship Wall. This truth explores the answers to these questions: *Why am I here? Why did God create me? Was God lonely? Did God need to create me in order to be happy?* As you will learn, God has never been lonely. He does not need you in order to be happy. He created you because it pleased Him to do so. And He created you so that you could praise and honor and glorify Him. Because God is the only perfectly excellent personal being, and because He is our Creator, He alone deserves to receive all of our praise. When we understand His perfect excellence, we will want to praise Him always and live to give Him glory.

Knowing that God created you tells you that your life is not an accident of nature. And knowing why He created you tells you that you have a very important reason for living.

WHAT YOU WILL DO

» You will learn how you can enjoy a relationship of fellowship with God.
» You will explore two reasons why God created you.
» You will learn the meaning of God's glory and identify nine ways you can bring glory to Him.
» You will erect the pillar for Biblical Truth 5 in the Fellowship Wall—*God created me to be His child and to give Him glory.*

FATHER DAMIEN

Leprosy is a chronic disease that can cause permanent damage to the skin, nerves, limbs, and eyes. People who have the disease are called lepers, and because the disease was once thought to be highly contagious, lepers were often confined to living areas set apart from the healthy population. In nineteenth-century Hawaii, anyone who had leprosy was moved to the island of Molokai to protect the rest of the people.

In 1873, a Catholic priest called Father Damien arrived from Belgium on the small island of Molokai. Father Damien wasn't worried about catching the disease. He wanted to help, so he asked his bishop for permission to live and work with the lepers. When he arrived, things were pretty bad. The lepers on Molokai didn't have any real houses or hospitals. No one was taking care of them. They were expected to take care of themselves, which was difficult because of the disease. Even things like planting crops and collecting water were hard for the lepers to do.

Day after day, Father Damien worked to build a church and houses for the people. He took care of the very sick, helping with their treatment. He taught the people about the Bible and helped them to live good lives. Eventually, Father Damien caught leprosy too. But by that time other missionaries had followed his example and had come to help. After sixteen years of work on Molokai, Father Damien died.

Now, many years later, doctors understand that bacteria causes leprosy and have developed effective treatments. Since 1987, more than 15 million people have been cured of leprosy. Yet Father Damien and his work are still remembered. In 2005, he was voted by his home country the greatest Belgian who ever lived, and a statue of him stands outside the state capitol in Honolulu, Hawaii.

Statue of Father Damien in Honolulu. Photo: blahedo

THE ANCESTORS

The mourning doves cooed softly as the sun rose slowly over the island mountains. Teki Nalatu lay sound asleep as the cool morning breezes from the ocean drifted through the window and across his bed. As the light crept gently through the open window, his cat Coco stretched, yawned, and brushed Teki's face with her furry black tail.

"Go away," scolded Teki, not yet ready to wake up. "Go outside!"

The cat only purred and continued pestering Teki.

"Oh, you're impossible, my furry friend." Teki slowly stood and stretched. "Come on, I'll go outside with you."

The waves were calm that Sunday morning as Teki and Coco walked along the beach. Fresh seaweed and a crop of new shells decorated the sand.

"Teki," he heard his mother call. "Come eat breakfast. We need to get an early start. We can't be late, you know. We don't want to keep Great-Great-Grandpa waiting. He may become angry if we're late."

Angry, thought Teki as he and Coco retraced their footprints in the sand and headed to the house. *I hear that every year. If it's not Great-Great-Grandpa, it's Great-Great-Uncle Joe or Great-Great-Great-Auntie Mopi who will be angry if we're late. I don't even know these ancestors, much less care if we're late to the cemetery.*

Nevertheless, Teki quickly ate his bowl of poi and a banana while his mother carefully wrapped gifts of oranges, mangoes, dried fish, and even a small sack of tobacco. His father loaded his backpack with bottles of water, dried fruit, and coconut.

"Let's go. We don't want to be late. The ancestors are waiting," said Mr. Nalatu as he loaded the gifts into his pack.

With the sun now shining above the mountain peaks, Teki and his parents followed the path through the village and up the hill toward the old cemetery. Soon they were joined by other families also carrying small gifts wrapped in banana leaves or old newspapers.

"Hey, Teki," shouted Koka. "Wait up. I'll walk with you."

As the two friends walked along, Teki complained, "I dread this day every year. I don't like cemeteries, and I don't remember these ancestors."

"I understand," said Koka, who shared Teki's feelings. "But we have to do this. It's the tradition of our people. We must honor our ancestors. We come from them. The only reason we are alive is because of them. We have to keep them happy, you know, or they'll become angry. And someday when we die, we'll go to live with them. And you sure want them to be good to you then, don't you?"

"I don't know," said Teki as he sipped from his water bottle. "It's like all we do is live for them. But our village leaders tell us that we're part of them and that we must honor them. So I guess we must."

Soon the villagers arrived at the cemetery. Teki's mother took out the gifts she had prepared for each family ancestor. She gave Teki oranges and dried fish. "Go place these on the grave of Great-Great-Great-Auntie Mopi. This is her favorite food. It will make her very happy."

Teki obeyed, and he and others began placing special gifts next to the gravestones. Teki's father placed bananas and the pouch of tobacco on Great-Great-Uncle Joe's grave, while Koka placed a fresh-cut bouquet of wild ginger lilies on his great-grandmother's grave.

After all the gifts were presented, the village leader spoke. "Today we bless our ancestors. We live for them. We live to honor them, for we came from them. May they be happy with our gifts. May they bless us for blessing them. May they live forever, and may we join them one day as part of their family."

Teki was happy when the ceremony was over. He wanted to spend the day at the beach, but he knew that would not be possible today. This was a special day, and only activities that brought honor to the ancestors were permitted.

"Lunch is ready," said Mrs. Nalatu as she opened the small sack of dried fish and pineapple she had carefully packed after breakfast. "Let's eat here under the mango tree and rest awhile before we head home."

Anxious to leave the cemetery, Teki ate quickly. "I'm going to run ahead home and check on Coco. She's probably wondering where we are by now," he said, trying to think of an excuse to leave.

"Be careful going down the hill," Mr. Nalatu warned. "We'll be home in just a bit."

As Teki wound his way down the hill toward the village, a mynah bird squawked and yakked from a palm tree above his head. A pair of mongooses scurried between the rocks in a broken wall next to the path. "Good morning, little friends. Enjoy the day," said Teki as he hurried along.

When he came to the edge of the village he stopped, stood quietly, and listened. The village church bells rang in the distance. He liked the bells. They always told him when it was Sunday. But Teki knew nothing about what the bells meant or why they rang every Sunday. In fact, he had never been inside the church. All he knew about it was that his friend Kalani Tai went there every Sunday morning with her family. As he continued down the path that led to the beach and his house, the bells rang once more. Teki stopped, thought a minute, and smiled. *I have to find out why Kalani and her family go there every Sunday. Maybe it's to see the bells or to listen to them more closely*, he thought.

Then instead of continuing down the path to the beach, he followed the path through the village to the edge of the churchyard. Not wanting to be seen, he hid in the shadow of an old avocado tree that grew behind the church. He saw Kalani and her family walk through the door of the church. Then others, most of whom he had seen in the village, entered. When it looked as if the last person had gone inside, Teki crept beside the building and sat quietly under one of the open windows to listen. This time what he heard was not bells, but the happy sound of singing:

> *Praise the Lord!*
> *Praise the Lord!*
> *Let the earth hear His voice.*
> *Praise the Lord!*
> *Praise the Lord!*
> *Let the people rejoice.*
> *O, come to the Father through Jesus the Son,*
> *And give Him the glory,*
> *Great things He has done.*

Photo: Forest and Kim Starr

Teki loved music, as did most of the people in his village, but there was something new about what he heard this day. *That's beautiful*, he thought, making sure he kept his head below the open window so no one could see him. *But I don't understand the words at all. Who are this Father and Son they are singing about? And what do they mean, "give him the glory"?*

Afraid that someone might see him, he moved away from the church and backed into the shade of the avocado tree. He sat quietly, thinking about the day and wondering why Kalani and her family had not gone to the cemetery with gifts for their ancestors. As the warmth of the sun began to erase the cool of the shade, Teki knew he needed to return home.

But something kept him there in the old churchyard. Once again he heard singing, and then the bells began to ring again. As people began leaving the church, Teki hid behind the tree. When he was sure everyone had left the church, he turned and headed back down the path toward his house.

"Teki," he heard someone call. "Is that you, Teki?" He turned and saw Kalani and her family behind him on the path.

"Uh, hi Kalani," Teki said, hoping they had not seen him at the church.

"Where are you going?" Kalani asked.

"Oh, just home. I need to check on my cat, Coco," replied Teki without slowing his pace.

"Where have you been on this beautiful Sunday morning?" Kalani asked.

"Oh, just walking on the beach and playing with Coco," Teki replied, not wanting her to know that he had been either to the cemetery or to the church. "I'd better get home now, or my parents will begin to worry."

As Teki hurried off, Kalani's dad said, "I think Teki didn't want you to know that he and his family went to worship their ancestors at the old cemetery up the hill. This is the day each year when they take gifts to them, hoping to bless them and keep them happy."

"Why do they do that?" Kalani asked, thinking about how much she loved her own grandmother.

"It's an old tradition," her father replied. "They believe that when their ancestors die, their spirits continue to live in the village. Because they believe that the spirits of the ancestors can bring blessings or curses on the village, people must do everything they can to keep them happy. That's why they worship them and bring them gifts each year. They also believe that their lives actually come from their ancestors."

"But our lives come from God," Kalani said emphatically.

"That's right," replied Mr. Tai. "Although we are descendants of our ancestors, and we remember and love them, we know that God is the one who gives us life. He is the only one we are to worship. Remember the song we sang in church today, "To God Be the Glory"? Well, we sing that because the Bible tells us that He alone is God. And if He is the only true and living God, He alone deserves to receive glory and honor."

"I wish Teki and his family believed in God," Kalani said as her family reached their house.

"It's not that they don't believe in God, but they believe in Him in a very different way than we do," replied Mr. Tai. "They know a great God exists, but they don't believe He has anything to do with their lives now. And they believe in lots of smaller gods who control everything in this world and live in different parts of God's creation."

"I've heard Teki talk about the great god of the volcano," said Kalani, looking up at the slope of the mountain that towered above their village. "He's afraid of him. And, well, I'm afraid of the volcano too."

"Being afraid of the volcano and being afraid of a god of the volcano who doesn't even exist are not the same thing," her father replied. "Remember, God is the one who created the earth, even the volcanoes, and we trust Him to care for us."

"I know," replied Kalani. "But I wish Teki knew that too."

That evening, as the sun seemed to drop into the sea, Kalani sat on the steps of her front porch. She watched in awe as God painted the evening sky with soft reds, glowing yellows, and magnificent purples. As the colorful canvas unfolded and changed with each second, she thought about one of her favorite verses from the Bible: *Let them give glory to the LORD and proclaim his praise in the islands* (Isaiah 42:12).

Down on the beach, Teki walked slowly with Coco. He thought about his family's visit to the cemetery. But these thoughts filled him with fear and doubt— fear that he might not have pleased his ancestors with his gifts and doubt that his gifts could ever truly please them.

As the last golden rays of the sun faded from the sky, Teki turned and headed up the beach toward home. He thought again about his secret visit to the church. And though he didn't understand why, these thoughts brought a smile to his face and peace to his heart.

THINK ABOUT IT

» What do you think draws Teki to the village church? Why do you suppose Teki doesn't want anyone to see him at the church?
» What tells you that Teki has doubts about his family's traditions? Does Teki's visit to the church have any effect on him? How do you know?
» The members of Teki's family live to honor their ancestors. Whom do you live to honor?

WALT DISNEY'S *MULAN*

The Disney animated movie *Mulan* tells the story of a Chinese girl who goes in her crippled father's place to fight a war. Enemies are attacking China, and each family is required to send one son to the army. But Mulan's family has no one to send but her aging father. So to save her family's honor and her father's life, Mulan cuts her hair and dresses like a boy and joins the army. In the end, she helps save China.

Ancestral Temple in Japan / Photo by Gisling

Before she goes off to war, Mulan visits the shrine behind her house, where her ancestors are buried, and prays. The ancestors, who act as guardians for the family, look like ghosts when they are awakened. Even though they cannot leave the shrine, they can still influence the lives of Mulan and her family. To help Mulan, they send a small dragon, Mushu, a disgraced guardian spirit who is trying to earn back his place among the ancestors.

Today, many Asian countries and Polynesian island cultures still practice ancestor worship. Sometimes it is because family honor and respect are very important to them. But sometimes it is also because the people are afraid their ancestors will become angry and damage their crops and homes if they don't worship them.

The Bible says Christians should worship only God. It also says that after people die they do not come back as ghosts or have any power to hurt people who are still alive. So we don't need to be afraid of our ancestors.

It is important to understand that people who worship their ancestors may not know the truth about God. We should be careful never to make fun of them but instead try carefully to show them the truth. The Bible says, "If someone asks about your Christian hope, always be ready to explain it. But do this in a gentle and respectful way" (1 Peter 3:15–16, NLT). We should always be respectful of others.

WORDS YOU NEED TO KNOW

- » **Fellowship:** Enjoying a relationship of harmony with God and others
- » **God's glory:** God's perfect excellence and majesty in everything He is, everything He says, and everything He does
- » **To give God glory:** To honor God through our praise and thanksgiving and in everything we do and say

» **Worship:** The love and devotion we give to God as an appropriate response to His awesome love for us
» **Joy:** A delight that comes not from our circumstances, but from living in fellowship with God as His child

Hide It in Your Heart

And before the world was made, God decided to make us his own children through Jesus Christ. That was what he wanted and what pleased him. . . . And we were chosen so that we would bring praise to God's glory. (Ephesians 1:5, 12, ICB)

I delight greatly in the LORD; my soul rejoices in my God. For he has clothed me with garments of salvation and arrayed me in a robe of righteousness. (Isaiah 61:10)

You and I Were Made to Worship

Based on an 1883 novel by Italian author Carlo Collodi, the classic animated film *Pinocchio* opens in the workshop of Geppetto, a lonely woodworker with only his cat, Figaro, and his goldfish, Cleo, to keep him company. Geppetto is putting the finishing touches on a puppet, a colorful marionette he names Pinocchio. As he prepares for bed, Geppetto sees a falling star outside his window and makes a fervent wish that Pinocchio could be a real boy. As he sleeps, the Blue Fairy visits Geppetto's workshop and causes Pinocchio to come to life, though he is still nothing more than a wooden puppet. The fairy tells him that if he wants to become a real boy of flesh and blood, he must prove himself to be brave and truthful and unselfish. Jiminy Cricket is assigned to act as Pinocchio's "conscience," and together they set out to prove Pinocchio worthy of becoming a real boy.

In this story, Geppetto is hungry for human companionship, specifically a child to call his own. As we have seen, on the sixth day of creation, God created a man and a woman to "fill the earth and govern it" (Genesis 1:28, NLT). But why did God make people in His own image? Was He lonely? Did He need someone to talk to after a long week of hard work? Did He need friends in order to be happy? No, God has never been lonely. The three Persons of the Trinity have always existed in harmonious fellowship. God is complete and doesn't need anything, so He didn't create us to fulfill a need:

"He is the God who made the world and everything in it. Since he is Lord of heaven and earth, he doesn't live in man-made temples, and human hands can't serve his needs—for he has no needs. He himself gives life and breath to everything, and he satisfies every need." (Acts 17:24, NLT)

Because God does not lack anything, He cannot be bribed with something He desires or blackmailed into doing something He doesn't want to do. God is free to do what He wants according to His good pleasure, and He takes pleasure in everything He does.

Most parents have children because they want to. Your parents didn't "need" children in order to survive or to complete themselves. Parents have children because they want to give their children love, and they are pleased by the love relationship they have with their children. The truth is that God created us to be His children simply because He wanted to! You are here because your existence brings God pleasure:

And before the world was made, God decided to make us his own children through Jesus Christ. That was what he wanted and what pleased him. (Ephesians 1:5, ICB)

You were created for the enjoyment of God. In fact, *everything* was created for the enjoyment of God. Why does an all-powerful God find enjoyment in the things He's created? Because His creations are an expression of His glory. That is, everything He creates—you, me, the crying baby who lives down the street, the trees, the clouds, the stars—reveals and reflects something of His majesty. **God's glory** is His excellence and perfection in everything He is, everything He says, and everything He does. And His glory is eternally deserving of our praise.

Indeed, this is your life's purpose: **to give God glory**. This doesn't mean you add to God's perfect glory. Rather, to give

Viganella

God glory means to *reflect* His glory. In the Italian Alps lies a tiny village called Viganella. Fewer than two hundred people live in the village, which sits at the bottom of a deep, deep valley. The mountain on the southern side of the valley is so sheer that on November 11 each year, the sun disappears and not a single ray of direct sunlight falls on the town until February 2. In 2006, the residents of Viganella mounted a giant "sun mirror" on the northern slope overlooking the village. A computer controls the mirror so that it follows the sun, always reflecting sunlight into the town square. You should be like a walking Son mirror, reflecting the light of God into the lives of everyone around you. How do you do this? You can reflect God's glory simply by praising Him, thanking Him, and honoring Him in everything you do or say.

Why should you honor God? Because of who He is and for the glory that is His alone. The Bible says, "We were chosen so that we would bring praise to God's glory" (Ephesians 1:12, ICB). In other words, you were made for the purpose of worshiping Him. **Worship** means to give honor and praise to someone or something. The word comes from the Old English *weorthscipe* and means "to declare the worth, or value, of something." Just look around you and you will see that everyone worships something. Some people worship money, while others worship their jobs or their possessions. Some people worship athletes or politicians or ideals or goals, while others worship pleasure.

Jack Hayford, pastor and composer of the classic worship song "Majesty," writes, "Whatever you value most highly or place the greatest worth upon, that is what you worship." Where do you spend your time? What do you value most? Do you worship at the altar of video games? Television? Music? Sports? Or do you give God first place in your life? Worship rightfully belongs to God and no one else because He alone is the creator of all things and all people. No one else but God can truthfully claim to be worthy of the most important position in any person's life.[1]

The Bible says:

"You are worthy, our Lord and God, to receive glory and honor and power, for you created all things, and by your will they were created and have their being." (Revelation 4:11)

You are going to worship something or someone, so it only makes sense to worship God, for He is the only one who has proven Himself worthy of all your praise and adoration. As we have seen, God made you, He always tells you the truth, He teaches you, He helps you, He is always faithful, He will never leave you or forsake you, and He loves you so much that He sent His only Son to die on the cross to pay the price for your sins so that you could live with Him forever.

MAKE A NOTE OF IT

Even though your parents did not decide to have children because their children could do things for them, what kinds of things do your parents enjoy receiving from you? Write down as many things as you can think of that you can do to show love and affection to your parents. Even though God does not need us in order to be happy or to do things for Him, including worship, why do you think He created us to praise His glory? Your parents are blessed to receive your expressions of love, so what kinds of things would God be blessed to receive from you as His child?

NINE WAYS WE CAN GLORIFY GOD

Psalm 34:3 says, "Glorify the LORD with me: let us exalt his name together." To give God glory and to glorify God mean essentially the same thing. Psalm 113:3 declares, "From the rising of the sun to the place where it sets, the name of the LORD is to be praised." This does not mean that you need to walk around all day singing hymns.

Singing songs of praise is not the only way we can worship God. Let's take a closer look at nine different ways in which we can glorify Him and bring praise to His glory.

WE GLORIFY GOD THROUGH PRAISE

In Psalm 50:23, God tells us, "Whoever offers praise glorifies Me" (NKJV). We are encouraged to "praise his name with dancing and make music to him with tambourine and harp. For the LORD takes delight in his people" (Psalm 149:3–4). God delights in the praises of His people! Finding things to praise about God isn't hard to do. First of all, we can praise Him for who He is:

> *Praise the LORD, all you nations; extol him, all you peoples. For great is his love toward us, and the faithfulness of the LORD endures forever.* (Psalm 117:1–2)

> *God is our refuge and strength, an ever-present help in trouble.* (Psalm 46:1)

> *Praise be to the God and Father of our Lord Jesus Christ, the Father of compassion and the God of all comfort.* (2 Corinthians 1:3)

We can also praise Him for what He has done:

Praise Him for His mighty deeds; praise Him according to His excellent greatness.
(Psalm 150:2, NASB)

You alone are the LORD. You made the heavens, even the highest heavens, and all their starry host, the earth and all that is on it, the seas and all that is in them. You give life to everything, and the multitudes of heaven worship you. (Nehemiah 9:6)

O LORD, you are my God; I will exalt you and praise your name, for in perfect faithfulness you have done marvelous things, things planned long ago. (Isaiah 25:1)

Do you want to see and understand God in a deeper way? Then spend time praising God for who He is and what He has done. When you do, your attention will be focused where it belongs—not on yourself or your problems, but on the Creator of all things! Try it, and you will find that your love for God grows more and more until it spills out onto other people.

> *Man is one of your creatures, Lord, and his instinct is to praise you . . . . The thought of you stirs him so deeply that he cannot be content unless he praises you, because you made us for yourself and our hearts find no peace until they rest in you.*
>
> **Augustine of Hippo**
> 354–430

WE GLORIFY GOD THROUGH THANKSGIVING

Nearly two thousand years ago the apostle Paul wrote to his young friend Timothy that "in the last days there will be very difficult times. For people will love only themselves and their money. They will be boastful and proud, scoffing at God, disobedient to their parents, and ungrateful" (2 Timothy 3:1–2, NLT). Today, most people think only about themselves, and they're dissatisfied with their lives. If they ever think about being grateful for all they have, it's only on Thanksgiving Day.

Instead of allowing ourselves to be influenced by the ungrateful attitudes of others, you and I are called to be forever thankful to God for the great many blessings He has poured out on us. In Psalm 69:30, King David wrote, "I will praise God's name in song and glorify him with thanksgiving." Colossians 3:16 commands us, "Sing psalms, hymns and spiritual songs with gratitude in your hearts to God." The Bible tells us we are to be so strong in our faith that we are "overflowing with thankfulness" (Colossians 2:7).

Be thankful for your family and your friends. Be thankful for your home and food and clothing. Be thankful for the leaders of your country and for all who are in authority over you, whatever their political affiliation (1 Timothy 2:1–2). Be thankful for the people in your church and for all who follow Christ (2 Thessalonians 1:3). Be thankful when you are happy or sad. Be thankful when you succeed or when you have the opportunity to learn from failure. Indeed, "give thanks for everything to God the Father in the name of our Lord Jesus Christ" (Ephesians 5:20).

Spend today looking for things to be thankful for. Express your thanks to God and to the people around you, and soon you will find that you are more positive, full of energy, and more at peace with yourself and others.

WE GLORIFY GOD THROUGH TELLING OTHERS ABOUT HIM

Psalm 63:3 says, "Because your love is better than life, my lips will glorify you." Psalm 96:3 tells us, "Declare his glory among the nations, his marvelous deeds among all peoples." Even creation itself is commanded to declare His glory:

Praise Him, sun and moon;
Praise Him, all stars of light!
Praise Him, highest heavens,
And the waters that are above the heavens!
Let them praise the name of the LORD,
For He commanded and they were created. . . .
Praise the LORD from the earth,
Sea monsters and all deeps;
Fire and hail, snow and clouds;
Stormy wind, fulfilling His word;
Mountains and all hills;
Fruit trees and all cedars;
Beasts and all cattle;
Creeping things and winged fowl.
(Psalm 148:3–10)

Even sea monsters are commanded to praise Him! How much more those of us with lips should declare His glory!

So talk to a hurting friend about what God has done for you. At the dinner table, tell your family what you learned today about God. Don't be shy about sharing His love. For when Jesus told us to "go and make disciples of all the nations," He made this very comforting promise: "I am with you always" (Matthew 28:19–20).

WE GLORIFY GOD THROUGH GIVING OUR POSSESSIONS

Proverbs 3:9 (NLT) says, "Honor the LORD with your wealth and with the best part of everything you produce." As we have seen, when we call God "Lord," we are naming Him the ruler and owner of all things. If He owns everything, then everything we have belongs to Him. Like the servants of the master in the Parable of the Talents (Matthew 25:14–29), we have been entrusted with the Lord's possessions and are expected to make wise use of them.

One of the ways we can glorify God with what He has given us is to give our money and possessions for the purpose of telling the world about Him. This can mean giving offerings or tithes to your local church to enable the church to minister to your community. It may mean providing money or supplies to a missionary family teaching people in a far-off land about God. It may mean donating money, food, or clothing to a family in need of a blessing from God. What are some of the ways you can glorify God with what He has given you?

WE GLORIFY GOD THROUGH SUFFERING AS A CHRISTIAN

The Bible tells us that many people will hate us for following Jesus Christ (Matthew 24:9) and that we may be made to suffer for our beliefs. Yet 1 Peter 4:16 (NRSV) assures us, "If any of you suffers as a Christian, do not consider it a disgrace, but glorify God because you bear this name." When you stand firm in your belief and do not waver when you are bullied or even beaten for following Christ, God will be glorified and you will be mightily blessed:

"Blessed are you when men hate you, when they exclude you and insult you and reject your name as evil, because of the Son of Man. Rejoice in that day and leap for joy, because great is your reward in heaven." (Luke 6:22–23)

WE GLORIFY GOD WITH OUR BODIES

Paul wrote to the church in Corinth, "Do you not know that your body is a temple of the Holy Spirit who is in you, whom you have from God, and that you are not your own? For you have been bought with a price: therefore glorify God in your body" (1 Corinthians 6:19–20). When Jesus died on the cross, He not only paid the price for your sins, but He also paid a ransom to free you from captivity to sin. As a follower of Christ, you belong to Him, and your body is the Spirit's home. Therefore, do not use the parts of your body to break the law, disobey your parents, harm yourself, tempt others, or sin against God.

This does not mean your body is supposed to be "perfect" (and certainly not according to the world's definition of the word). You don't have to slim it down, bulk it up, or dress it up. You can glorify God in your body simply by using it at all times to honor Him. To the church in Rome, Paul wrote, "I urge you, brothers, in view of God's mercy, to offer your bodies as living sacrifices, holy and pleasing to God—this is your spiritual act of worship" (Romans 12:1). Here are a couple of ways you can make your body a living sacrifice:

1. *Physical worship.* King David, whom God called "a man after his own heart" (1 Samuel 13:14), worshiped the Lord with every fiber of his being. David

"danced before the LORD with all his might" (2 Samuel 6:14) and wrote, "I will praise you as long as I live, and in your name I will lift up my hands" (Psalm 63:4). He sacrificed his inhibitions and kingly dignity to worship the Lord with his whole body.

2. *Fasting.* Fasting is a spiritual discipline in which a person refrains from eating or other activity for a period of time as a way of putting God first above all other things. Moses fasted from food for forty days while he was on the mountain with God (Exodus 34:28). Jesus fasted for forty days in the desert before He was tempted by Satan (Luke 4:2). Paul and Barnabas appointed elders with prayer and fasting (Acts

Medieval painting of King David worshiping

14:23). Today, some people choose to fast from television for a time, while others may fast from the Internet or the phone. Many Christians still fast from food when they feel God leading them to do so. However, until you are an adult, never fast from food without the supervision and direction of your parents.

WE GLORIFY GOD THROUGH DOING GOOD WORKS

Glorifying God isn't just something you do in church; it's a way of living your life. Matthew 5:16 (NKJV) says, "Let your light so shine before men, that they may see your good works and glorify your Father in heaven." Although doing good works cannot earn you a reservation in heaven (Galatians 2:16), your good deeds will proclaim the Christian faith that lives within you (James 2:17–18).

In the New Testament, a woman named Dorcas is praised as one who was "full of good works and charitable deeds" (Acts 9:36). Because of her generous spirit, she was known throughout the port city of Joppa. So when she was overcome by illness and died and the apostle Peter raised her from the dead, the news spread quickly and "many believed in the Lord" (Acts 9:42). Are you known for your good works? What are some things you can do for others that will lead them to glorify God?

WE GLORIFY GOD THROUGH DOING WHAT IS RIGHT

Because you have been chosen by God to be one of His own, "you can show others the goodness of God, for he called you out of the darkness into his wonderful light" (1 Peter 2:9, NLT). The apostle Peter wrote these words to Christians living in foreign lands, where most people did not share their beliefs. He said, "People who do not believe are living all around you. They might say that you are doing wrong. So live good lives. Then they will see the good things you do, and they will give glory to God on the day when Christ comes again" (1 Peter 2:12, ICB).

Many of America's founders were men and women who believed and followed God. For much of the nation's history, the values and ideals held by most of its people were very much like those held by the Christian church. Those days are quickly coming to an end. Today, Christian views and values are largely scoffed at as being old-fashioned or even hateful and bigoted. Many people even think that America would be better off without Christians! This change would

not have taken the apostle Peter by surprise; in fact, he would have expected it. Peter told us that although we are to live godly lives while living among ungodly people, we should not expect to be praised for it. Indeed, he said, many will hate us for what we believe. Yet we must not change our behavior because of how people respond to us, good or bad. Instead, we must remain faithful, certain in the hope that our godly behavior will bring praise and glory to God when Christ returns. The Bible promises that one day God will be praised even by those who have rejected Him and those who made life difficult for His servants.

In the meantime, Peter says, we are to follow the example set by Jesus: "For God called you to do good, even if it means suffering, just as Christ suffered for you. He is your example, and you must follow in his steps. He never sinned, nor ever deceived anyone. He did not retaliate when he was insulted, nor threaten revenge when he suffered. He left his case in the hands of God, who always judges fairly" (1 Peter 2:21–23, NLT). When you are called hateful because of your beliefs, do not prove your accusers right by responding with hateful words or a promise that they will spend eternity in hell—such ungodly behavior will not change anyone's mind about you or about your God. Remember, your unbelieving neighbors do not know Jesus, and they may never have read the Bible. Most of what they know about God comes from watching you and those of us who say we believe. Telling others about Jesus is at least as much about what you do as what you say. As it is often said, actions speak louder than words.

We Glorify God Through Everything We Do

By now you have probably figured out that glorifying God is about much more than singing a song in church or saying a prayer of thanks before you eat. Everything you do should bring glory to God! The Bible says, "Therefore, whether you eat or drink, or whatever you do, do all to the glory of God" (1 Corinthians 10:31, NKJV). Whatever you do, do *all* to the glory of God.

All of life and not just some of life can be lived for God's glory. God is glorified not only when we worship, but also when we eat and drink in a way that pleases Him. God is glorified not only when we pray, but also when we help our neighbor. God is glorified not only when we study our Bible, but also when we do a job well. When you are a given a job to do, whether or not you are being paid to do it, you can glorify God by doing that job thoroughly, completely, and to the very best of your ability—as though you were doing it for God Himself! In this way God is glorified not only by the work of pastors and missionaries, but He is also glorified by parents, students, mechanics, teachers, construction workers, nurses, truck drivers, babysitters, and gourmet chefs.

We can also glorify God during our leisure time—that is, when we're playing, resting, or relaxing. When you play sports, do you play fair and cheer when others do well? Or do you lose your temper easily when your team falls behind or you're called for a foul? When you play a board game, do you play by the rules? Or do you want so badly to win that you're willing to cheat "just a little"? Do you include the younger kids in your activities? Or do you push them aside so you and your friends can have fun together?

Make a Note of It

How can you glorify God when you are eating and drinking? How can you glorify God while doing your school work? How can you glorify God while playing sports? How can you glorify God while watching TV or going to the movies?

A Prayer

Dear God, thank you for creating me and for choosing me to be your child. Thank you for sending your Son to die for my sins so that I may know you and talk with you and have a relationship with you. Help me to be joyful every day and to bring you glory through everything I do and say. In Jesus' name I pray. Amen.

WHAT SHOULD I DO?

God wants to have a close relationship with His children. And He wants the world to see how this relationship has changed our lives for the better. Does this mean we should always dress like we're going to a funeral, never have any fun, and walk around grumbling about sinners and hypocrites? No way! The Bible tells us, "Be joyful always; pray continually; give thanks in all circumstances, for this is God's will for you in Christ Jesus" (1 Thessalonians 5:16–18).

God wants us to be filled with **joy** always. That doesn't mean we're supposed to be constantly giddy, walking down the sidewalk laughing like lunatics all day long. Joy is a deeper pleasure, a constant delight that comes not from our circumstances but from living in fellowship with God as His child. Joy means being continually aware of God's loving presence, whatever we're doing and whatever is happening around us.

True joy is a natural response to a life of harmonious fellowship with our heavenly Father. We experience this joy when we know that our sins are forgiven and we will live eternally with God. Isaiah 61:10 says, "I delight greatly in the LORD; my soul rejoices in my God. For he has clothed me with garments of salvation and arrayed me in a robe of righteousness."

When you live a life of joy, the world will take notice. People will begin to wonder what you have that they don't have. They may even ask about your faith. Be on the lookout this week for someone who could use a smile or an encouraging word from you.

Be filled with the Holy Spirit, singing psalms and hymns and spiritual songs among yourselves, and making music to the Lord in your hearts. And give thanks for everything to God the Father in the name of our Lord Jesus Christ. (Ephesians 5:18–20)

A World of Worldviews

You have learned that a worldview is a set of beliefs through which you view and interpret life and the world and that this worldview guides your choices and behaviors. You've learned that a worldview is like a pair of glasses that helps you bring life and the world into focus. You've also learned that people do not all hold the same basic beliefs. In other words, people don't all wear the same kind of "belief glasses" to help them bring the world into focus. People hold different beliefs about God, the universe, people, truth, and right and wrong. These different beliefs lead people to behave or act in different ways.

With so many ways of looking at life and the world and so many ways to behave, have you ever wondered which worldview is the correct one? Does any one worldview provide a more accurate or truthful understanding of the world than other worldviews do? As we have seen, most people don't think much about their worldview or ask important worldview questions. Many people think like Amanda, who told Joshua, "I think it's boring to think about life and the world and all that kind of stuff. I just do what I like to do."

But is such thinking really boring? Is it not important to think about what you believe and to know if your beliefs give you a true picture of your life and the world? Throughout history people's beliefs have always led to action. If what a person believes isn't true, his or her choices and behaviors can have tragic consequences, not only for themselves, but also for entire communities, nations, and the world. Remember—beliefs lead to choices, and choices always have consequences.

Looking at a World of Worldviews

Even in your own community, you know that people have different views about God, the universe, people, truth, and right and wrong. And although they don't wear signs announcing their worldview, we can know something about their worldview by observing them. First, individual behaviors provide clues about people's beliefs and their view of the world. Although we must be careful not to judge or label others by what they look like or what they do, behaviors such as how they dress and speak often reveal how they interpret life and the world.

Second, when large numbers of people hold the same worldview, we often see evidence of that worldview within the nation and communities where they live. For example, in nations and communities where many people are Christians and hold a biblical Christian

worldview, we would expect to see many churches. We would also expect to see Christian schools and bookstores and different kinds of Christian organizations that serve the local community and other parts of the world. In countries where most of the people hold other worldviews, we might expect to see temples or mosques where they worship beings they believe to be their gods or God. We would also expect to observe festivals, clothing, and customs that would tell us about their beliefs as a community. In some countries, the worldview of the government leaders may not include a belief in God at all or a belief in the value of each citizen as one who is made in the image of God. In these countries, we may not see any places of worship because they may be illegal. Even in these countries, however, Christians and others may be worshiping in secret.

THEISTIC WORLDVIEWS

So many kinds of worldviews exist today that it's hard to identify all of them by name. One way to help us study them is to organize them into categories according to their beliefs about God and nature or the universe. When we look at the different worldviews this way, we find three major groups or categories. We will explore the first category in this lesson.

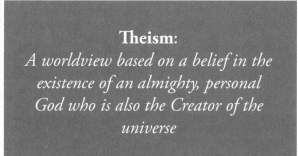

Theism:
A worldview based on a belief in the existence of an almighty, personal God who is also the Creator of the universe

Some people hold a worldview that includes a belief in one personal and living God. This God is the Creator of the universe, including the world and everything in it. This God is separate from His creation, though He is very much involved in sustaining it. He is an all-powerful spiritual being who is omnipresent, omniscient, and absolutely holy. This God is eternal, unchanging, and worthy of our worship.

A worldview that includes a belief in one personal and living God is called a *theistic* worldview, or *theism*. The word *theism* comes from the ancient Greek *theos*, meaning "god." A theistic worldview forms the basis for three of the world's major, or great, religions: Judaism, Christianity, and Islam. Although each of these religions is theistic, we will see that there are differences in what each believes about a personal God.

JUDAISM

Judaism is the great world religion that was practiced by the ancient Hebrew people, whom God chose and formed into the nation of Israel from the descendants of Abraham. The people who practice this theistic worldview religion are often called Jews. Although they believe that God is a personal being and that He created the world, Jews do not believe that God is one God in three Persons—God the Father, God the Son and Messiah, and God the Holy Spirit.

Jews believe that their theistic worldview is based on revelation from God. In other words, God has shown His people that He exists and what He is like. First, Jews believe that God has spoken to people through the creation. Just by looking at the world, all people can know there is a wise and all-powerful Creator. Jews also believe that God has revealed special truth to people about Himself through the Old Testament books of the Bible, including the first five books—Genesis, Exodus, Leviticus, Numbers, and Deuteronomy. Jews refer to these five books as the Torah. Those who follow Judaism, however, do not believe that God revealed Himself through His Son, Jesus, or through the New Testament books of the Bible.

Abraham by Molnár József

CHRISTIANITY

Christianity is another of the world's great religions. People who embrace this theistic worldview religion are called Christians. Christians believe that God is the one personal, living Creator. However, unlike Judaism, Christianity views and understands God as being one God existing in three Persons. You may remember from lesson 5 that Christians refer to this important biblical truth as the doctrine of the Trinity. While Christians believe in one God, they understand Him to be one God in three equal but unique Persons—God the Father, God the Son, and God the Holy Spirit. They also believe that God the Father sent God the Son, Jesus Christ, to live on the earth to redeem people and the earth from the curse of the Fall.

Christians also believe that their theistic worldview is based on revelation from God. Like Jews, Christians believe that God speaks to people through what can be observed in the creation. Like Jews, Christians believe that God reveals special truth about Himself through the Old Testament books of the Bible. Unlike Jews, however, Christians believe that God reveals Himself through Jesus Christ. Christians also believe that God reveals truth about Himself in the New Testament books of the Bible.

ISLAM

Islam is the third great world religion based on a theistic worldview. People who practice Islam are called Muslims. Like Christians and Jews, Muslims believe in one living Creator God. Like Jews, they believe that God is one Person, not one God in three Persons as Christians believe. Muslims, like Christians and Jews, believe that their theistic worldview is based on revelation from God, whom the Muslims call Allah. However, Muslims believe that in the seventh century Allah spoke through the angel Gabriel to a man named Muhammad over a period of several years. Muslims believe Muhammad received Allah's messages while he was alone in the

desert. Muhammad was called God's prophet because he told others the messages Muslims believe he received from Allah.

Many years after Muhammad died, his teachings were written down in a book called the Koran, or Qur'an. Muslims have also developed their theistic worldview from the first five books of the Old Testament, the Psalms of David, and the Gospels of the New Testament. However, Muslims do not believe everything in these books of the Bible. Muslims believe that Jews and Christians have changed or corrupted the original versions of these books of the Bible.

As you can see, Judaism, Christianity, and Islam are all based on a theistic worldview—that is, they believe in the existence of an almighty, personal Creator. However, you can also see that these worldviews do not believe the same things about the one true God. Likewise, each holds many different beliefs about the universe, people, truth, and right and wrong.

THE HOUSE OF TRUTH: THE FIRST PILLAR

During the next few lessons, you will complete the first wall in your House of Truth. This wall represents the relationship God created you to have with Him. It is called the Fellowship Wall, and you will construct it using four pillars of biblical truth. The first two truths will explain what God intended your relationship of fellowship with Him to be like. The third truth will explore what the Fall did to your relationship with God. The fourth truth will explain God's plan for redemption that opens the way for your relationship of fellowship with God to be restored.

In this lesson, you erected the first of these pillars:

BIBLICAL TRUTH 5:

God created me to be His child and to give Him glory.

WILL GOD MEET ALL MY NEEDS?

> "EVEN TO YOUR OLD AGE AND GREY HAIRS I AM HE, I AM HE WHO WILL SUSTAIN YOU. I HAVE MADE YOU AND I WILL CARRY YOU; I WILL SUSTAIN YOU AND I WILL RESCUE YOU."

ISAIAH 46:4

THE BIG IDEA

So far you have learned that God created you to be His child and that your purpose is to give Him glory. You've learned that this means you are to give Him glory and honor because He is the only true and perfectly excellent God. But God also created you to depend completely on Him. Depending on God for all your needs doesn't mean He created you to be a marionette, a mere puppet in His hands. What it does mean is that your life is dependent upon God. He created you, and He will give you everything you need for life on this earth.

You may be wondering what kinds of things you need God to provide for you. Think back to when you were very young and you had to depend on your parents to feed you, bathe you, dress you, and even carry you around until you were old enough to walk. Now you can do these things for yourself. But you still need your parents to provide you with food, clothing, and shelter, and you need them to take care of you when you're ill. These kinds of needs are called physical needs. You couldn't survive if there were not someone to meet your physical needs.

God meets your physical needs by providing you with parents and other adults who have the ability to do so. Even Jesus had His physical needs met by parents when He was born as a baby on this earth. Does this sound strange to you that our omnipotent God would ever need mere humans to meet His physical needs? Yet that was God's plan. He entrusted His only Son to be born to earthly parents who fed Him, clothed Him, and met His every physical need.

Now think ahead to the future, when you will be older still and able to provide for your own physical needs. Do you suppose you will no longer need God to meet those needs? When you can work and earn money to buy food, clothing, and shelter, will you no longer be dependent upon God for those things? Some people think so. But ask yourself this question: Who provides your parents with work and gives them the talent and ability to earn money to buy the things your family needs? You see, we must depend on God for everything, even the ability to work to provide for our own physical needs!

Now think about the things you depend on your parents to provide that are not physical. You count on your parents to provide you with such invisible things as love, encouragement, teaching, and yes, even discipline. You cannot shop for these things in a store like you shop for food and clothing, and yet they are very real needs. These are the needs of your heart, your mind, and your spirit. We call them nonphysical needs. When you are young, God meets most of your nonphysical needs through your parents. But He also brings others into your life, friends and family and people in authority who care about you, teach you, and love you.

What we must remember, however, is that people, including our parents and those who love us most, can never meet our nonphysical needs fully and perfectly. Why? Because no one but God is perfect. Because of the Fall, every one of us has sinned, even the most faithful followers of Christ. But there is One who can and will meet your nonphysical needs perfectly. He is God, your Father, who created you and knows your every need even better than you do. He is the Perfect One who will provide the love, encouragement, help, comfort, and even the discipline you will need all through your life.

Knowing that God created you to depend on Him to meet all your physical and non-physical needs may sound a bit scary. You may be wondering now what would happen to you if He did not meet your needs. But God *does* meet them! He created you to depend on Him, and He will never let you down, even in the most difficult situations. Knowing that God will meet every one of your needs should encourage you to live each day to the praise of His glory.

Now to him who is able to do immeasurably more than all we ask or imagine, according to his power that is at work within us, to him be glory in the church and in Christ Jesus throughout all generations, for ever and ever! Amen. (Ephesians 3:20–21)

WHAT YOU WILL DO

» You will define your physical and nonphysical needs and identify how God meets your every need.
» You will define *trust* and be encouraged to demonstrate it in your life, knowing that God promises to meet every need you have.
» You will erect the second pillar in your Fellowship Wall—*God created me to need Him for everything.*

RAINDROPS KEEP FALLING ON MY HEAD

Rain is absolutely necessary for sustaining life on earth. Without it, crops and forests wouldn't grow, and people and animals would soon die. God designed all living things to need water to survive, so He also created the water cycle to provide for His creation.

The water cycle constantly moves our water from oceans to land and back again. The sun heats the surface of lakes and oceans and evaporates water, which then rises into the air as water vapor, a gaseous state. The water vapor ascends on rising air currents into the atmosphere, where cooler temperatures allow the vapor to condense into clouds. As strong winds move the clouds around the world, the water eventually falls back to earth as rain or snow. Then the rain or melted snow travels along rivers and streams back to the ocean to start the cycle all over again.

Ultimately, since God created the water cycle and sustains it, He is responsible for where, how, and on whom the rain falls. Matthew 5:45 (NKJV) says that our Father in heaven "makes His sun rise on the evil and on the good, and sends rain on the just and on the unjust." Any time it rains or snows, God is making it happen, giving water to the earth so that we may live. It's comforting to know that our all-powerful Creator is always watching over us, ready and able to provide everything we need.

ISLAND GOLD

It's time to come in and get ready for bed, Kalani," said Mr. Tai as the last red streaks of the sunset finally disappeared from the sky. "We've got a busy day of planting ahead."

"Are we planting sweet potatoes again this year, Dad?" Kalani asked as she came in from the front porch.

"Not this year." Dad poured himself a cup of tea. "This year we're going to plant a new crop. We're going to plant sweet corn."

"Sweet corn?" Kalani asked with surprise. "I've never seen corn growing. The only corn I've ever seen is the kind we buy in a can at the village market."

"Well, you're going to get to see it grow this year," her dad said with a smile. "From what I hear, our island soil and climate are perfect for growing corn. And because we don't have a cold season, we can probably grow it all year long."

"Wow," exclaimed Kalani. "That sounds exciting. Are we going to sell our corn in the farmers market where we sell our sweet potatoes?"

"That's our plan," replied her dad, taking the family Bible off the shelf. "We just need to pray that the tractor keeps running. She's getting pretty old, you know."

Kalani snuggled up next to her mom on the sofa as her dad sat down in his old wooden rocking chair and opened the Bible. "Are you going to read the same psalm you read every year before we plant the sweet potatoes?" she asked, hoping her dad would not break the family tradition.

"Of course," he replied as he turned to Psalm 65. "This is God's promise to us, and He has always met all of our needs."

Kalani smiled as he began to read:

You take care of the earth and water it,
making it rich and fertile.
The river of God has plenty of water;
it provides a bountiful harvest of grain,
for you have ordered it so.
You drench the plowed ground with rain,
melting the clods and leveling the ridges.
You soften the earth with showers
and bless its abundant crops.
You crown the year with a bountiful harvest;
even the hard pathways overflow with abundance.
The grasslands of the wilderness
become a lush pasture,
and the hillsides blossom with joy.
The meadows are clothed with flocks of sheep,
and the valleys are carpeted with grain.
They all shout and sing for joy!

After reading, Mr. Tai closed the Bible, moved in front of the sofa, and knelt down. He took Kalani's and her mother's hands and held them in his own dark leathery ones. "Dear Father, we thank you for every blessing you have given to us," he prayed. "We thank you for our family, our friends, our home, and this beautiful island where we live. We ask you to bless the crops this year, for we know that we depend on you to meet all of our needs. And as we plant tomorrow, may we bring you glory in everything we do and say. In Jesus' name. Amen."

Kalani gave her parents a big hug and started toward her room.

"Oh, I almost forgot to tell you," Mr. Tai said. "After we plant our corn, I'm going to help Mr. Nalatu plow the new field he bought just up the mountain from ours. He's going to plant corn this year, too, but he doesn't have a tractor."

"Can Teki and I ride on the tractor with you?" asked Kalani expectantly.

"If you want to," he replied. "But you'll have to take turns. It's only a two-seater, you know."

Kalani had a hard time going to sleep as she anticipated the excitement of helping her dad plow the fields and plant the corn. For a long time she watched silver ribbons of moonlight dance on her bedroom wall as the full island moon shone through the swaying palms outside her window. Finally, she closed her eyes and fell asleep.

Early the next morning, Kalani heard the same wake-up call she heard every morning. "Time to get up, Sleeping Beauty," her dad called affectionately. Then he added, "We've got a full day of plowing and planting ahead."

At almost the same time, down the hill near the beach, Teki also heard a familiar wake-up call. "Rise and shine, sleepy head," Mr. Nalatu called. "We've got a full day of plowing and planting ahead, and Mr. Tai is going to help us with his tractor."

"Can I ride on the tractor?" Teki asked with a yawn as he climbed out of bed.

"If it's okay with Mr. Tai, I don't mind," his dad answered. "But remember, today is a work day. Now hurry and get dressed and come eat a good breakfast. You'll need lots of energy."

Teki's mom set a large bowl of fresh mangoes, oranges, and papaya on the table. Then she looked seriously at Teki and said, "Now remember. Be sure to wear your lucky necklace while you're planting. And don't forget to ask Kumu to send good rains at just the right time this year. And don't forget to—"

"I know," answered Teki with a yawn. From memory he added, "And don't forget to put three sacred lava rocks at each corner of the field to keep away the evil spirits."

"That's right," his mother said. "And because this is the first year we've ever planted corn, we don't know what kinds of evil spirits might want to steal it and eat it. So we must protect it well."

"I also think Great-Great-Great-Auntie Mopi will help us by watching over our field this year," said Mr. Nalatu. "That's one reason we honored her with everything she likes at the cemetery yesterday."

Teki didn't want to talk about the cemetery visit again, so he finished his last bite of papaya, excused himself from the table, and went to finish getting ready for planting day. *I love to help my dad plant and harvest each year,* he thought to himself, *but I don't like all of other stuff we always have to do, like wearing this silly necklace for good luck and piling lava rocks around the field to keep out the evil spirits. I wonder what Kalani and her dad do to keep the spirits away.*

By mid-morning, Kalani's dad had plowed most of his field, and the island sun had warmed the freshly turned soil.

"I love the smell of the plowed soil," said Kalani, sitting next to her dad on the tractor. "I just can't wait to see the first shoots pop up."

"It won't take long with a good rain or two," her dad replied. "Here, sit in my lap and help me drive the tractor down the last two rows. Then we need to get on up the hill. I told Teki's dad we'd be there by noon."

By late afternoon, Mr. Tai had finished plowing his neighbor's field, and the seed corn had been planted. Teki and Kalani had shared the tractor rides, although Teki had convinced Kalani to let him ride longer because it was his first time on a tractor.

"Thank you, my good neighbor," Mr. Nalatu said. "I couldn't have done this without your help. Now it will be up to Kumu and Great-Great-Great-Auntie Mopi to produce a good crop."

Kalani glanced up at her dad but didn't say anything. With a puzzled look on her face, she thought to herself, *Who in the world are Kumu and Great-Great-Great-Auntie Mopi?*

"God, our Father, will bless our crops," Kalani's dad said with a kind smile. "And we will give Him the glory for the good harvest. Now I think we all need to get home. It's been a very long day."

"You two go ahead," said Mr. Nalatu. "My son and I still have one more thing to do before we head home. And thanks again for all your help."

"What do you still have to do?" Kalani asked Teki.

"Oh, just look around to be sure there aren't any rocks in the field," said Teki, not wanting to talk about the sacred lava rocks.

"Come along, Kalani," her dad said as he hopped up on the tractor. "Your mom will have supper ready and waiting for us."

"What did Teki and his dad have to do?" Kalani asked as the tractor bounced down the dusty road toward their house.

"I'm not sure. But from the look on Teki's face, I don't think it was something he wanted to talk about."

"Do you think it might have something to do with the ancestors or spirits they believe in?" she asked, remembering what her dad had explained on the way home from church the day before.

"Maybe so," her dad replied.

Meanwhile, Teki and his dad began gathering several large, black lava rocks from the surrounding fields. Carefully, they stacked three rocks at each corner of their field.

"That should do it," said Mr. Nalatu, wiping the sweat from his face. "No evil spirits will dare come into our field now."

"Can we go home now?" asked Teki, who was hot and tired after the long day. "I'm hungry."

"Say your prayers to Kumu, and ask him to send the rains at just the right time. Then we'll go."

Teki mumbled a few words softly to himself, then hopped in the truck. He heard his dad say, "Oh Great Kumu, god of the rains, send the good gentle rains. Water our crops. Be good to us."

Early the next morning, Teki and Kalani awoke to the sound of a gentle rain falling on the tin roofs of their different houses.

"Thank you, God," whispered Kalani as the fragrance of rain-fresh air filled her little room.

"Thank you, Kumu," said Teki quietly as he climbed out of his bed and looked out the window. "I guess you really do hear us. Thank you for watering our fields."

The gentle rains came each afternoon that week. And urged on by the warm tropical sun, the newly planted corn fields began to show the first signs of growth.

"I'm going to walk up and check on the corn today," Teki told his dad. "I'll be back after lunch."

"Check the sacred stones while you're up there," said his dad. "And let me know if everything is okay. I have to go into the village this morning."

"I will," said Teki as he headed out of the house and up the road.

As he came to the field belonging to Kalani's family, he stopped, knelt down, and looked closely at the row next to the road. Just as he had hoped, he saw young shoots of corn pushing up through the warm, moist soil. Encouraged by what he saw, Teki got up and began to run up the hill toward his family's field.

"Hey, Teki. Wait for me!" a familiar voice called.

Teki turned and saw Kalani running after him.

Photo: Freestyle nl

"The corn's already coming up," she said excitedly as she caught up with him.

"I know," he said. "I hope our corn is coming up, too."

As they approached the Nalatus' field, Kalani stopped. She saw the piles of black lava rocks at each corner.

"What are those for?" she asked curiously.

"Oh, just rocks so we'll know which field is ours," answered Teki with some embarrassment.

"Really?" asked Kalani. "Everyone in our village knows whose field is whose. What are they really for?" she persisted.

"Well," said Teki, "they're supposed to keep out the evil spirits. They're sacred rocks—you know, from the sacred volcano. When evil spirits see them, they'll run away and not eat our corn."

"Really?"

"Well, that's what our ancestors have told us," said Teki. "And I guess it's true. And I guess it's also true that Kumu heard my prayer and sent the rain this week."

"Who's Kumu?" asked Kalani, remembering that Teki's dad had mentioned the name the day they plowed and planted.

"He's the rain god," replied Teki, beginning to show his irritation at Kalani's persistent questions. "If you pray to him, he'll send the rain—maybe."

"Oh, I see," said Kalani. "And what's that necklace you're wearing? I've never seen you wear that before."

"You've sure got lots of questions this morning," said Teki, trying not to let his anger show. "But if you must know, it's a good-luck necklace. I'm supposed to wear it so that we'll have a good corn crop."

"Oh," said Kalani, suddenly remembering her dad's warning about not asking Teki questions about his family's beliefs.

"So what did you and your dad put around your field to keep out the evil spirits?" Teki asked sarcastically. "And don't you have something to wear for good luck?"

Kalani could see that her curiosity was irritating Teki and wished that she had remembered her dad's advice. After thinking for a moment, she said quietly, "I'm sorry I ask so many questions. I didn't mean to be nosey or to make you angry."

"That's okay," he said, feeling sorry that he had gotten angry. "It's just that I'm not really sure I believe in all this stuff about how to have a good crop or to keep the ancestors happy all the time." Then he asked, "Do you pray to Kumu? Do you have a lucky necklace?"

"We don't do any of those things," Kalani replied kindly.

"Then what did you do?" asked Teki, becoming more curious. "It rained, and your corn is coming up just like ours."

"Teki," she said, "I believe in God. Not a rain god or a god of the volcano or just any old god. God is the one who created everything, including you and me. He's the one who sends the rains. He makes the corn grow and provides everything we need."

"Maybe so," said Teki. "But just in case your God doesn't do all of that, you'd still better put sacred stones around your fields, or evil spirits might steal the corn before the harvest."

"Oh, Teki," Kalani said with a sigh. "If anyone steals the corn, it won't be evil spirits. It might be a crow or some wild boars from up the mountain, but not an evil spirit. Each night our family prays to God to bless us, protect us, and provide for us. We trust Him. He really is the only One we depend on for everything we need."

"Well, we'll see," said Teki, wanting to believe more in what Kalani had said than in sacred lava rocks or lucky necklaces. "But I still think you'd better do something to protect your crop."

Kalani realized there was no need to discuss the matter further. As she turned to head back home, she said, "Teki, would you like to have a Bible? It's a book God gave us. It tells us about Him. It tells how He created us and how He provides for us. And because He is such a wonderful Father, we want to love Him and give Him the glory He deserves."

Teki listened carefully. Once again he was hearing words about giving glory to this God who is a Father. Like the first time he heard them, a peace filled his heart. Still, he didn't understand what the words meant. "Perhaps I would like a Bible," he finally answered. "But you know, this summer I'll be pretty busy helping my dad with the fields. Maybe when school begins you can give me one. I'll probably have more time to read it then."

Teki thanked Kalani again for letting him ride the tractor, said good-bye, and headed down the slope of the mountain to his house on the beach.

That summer as the good rains continued, the corn grew tall in the fields on the slope of the old volcano. The stalks were heavy with ears whose lush green husks hid the golden kernels beneath. People from all over the island talked about the new crop that flourished in the rich island soil and warm sunshine.

"It's our island gold," they would say.

To Teki's family, the new island gold was a gift from the ancestors. To Kalani's family, it was a gift from God the Father.

From time to time that summer, as Teki helped his dad work in the field, he would find an excuse to walk down the slope of the mountain to see if the Tai family's field of corn was growing as well as his family's. There he also saw tall stalks filled with ripening golden ears. But as often as he looked, he never found any black lava rocks in the Tai field. And every time he met Kalani that summer, he looked to see if she were wearing something for good luck, but she never was.

» Both Teki and Kalani prayed for rain for their corn crops. So why do you think it rained?
» Why do you think Teki keeps checking to see how the corn in Kalani's field is growing?
» What do you think is going on in Teki's heart and mind? How do you know?

POPPING OFF ABOUT CORN

Have you ever bitten into a freshly cooked ear of corn, drizzled with butter and salt? It's one of the best parts of summer! But do you know how important corn is around the world? Each year more corn is grown worldwide than either rice or wheat—about 800 million metric tons. The United States grows twice as much corn as any other country. In fact, corn has been growing in North and South America since before Columbus arrived. Archeologists have even found ears of corn in the Americas that are over 5,000 years old!

Corn is popular because there are so many things you can do with it. Try thinking of all the ways corn can be prepared, like cornmeal mush, grits, cornbread, even popcorn. Corn can also be made into cooking oil, corn syrup, and corn starch to thicken sauces. Corn is also used to feed farm animals including cows, pigs, and chickens. Now people are even finding ways to use corn instead of gasoline to power their cars!

So why don't you try growing corn yourself? This experiment may take several weeks, so be prepared to be patient!

Here's what you'll need:

» Corn seeds (available at a local nursery or garden supply store)
» Plastic sandwich bag
» Paper towels

Dampen the paper towels and place them inside the bag. Put a few corn seeds inside too, making sure each seed is pointing down. (The roots will grow out of the pointed end, not the flat end.) Then seal the bag, place it in a sunny window, and wait for the seeds to sprout. Check each day that the towels are still damp. When the seeds have sprouted, you can even transplant them into a garden! From planting to harvest takes from 55 to 95 days, depending on the variety of corn and, to some extent, the weather. Your corn is ready to harvest when the kernels are soft and plump and their juice is milky.

» **Physical needs:** The visible things I need for growing and keeping a healthy body

» **Nonphysical needs:** The invisible things I need for growing and keeping a healthy mind, spirit, and emotions

» **Intangible:** Something that cannot be seen or felt by touch

» **Trust:** A complete confidence in God that He will always do everything He promises

HIDE IT IN YOUR HEART

This God is the One who gives life, breath, and everything else to people. He does not need any help from them. He has everything he needs. (Acts 17:25, ICB)

Trust in the LORD with all your heart and lean not on your own understanding; in all your ways acknowledge him, and he will make your paths straight. (Proverbs 3:5–6)

WHY DOES GOD WANT US TO DEPEND ON HIM?

God wants you to know Him as your Creator and Father and to understand His desire to have a close personal relationship with you. He wants you to know that your life is not an accident. Rather, before time even began He designed this life specifically for you so that you can enjoy intimate fellowship with Him. For reasons known only to God, He chose to take up residence within you, calling you "a temple for the Holy Spirit" (1 Corinthians 6:19, NCV) and a child of God (1 John 3:1).

Because God is infinite and we are not, the wondrous nature of this relationship can be difficult for us to grasp. Although we were made to fellowship with God, we were also designed to be absolutely dependent upon Him for everything (Acts 17:25). Our lives, our daily existence, our talents, and everything we hope to accomplish are totally dependent upon our Creator. When Jesus said, "Apart from me you can do nothing" (John 15:5), He wasn't boasting. He was teaching us an important and valuable truth: We need God and His provision in order to become what we were meant to be. If we choose not to depend on Him, we will never be happy, nor will we be able to accomplish anything that has lasting value.

God loves you. He loves you wildly and all the time. He loves you without reserve and without condition. "Every good and perfect gift" comes from your heavenly Father (James 1:17), and He wants you, a child of God, to have the very best of everything. That is why He made you to depend on Him—so that you will never lack anything, so you will always have the best, and so you will never have to settle for the pale imitations the world has to offer. Yes,

Jesus said, "Apart from me you can do nothing." Then He went on to say, "But if you remain in me and my words remain in you, you may ask for anything you want, and it will be granted!" (John 15:7, NLT).

"Like a baby with its mother" (Psalm 131:2, NCV), when we acknowledge our dependency upon God and choose to rest in his arms, we will be calm, quiet, and at peace no matter how much the world rages around us.

> *Abraham never wavered in believing God's promise. In fact, his faith grew stronger, and in this he brought glory to God. He was fully convinced that God is able to do whatever he promises.*
>
> Romans 4:20–21, NLT

WE ARE PHYSICAL AND NONPHYSICAL BEINGS

Before we can understand the marvelous scope of the many ways God provides for our every need, we must first understand the dual nature of how we as human beings are made. A human being is a wonderfully complex creation. On the one hand, we have many things in common with parts of the animal kingdom. Our bodies have skeletons, muscles, stomachs, brains, nerves, blood, lungs, and other systems that work together in amazing harmony. And in order to survive we must have air, food, water, sleep, a capability for reproduction, and some protection from the elements and other, more dangerous creatures.

On the other hand, our Creator has also gifted us with qualities much more in common with His own nature. He has endowed human beings with thought and reason, emotions, a will, and a spirit. These qualities separate us from the animal kingdom and set us above all other creatures on earth. This is what it means to be created in God's image.

Our physical nature is sometimes called "the flesh" or "the sinful nature," while our nonphysical nature is referred to as "the spirit" and is characterized by the Holy Spirit who lives within us. The Bible says that these two parts of a Christian are always at war and competing for our loyalties. Although our physical needs are important and must be met, the Bible is very clear about where our ultimate priorities must lie (Galatians 5:16–18). The apostle Paul calls Christians people "who put no confidence in the flesh" (Philippians 3:3).

This doesn't mean that the human body is necessarily evil. It's what we do with our bodies that counts. When we put the desires of our flesh first, people tend to be beastly toward one another, even devilish; when we follow the leading of the Holy Spirit, we cannot help but be loving, patient, kind, and at peace. When we live according to the flesh, we are small and weak and helpless and unworthy; but when we put first the things of God, we can rise up by His grace and power and say, "I can do all things through Christ who strengthens me" (Philippians 4:13, NKJV). When we live according to the ways of the flesh, we are the vilest of all creatures, doing what we feel like at any given moment while openly rebelling against our loving Creator; but when we walk in the ways of the Spirit, embracing Christ as our Lord and Savior, we take our place as the noblest of God's creatures. Then we may joyfully cry out to the throne of God, "I will praise You, for I am fearfully and wonderfully made; marvelous are Your works!" (Psalm 139:14, NKJV).

WE DEPEND ON GOD TO MEET OUR PHYSICAL NEEDS

The physical world is composed of matter. Matter is anything that is composed of atoms and occupies space. It includes solids, liquids, and gases. Some kinds of matter can only be observed with the aid of a microscope or other special instruments, but through scientific investigation and instrumentation they can be "seen" and known to exist. The physical world includes everything God created that we can know through our five senses—sight, hearing, smell, taste, and touch.

Iluustration: Miraceti

Your physical needs are those visible things you need to grow and maintain a healthy body, including food, water, clothing, and shelter. God provides and sustains all the basic resources for meeting your physical needs—He causes plants and trees to grow, animals to be born, the sun to shine, and the rain to fall. He causes the earth to produce materials we use for construction and fuel. God causes plants to take in carbon dioxide from the air and give off oxygen, while He causes you to take in oxygen from the air and exhale carbon dioxide. The Bible tells us that "in his hand is the life of every creature and the breath of all mankind" (Job 12:10).

Indeed, God has been providing for your needs since before you were even born!

You made my whole being.
You formed me in my mother's body.
I praise you because you made me
in an amazing and wonderful way.
What you have done is wonderful.
I know this very well.
You saw my bones being formed
as I took shape in my mother's body.
When I was put together there,
you saw my body as it was formed.
All the days planned for me

*were written in your book
before I was one day old.*
(Psalm 139:13–16, ICB)

From the moment you began to grow in your mother's womb, God knew exactly how long you would live on this earth, He knew every need you would ever have, and He promised to provide for every one of them:

I will be your God throughout your lifetime—until your hair is white with age. I made you, and I will care for you. I will carry you along and save you. (Isaiah 46:4, NLT)

You may ask, "What about the cereal, yogurt, cheese, pizza, and other kinds of food we buy at the grocery store? If God doesn't make the foods we buy at the store, are we really dependent on Him for our food?" As we have already learned, only God can make something out of nothing. Cereal, yogurt, cheese, and pizza are examples of derivative food products,

meaning they were made from other kinds of food. If God did not provide cows and goats to give milk, we would have no cheese or yogurt. If He did not cause the grain to grow, we could not make bread or pizza crust. We can only create food from that which God created out of nothing.

King David wrote, "I was young and now I am old, yet I have never seen the righteous forsaken or their children begging bread" (Psalm 37:25). So if God has promised to meet our every physical need, why is it that when the so-called experts wring their hands and make dire predictions about the economy do so many Christians still worry about where their next meal is coming from? Or their next car payment? Or their next paycheck? Jesus made it very clear that worrying won't do a thing to help us:

"I tell you not to worry about everyday life—whether you have enough food to eat or enough clothes to wear. For life is more than food, and your body more than clothing. Look at the ravens. They don't plant or harvest or store food in barns, for God feeds them. And you are far more valuable to him than any birds! Can all your worries add a single moment to your life? And if worry can't accomplish a little thing like that, what's the use of worrying over bigger things?" (Luke 12:22–26, NLT)

So what does Jesus tell us to do instead? Are we supposed to stop complaining, pull ourselves up by the bootstraps, and make our success happen? Are we supposed to make our clothes from used grocery sacks? Are we supposed to buy a handful of lottery tickets and pray really hard? No, no, and no. Jesus tells us simply to have faith. Believe God. Believe Him and His promise to provide for us:

> *"Look at the lilies and how they grow. They don't work or make their clothing, yet Solomon in all his glory was not dressed as beautifully as they are. And if God cares so wonderfully for flowers that are here today and thrown into the fire tomorrow, he will certainly care for you. Why do you have so little faith? And don't be concerned about what to eat and what to drink. Don't worry about such things. These things dominate the thoughts of unbelievers all over the world, but your Father already knows your needs. Seek the Kingdom of God above all else, and he will give you everything you need."*
> (Luke 12:27–31, NLT)

You were made in God's image! The Bible says you are "crowned" with "glory and honor" (Psalm 8:5). And if you will make God the priority in your life, He will provide for every physical need you will ever have. For now, He will continue to meet your needs through the service and skills of your parents and those in authority over you. Later, He will provide for you through the abilities and talents He gives you or your spouse for earning a living. He may even use other Christians to help you in special times of need.

MAKE A NOTE OF IT
Write about a time when God used you or your family to provide for someone else's needs. Can you think of someone else in need whom God can use you to help?

WE DEPEND ON GOD TO MEET OUR NONPHYSICAL NEEDS

As we said, human beings have two sides—the physical and the nonphysical. The physical world includes everything God created that is composed of matter and we can know through our five senses. The nonphysical is everything else. We call these things **intangibles**, meaning we cannot see, hear, taste, smell, or touch them. Our nonphysical needs are those things we must have to grow and maintain a healthy mind, spirit, and emotions. These nonphysical needs include such intangibles as love and acceptance, comfort and encouragement, peace and emotional security, spiritual training, wisdom and understanding, and yes, even correction and discipline.

THE MIRACLE OF LIFE BEFORE BIRTH

God designed human babies to grow inside their mothers for nine months before being born into the world. He makes the mother's body a special place for babies, giving them everything they will need to grow and mature. Within the first month, the baby will grow 10,000 times its original size as it begins to develop its circulatory, nervous, and digestive systems. By the end of the second month, the baby has eyes, a nose, lips, a tongue, ears and the beginnings of teeth. A week later, the mother's doctor can hear the baby's heartbeat. By the end of the third month, the baby will have his or her own unique fingerprints.

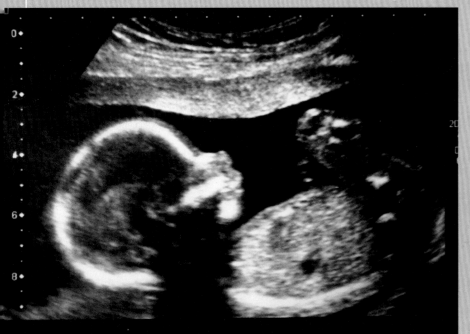

Almost before the mother knows she is pregnant, the baby is already able to move. As the baby reaches five months, he or she can stretch and kick so much that the mother can feel her child inside her. At this point the baby has hair, eyebrows, eyelids and eyelashes and may startle at sounds and respond to the voices of its mother and father. Ultrasound pictures at this stage may catch the baby sucking its thumb, yawning, or even what appears to be walking!

No one really knows exactly when babies begin thinking about things or feeling pain, but we do know that God has designed babies to start being people from the time they are conceived. God told the prophet Jeremiah, "Before I formed you in the womb I knew you, before you were born I set you apart" (Jeremiah 1:5). Just like you are different from anyone else in your family, God creates each baby to be special and unique long before he or she is born. The book of Luke tells of when Mary, the newly pregnant mother of Jesus, visited her pregnant cousin Elizabeth. When the baby Elizabeth was carrying heard Mary's voice, he jumped! Elizabeth said, "As soon as the sound of your greeting reached my ears, the baby in my womb leaped for joy" (Luke 1:44). Elizabeth's baby would grow to be John the Baptist, who recognized the coming Messiah before either of them was born!

How God meets our nonphysical needs is not always easily understood. Often people don't even see the working of God's hand until after the need has been met. Then they may say, "Oh, now I see how God was working." God is always faithful to meet our needs, so even when we don't "see" an immediate answer to our prayers, we must trust that God is always working in our lives. In His way and in His time, He will meet our needs.

God meets our nonphysical needs through His Holy Spirit dwelling in us, through the power of His Word, and through other people. Here are some of the needs you will experience that God promises to provide for.

LOVE AND ACCEPTANCE

Have you ever felt unloved or rejected? It hurts, doesn't it. Why do you suppose our need for love and acceptance is so important? It's because God is love (1 John 4:8) and He created us in His image to love and be loved. When ordinary people fail to love us, we can always find love and acceptance in His arms:

> *How great is the love the Father has lavished on us, that we should be called children of God! And that is what we are!* (1 John 3:1)

> *"I love you . . . with a love that will last forever. I became your friend because of my love and kindness."* (Jeremiah 31:3, ICB)

Crucifixion of Christ by Zurbaran

> *"Be strong and courageous. Do not be afraid or terrified because of them, for the LORD your God goes with you; he will never leave you nor forsake you."* (Deuteronomy 31:6)

> *Give all your worries and cares to God, for he cares about you.* (1 Peter 5:7, NLT)

God understands what it feels like to be unloved and rejected by people. Imagine what it must have been like for Jesus to come to earth. His prophets told the people He was coming. He even told them exactly where He would be born and what would happen to Him. He showed people the Father's love and did miracles to prove that He was, in fact, God's Son. He taught only what the Father wanted Him to teach, and He never sinned. He saved us from a life of slavery to sin. And how did we repay Him? We sentenced Him to die on a cross like the lowest of criminals.

And how did God respond? He promised to love you "with a love that will last forever" and that He would "never leave you nor forsake you." So how do you think God wants you to treat others who feel unloved and rejected? He wants you to share with them the love and acceptance He so freely gives to you (Matthew 25:31–40).

COMFORT AND ENCOURAGEMENT

How do you feel when someone hurts your feelings? What about when you try and fail at something? Have you ever lost a pet or had a friend move away? Have you ever had a grandparent die? At such times, there is little that someone can say or do to make the hurt go away. A friend may even be uncomfortable in the situation and not even try. But there is One who will always come to our aid:

> *God is our merciful Father and the source of all comfort. He comforts us in all our troubles so that we can comfort others. When they are troubled, we will be able to give them the same comfort God has given us.* (2 Corinthians 1:3–4, NLT)

Our need for comfort in times of grief or loss is seldom if ever met instantly. But over time the Holy Spirit will work deep within your heart to apply the truths of God's promises. And God will bring others into your life to listen to your troubles and bear your grief with you. Then, when a friend or family member is grieving, He may send you to comfort them.

PEACE AND EMOTIONAL SECURITY

Have you ever been afraid of the dark? A fear of the dark can make it pretty hard to get to sleep at night! What are some other things that frighten or trouble you? A math test? A piano recital? A big game? We all worry about something at some time. At such times, we need more than just comforting. We need peace. We need to be secure in the knowledge that everything is going to work out for the best. And God alone can provide us with perfect peace:

> [Jesus said] *"I am leaving you with a gift—peace of mind and heart. And the peace I give is a gift the world cannot give. So don't be troubled or afraid."* (John 14:27, NLT)

> *And we know that God causes everything to work together for the good of those who love God and are called according to his purpose for them.* (Romans 8:28, NLT)

> *I will lie down and sleep in peace, for you alone, O LORD, make me dwell in safety.* (Psalm 4:8)

Pay attention when Jesus says that the peace He gives is something the world cannot provide you. This doesn't stop the world from making promises it can't keep. Watch TV for just a few minutes during any standard commercial break. Advertisers are spending millions of dollars to tell you that if you will only drive their car, use their air freshener, listen to their music, eat their food, and make calls on their phone that you will be happy, prosperous, loved, and at peace with the world. It all sounds nice, but none of it is true!

God alone keeps all His promises, and He alone can cause everything to work together for your good!

HELP IN TIMES OF NEED

What are some things you need help doing? Schoolwork? Cleaning your room? Memorizing Bible verses? Resisting temptation? There is One who is always there, never sleeps, and is always ready to help you:

> *I lift up my eyes to the hills—*
> *where does my help come from?*
> *My help comes from the LORD,*
> *the Maker of heaven and earth.*

He will not let your foot slip—
he who watches over you will not slumber.
(Psalm 121:1–3)

"So do not fear, for I am with you; do not be dismayed, for I am your God. I will strengthen you and help you; I will uphold you with my righteous right hand."
(Isaiah 41:10)

God is our refuge and strength, an ever-present help in trouble. (Psalm 46:1)

Sometimes the help we need may be physical, but it may also be nonphysical such as dealing with a problem, knowing the right thing to do, or building godly friendships. When you have a problem you can't solve, take it to God in prayer. God may help you by speaking to the heart of another person. He may send His help in the form of a person to assist you or encourage you. Or He may intervene in your situation by providing you with remarkable healing, wisdom, or strength. And don't forget to read your Bible! God's Word is always a help that is made alive in you through the Holy Spirit, your Helper and Counselor.

WISDOM AND UNDERSTANDING

Simply defined, wisdom means applying the knowledge of how to live well. Some problems can only be solved through the application of godly wisdom, while many problems can be avoided altogether if we will seek God's wisdom daily and live it. The good news is that God's wisdom is readily available to you. All you have to do is ask:

If any of you needs wisdom, you should ask God for it. God is generous. He enjoys giving to all people, so God will give you wisdom. (James 1:5, ICB)

For the LORD gives wisdom, and from his mouth come knowledge and understanding. (Proverbs 2:6)

[Jesus said] "But the Counselor, the Holy Spirit, whom the Father will send in my name, will teach you all things and will remind you of everything I have said to you." (John 14:26)

God's wisdom is not hidden knowledge. You don't need to be Indiana Jones to discover it and dig it up. You don't need a secret password or a "cheat code" to access it. God wants you to have full and free use of His wisdom. In fact, He's written it all down for you in the best-selling book of all time! You probably have a copy of it somewhere in the house. Most of us know it as the Bible. Be sure to check out the part titled "Proverbs." It's full of good advice.

CORRECTION AND DISCIPLINE

You probably don't enjoy being disciplined by your parents. No one does. However, discipline and correction are important to our long-term growth and learning. Loving parents will correct their children for wrong behavior so that the children will learn to choose right behaviors in the future. God is also a loving parent and does the same for His children:

> *My son, don't think the Lord's discipline of you is worth nothing. And don't stop trying when the Lord corrects you. The Lord corrects those he loves.*
> (Hebrews 12:5–6, ICB)

> *We have all had fathers here on earth who punished us. And we respected our fathers. So it is even more important that we accept punishment from the Father of our spirits. If we do this, we will have life. . . . God punishes us to help us, so that we can become holy as he is. We do not enjoy punishment. Being punished is painful. But later, after we have learned from being punished, we have peace, because we start living in the right way.* (Hebrews 12:9–11, ICB)

God disciplines everyone He calls His children, even parents! He does this so that we will grow to be holy like He is. He does this so that we will learn that sin does more than hurt His feelings—every sin has consequences for our own physical and spiritual health. And when we learn from His correction, we can have true peace and begin walking once more the correct path that He has set before us.

A PRAYER

Dear God, thank you for meeting every one of my needs, both physical and nonphysical. Thank you for teaching me to depend on you for everything. Thank you that you are faithful and will never let me down. Help me to trust you more and more every day. In Jesus' name. Amen.

Write about a time when you received discipline or correction for something you did wrong. Did you deserve to be punished? What did you learn from the correction? Did you experience other consequences as a result of what you did wrong?

WHAT SHOULD I DO?

God gave clothing to Adam and Eve after they sinned against Him (Genesis 3:21). He provided water for the Israelites in the desert (Exodus 15:22–24). He fed the prophet Elijah in the midst of a famine (1 Kings 17:6). He provided shelter for Joseph and Mary when there was no room at the inn (Luke 2). God created us to depend on Him, and He has promised to provide for all our needs.

So the question is this: Do you trust God? **Trust** means having confidence in someone else. Specifically, trusting God means having complete confidence that He will always do everything He promises. Trust is an important part of any relationship—it sets us free from worrying about whether the other person will care for us and not hurt us. Without trust, we cannot be in harmony with that person.

Because God is who He is, we can trust Him completely! You've learned already that God is truth and that He always keeps His promises. You've learned that you are His child and that you can always depend on Him. Even when we cannot see a solution to our problems, even when we're not sure how God will provide, we must choose to trust Him:

The Prophet Elijah by Volterra

Trust in the LORD with all your heart and lean not on your own understanding; in all your ways acknowledge him, and he will make your paths straight. (Proverbs 3:5–6)

He will always provide because He is a faithful God. Therefore, we need to trust God for everything. We need to trust God if we are to please Him (Hebrews 11:6). When we trust God, He will answer our prayers (Matthew 21:22), give us peace (Isaiah 26:3), and ensure our victory over the devil (Mark 9:23).

MAKE A NOTE OF IT

Think about a need you have that you sometimes worry about. It may be a physical need, or it may be a nonphysical need. Write a letter to God telling Him about your need. Then thank Him for His promise to meet this need. At the end of your letter, write out one of the scriptures from this lesson that gives you hope and encouragement that God will indeed meet this particular need.

WHO PUT THE WORLD IN YOUR WORLDVIEW?

Some worldviews hold that nature, or the physical earth and universe, is all that exists and that there is no God. Other worldviews insist that nature is God and God is nature.

Let's take a closer look at these different worldviews.

WORLDVIEWS THAT BELIEVE ONLY NATURE EXISTS

Some worldviews do not include beliefs about a personal God except the belief that God does not exist. These worldviews are called *atheistic* worldviews. If you look carefully at the words *atheistic* and *atheism*, you will see the root words *theistic* and *theism*. As you have learned, these words come from the Greek word *theos* meaning "god." Adding the letter *a* to these words changes their meaning. The prefix *a-* means "without" or "not." Therefore, *atheism* is a word used to describe a worldview that believes God does not exist.

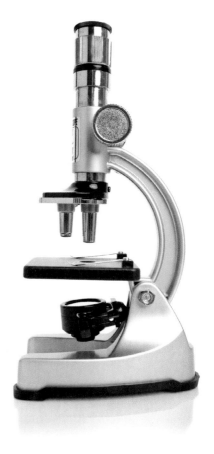

A worldview that holds that nature, or the physical earth and universe, is all that exists and that there is no God, is sometimes called *naturalism* or *materialism*. Each of these has some similar and some different beliefs about God, the universe, people, truth, and right and wrong.

You can see the root word *nature* in the word *naturalism*. This worldview holds that only things that can be seen or proven to exist in nature are real. You can see the root word *material* in the word *materialism*. This worldview is very similar to naturalism. It holds that only material, or physical, things are real. If something is immaterial, or intangible, such as God or your spirit, then it is not thought to be real. Because we cannot touch or see God or conduct a laboratory experiment to prove He exists, people who hold a naturalistic or materialistic worldview are usually atheists.

The naturalistic worldview, or naturalism, is based only on what we can discover and understand with our minds and our senses. It does not accept the belief that God exists and reveals or speaks truth to people about the world. People with a naturalistic worldview believe that the truth about what exists can be known only through science. They believe that science proves that the natural or material world is all there is and all there ever will be.

WORLDVIEWS THAT BELIEVE NATURE IS GOD AND GOD IS NATURE

Some worldviews hold that there is no difference between God and things that exist in nature. These worldviews do not believe that God is a personal being. In these worldviews, "God" is thought to be an impersonal force or spiritual energy. People who hold these worldviews believe that everything that exists is part of this impersonal spiritual or energy force which they may call "God." In other words, they believe the earth is God, I am God, and you are God. Everything is part of this one, impersonal "God-force."

These worldviews are called by many names, but perhaps the most familiar include *New Age* and *spiritualism*. The religions of Hinduism and Buddhism also include the belief that God is everything, and everything is God. The word *pantheism* is sometimes used when referring to the New Age worldview. The prefix *pan-* means "all." Pantheism is a worldview that believes that *all* things are "God," and this includes you and rocks and trees and everything in the universe.

The name "New Age" may sound at first like a strange one for this mystical worldview that believes everything is God and God is everything. But people who hold this worldview believe that a new age, or time of peace and harmony on earth, will begin when enough people come to understand that everything that exists is part of one spiritual or energy force called God. There is nothing "new" about this worldview; it includes beliefs held by people from earliest history.

The New Age beliefs about God, the universe, people, truth, and right and wrong are not based on special revelation from God. Many of this worldview's beliefs are based on ancient writings of philosophers and magicians. Some are based on the writings of people called *astrologers*, who believe they can understand the truth about the world by studying the position and movement of planets and stars. Other beliefs of the New Age worldview are based on human imagination and superstition.

MAKE A NOTE OF IT

Write the following passage in your notebook: "For ever since the world was created, people have seen the earth and sky. Through everything God made, they can clearly see his invisible qualities—his eternal power and divine nature. So they have no excuse for not knowing God" (Romans 1:20, NLT). Now answer these questions: How do we "see" God's invisible qualities in the world? What can we know for sure about God from the things we see in creation?

THE HOUSE OF TRUTH: THE SECOND PILLAR

In this lesson, you added another important pillar to the Fellowship Wall in your House of Truth:

BIBLICAL TRUTH 6:

God created me to need Him for everything.

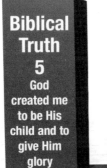

Biblical Truth 5
God created me to be His child and to give Him glory

Biblical Truth 6
God created me to need Him for everything

FELLOWSHIP WALL
My relationship with God when I believe that Jesus is God's Son and my Savior

Biblical Truth 1
God always tells me what is right and true

FOUNDATION OF WISDOM
Knowing, loving, and obeying God my Rock

**THE ROCK
God and His Word**

WHY DOES SIN KEEP ME FROM KNOWING GOD?

YOUR EYES ARE TOO PURE TO LOOK ON EVIL; YOU CANNOT TOLERATE WRONG.

HABAKKUK 1:13

THE BIG IDEA

So far you have learned many things about what God is like. One of the most important things you learned is that God is holy. Do you remember what it means to be holy? It means that God is totally sinless. He is absolutely just and always does what is right and good. God will never do something that is wrong. You've also learned that the only true and holy God is our Creator and that He created us in His image. If God is holy and if He created us in His image, then He created us to be holy like He is holy. God never intended for us to be anything less than holy. And if we were holy like God is holy, God would have perfect, close fellowship with us as He originally intended. A holy God can fellowship only with those who are also perfectly holy.

However, being created in God's image also means that man was given a will and the freedom to choose. Sadly, the first man and woman, Adam and Eve, used their free will to make a tragic choice. They deliberately disobeyed God's command to not eat from the tree of the knowledge of good and evil. Yes, Satan tempted them to disobey, but they did not have to give in to temptation. They made their own choice, and they chose to disobey. Once they made that choice, they were no longer holy as God created them to be. Thus they were separated from fellowship with God.

All people born since the Fall have been born unholy. Even before we commit our first sin, we are born into this world as sinners. This is important to understand: We are not sinners because we sin; we sin because we are born with a built-in tendency to disobey God. And it is our sinful nature that separates each of us from God.

Does this make you feel sad or depressed? At first it may, but it is important to remember that God did not abandon His creation after the Fall. Instead, He continued to provide His children with everything they needed to live on this earth. Most importantly, He also provided a plan to restore us to holiness so we can one day live eternally with Him on a new earth. Instead of punishing us with eternal separation from Him, He sent His Son, Jesus, to take the punishment we deserve.

We will study God's great plan of redemption in the next lesson. However, before we can appreciate what God did for us through His Son, we must truly understand how sinful we are and how our sins separate us from a holy God. We must understand the bad news before we can understand and be grateful for the wonderful Good News!

Expulsion from Eden by Dore

WHAT YOU WILL DO

» You will identify the consequences of sin and how all people inherit a sinful nature from Adam and Eve.

» You will describe what our sins do to our fellowship with God.

» You will be encouraged to demonstrate humility as you realize that you and all people are sinners who need Jesus Christ to restore their fellowship with God.

» You will erect the third pillar in your Fellowship Wall—*Sin causes separation and disharmony between me and God.*

MOUNT ST. HELENS

Have you ever seen pictures of an erupting volcano, with red-hot lava and clouds of steam and gas? Volcanoes form in places where the earth's crust is thinner and the hot rock underneath can push through. Just like the whistle on a teakettle releases pressure, a volcano can help vent pressure and heat from deep inside the earth.

Photo: USGS

Sometimes volcanoes erupt slowly with steam and seeping lava, like Kilauea in Hawaii. Other times volcanoes explode violently, sending a cloud of hot gasses racing along the ground and throwing ash high into the air. Mount Vesuvius, which erupted in A.D. 79, buried the Italian city of Pompeii. In 1883, the volcanic island of Krakatoa, in what is now Indonesia, erupted in a series of explosions so violent they were heard 3,000 miles away. Krakatoa threw so much ash into the air that the sun was blocked for months, causing temperatures to fall worldwide.

More recently, in the state of Washington, a volcano in the Cascade mountain range erupted. On May 18, 1980, Mount St. Helens exploded, sending hot ash miles into the air. The eruption broke off a huge piece of the mountainside, which slid down into Spirit Lake, uprooting the forest and sending mud and debris down the river for miles. Fifty-seven people died, and ash was carried east by the wind into ten other states. The volcano erupted for nine hours before finally quieting down.

Natural disasters like volcanoes are part of the curse God put on the earth when Adam and Eve sinned. The apostle Paul said, "Against its will, all creation was subjected to God's curse. But with eager hope, the creation looks forward to the day when it will join God's children in glorious freedom from death and decay" (Romans 8:20-21, NLT). God has promised that the consequences of the Fall will not last forever. One day, He will create a new heaven and earth where His children will live with Him forever in peace.

ISLAND FIRE

"Where's dad?" Kalani asked as she sat down for her favorite Saturday breakfast of pancakes.

"He's already up at the field," her mom said. "He thinks the corn is just about ready to harvest, perhaps as soon as next week."

As Kalani poured warm coconut syrup over her pancakes, her dad bounded up the front steps. "It's beautiful," he beamed. "Next Saturday for sure. I saw Mr. Nalatu, and he said his crop would be ready to pick by then too."

Kalani smiled, swallowed her first delicious bite, and said, "I can't wait! Maybe we can even have corn on the cob for supper after the harvest."

"Maybe?" replied her mom. "No *maybe* about it. I've already planned the meal—pulled pork, fresh greens, sweet potatoes, and corn on the cob. And for dessert, sweet rice pudding. Now finish your breakfast, Kalani. Today's market day in the village, and I need you to carry one of the baskets."

Kalani loved market day. It seemed as if everyone on the island was there. She especially loved sampling the vendors' fresh tropical fruits.

"Here, Kalani," said Mr. Omotani, handing her a slice of juicy pineapple as she and her mother approached his fruit stand. "And how are you both today?"

"Thank you," Kalani said. "I'm really excited. My dad thinks the sweet corn will be ready to harvest by next Saturday."

"Everyone's excited," he said. "We've never grown corn on this island, and from what I hear, we're going to have a bumper crop. It's our island gold, you know."

"I'll take two pineapples," said Mrs. Tai. "And by market day next week I hope to bring a dozen ears of corn for you and your family, Mr. Omotani. Have a good day."

As Kalani followed her mom through the crowded market, she felt a tug on her basket from behind. She turned around quickly and saw Teki smiling mischievously.

"Hi, Kalani," he said. "Do you want to come with my family to a beach picnic this afternoon when you're finished shopping?"

"Oh, Teki," laughed Kalani. "I thought someone was trying to steal one of our pineapples. Yes, I'd love to go the beach if it's okay with my mom."

"You may go," said Mrs. Tai who had overheard the conversation. "Just remember to play safely, and don't go too far out in the water."

"My dad will make sure of that," Teki said. "And besides, he's a good swimmer if anything should happen. Hey, I need to go! My mom will be looking for me. See you this afternoon!"

"Let's pick up some chocolate-chip macadamia-nut cookies from Auntie Ruth's bakery for you to take to the picnic," Mrs. Tai suggested.

"Oh, Mom," Kalani said, "you always think of everything."

Photo: Ralf Beier

After helping put away the groceries, Kalani changed into her swimsuit and packed her beach bag with a towel and the cookies. "I'll be back before dark. Teki's dad will walk me home," she called as she headed out the door.

"Have a good time, Kalani," her mom said. "And thanks for helping me with the shopping."

The weather was picnic perfect. A warm tropical sun and gentle island breeze both warmed and cooled the beautiful beach. While Teki's mom spread a blanket under the shade of two palm trees and began to unpack the picnic basket, Kalani and Teki built sandcastles on the beach.

"I wish our castles would last forever," said Kalani, as she built a sand wall to protect the fragile structures from the waves. "But high tide will wash them away by morning."

"Me too," said Teki wishfully. "But we can always build another and another and another anytime we want to."

"Time to eat," said Mr. Nalatu as he came in from a swim. "I'll race you. First one to the palm trees gets an extra cookie for dessert!"

"No fair, Dad," Teki called as the three made a dash up the beach toward the picnic blanket. "We can't run faster than you."

"Of course you can!" Mr. Nalatu laughed as he slowed his pace to allow Teki and Kalani to pass him.

Kalani and Teki dashed up the beach and reached the palm trees at the same time. Mr. Nalatu, pretending to be out of breath, arrived five steps behind them.

"You just let us win." Teki laughed.

"You think so?" his dad replied, trying not to smile. "Now why would I do that?"

Mrs. Nalatu unpacked the picnic basket and set out a feast of crispy sweet-and-spicy fried chicken, potato salad, sticky rice, and fresh pineapple, papaya, and mango.

"It's so beautiful here," said Kalani, taking a sip of cold fruit punch. "This has to be the most peaceful and beautiful place in all of God's creation."

Mrs. Nalatu smiled. "Yes, we know the legend of the great Creator who many, many years ago made everything. He is the highest of many gods, but sadly he no longer cares about what he made. He never speaks to us now because he is angry with us. He's angry because of all the bad things people do."

Kalani sat quietly, trying to understand what Teki's mom was saying.

"Of course, there are gods who *do* listen to us," Mr. Nalatu said. "These are the gods we pray to and try to make happy. You know, like the rain god, Kumu. He must be happy with us because he has sent good summer rains to make the corn grow."

Oh, my, Kalani thought to herself. *What should I say?*

Suddenly everyone's attention shifted to something very different than corn crops and rain gods. Without warning, a strange rumbling noise raced down the slope of the mountain toward the beach.

Mr. Nalatu stood up and turned toward the mountain. The beach rose like a sandy wave and began to shudder. Mr. Nalatu lost his balance and fell back on the sand. Then, just as suddenly, all was quiet and calm.

"Dad!" screamed Teki.

"I'm okay," he said. "Everything's fine."

"I'm scared," Teki said. "The last time we felt an earthquake like that, everyone thought the volcano would erupt."

"It hasn't erupted for many years," said Mr. Nalatu, trying to keep everyone calm. "I just hope Lomoko is not angry with us for some reason. If he is, there won't be anything we can do to stop him from erupting."

"Lomoko?" asked Kalani in a frightened voice. "Who's that?"

"Why, he's the god of the volcano," answered Mrs. Nalatu, surprised that Kalani didn't know this. "If he's not happy, he can punish us with great destruction. The dry lava flows around this island remind us always what he is capable of. My grandmother told me stories about how the last eruption covered part of her village when she was a young girl."

"Okay, that's enough talk about the volcano," cautioned Mr. Nalatu. "It's getting late. We need to pack up and get home. I'm sure the little quake we felt today will be the last."

As they were packing up the picnic things, Mr. Tai came running down the beach. "Is everyone okay?" he asked anxiously.

"We're all fine," replied Mr. Nalatu. "A little frightened, but we're okay. I guess no one will sleep well tonight just wondering what will happen."

"God will protect us," said Mr. Tai with an assuring smile. "He's our Creator and Protector. Thank you for inviting Kalani to the picnic. I'm sure she had a wonderful time."

"Good-bye," said Kalani. "And thank you. I did have a good time—well, mostly."

That night, everyone on the island slept lightly, if at all, as small tremors continued to ripple across the island. Unable to sleep, Kalani left her room and climbed into bed with her mom and dad. Mr. Tai said a short prayer, hugged Kalani and her mom, and all three fell into a light sleep.

Before the sun rose, Mr. Tai slipped quietly out of bed so as not to awaken Kalani. He whispered to his wife, "I'm going into the village to see if there is any news about the volcano. While I'm gone, pack up a few clothes, our important papers, and our photo albums. I don't know that anything will happen, but just in case the old volcano does erupt, we need to be ready to evacuate."

The marketplace was already filled with anxious villagers by the time Mr. Tai arrived. Everyone was pacing and talking nervously. As the sun began to rise over the horizon, it cast an eerie pink glow on the towering volcano. In those first rays of light, everyone saw what they had hoped they would not see—clouds of steam belching from the top of the mountain.

"She's going to erupt for sure," said one old man nervously. "The last time I saw steam like that was when I was a boy, and it wasn't long before   Lomoko let his anger be known. And did he blow!"

"But we also know how this mountain erupts," said Mr. Tai a bit more optimistically. "It doesn't just spew fire and ash everywhere. Usually it just sends slow rivers

of lava down the sides, like rivers of syrup. We'll have plenty of time to get out of the way once we know which way the lava is going to flow."

As the villagers continued to guess whether the volcano would erupt or not, Mr. Tai headed back up the path that led away from the village and toward his house. As he came to the edge of the village, he met Mr. Nalatu. "Good morning, Mr. Nalatu," he said. "Why don't you pack up what you need and bring your family up to our house. That way you will be away from the beach in case there are more earthquakes or a tsunami."

"Thank you, my friend," replied Mr. Nalatu. "Teki and his mom are quite worried. To be honest, I am too."

"That's what neighbors are for," Mr. Tai said. "And on this island, everyone's a neighbor."

By mid-morning, the Nalatu family had packed their truck. As they started up the road to the Tai house, a violent explosion shook the island.

"Dad!" Teki screamed. "The volcano!"

"Hang on!" His dad hit the gas and sped up the road toward safety. When they arrived, a group of neighbors was standing outside, looking up toward the steaming mountain where red ribbons of lava were flowing slowly down its flank.

"Is everyone okay?" asked Mr. Tai, holding Kalani's hand as he greeted the Nalatu family.

"So far," said Teki's dad. "Now that he's blown his top, maybe old Lomoko will just let the lava flow without more earthquakes or explosions."

"I think you're right," said Mr. Tai. "Now come on inside. There's nothing we can do until later. After breakfast, we'll go up to the corn fields and see if we can tell which way the lava is flowing. You never know the direction it will take. Hopefully, it will miss the fields and our village and just flow into the ocean."

As the two families sat around the big kitchen table, Kalani's mom served mango tea and banana bread.

"Thank you for your hospitality," said Mrs. Nalatu. "We're most grateful."

"And you're most welcome," replied Mrs. Tai. "We're just glad that you're safe and here with us."

"Dad?" said Teki with a worried look on his face. "Do you think Lomoko is really angry with us? What do you think we've done wrong? Why would he want to punish us?"

"He must be angry," Mr. Nalatu said. "Maybe someone did something wrong that we don't know about. Maybe someone didn't bring him the right gift. There could be any number of reasons why he's angry."

"Bring the right gift?" asked Kalani, who rarely hesitated before asking a question.

"Why, yes," said Mr. Nalatu. "People take gifts up to the volcano to keep Lomoko happy and peaceful. Don't you? Last year we took flowers way up on the slopes and left them there."

Before Kalani could answer, Mr. Tai wisely interrupted. "May I tell you why we don't take gifts to Lomoko?"

"Yes, please do," said Mrs. Nalatu with a questioning look. "Maybe that's why Lomoko is angry."

Mr. Tai smiled, reached for his Bible, and opened it to the book of Genesis. "The Bible tells us there is only one true and living God. He is God our Father who created everything, including this beautiful island." Then he began to read the creation story.

When Kalani's dad finished reading, Mr. Nalatu said, "That's what we believe too. We believe in the great Creator who made everything. But our ancestors have told us that, one day, something made him angry and now he won't have anything to do with us or the world he made."

"Let me explain further," said Mr. Tai patiently. "When God created the first man, Adam, and the first woman, Eve, He made them in His image. This means He created them with a mind so they could know Him and a heart so they could love Him. But He didn't create them to be like puppets. He created them with a will so they could choose either to obey Him or not obey Him. Only by choosing to obey God could they really show they loved Him. Sadly, Adam and Eve chose to disobey God."

"What did they do?" asked Teki, who wanted to know more about this Father he had heard Kalani speak about.

"They ate fruit from the tree of the knowledge of good and evil. God had told them they could eat fruit from any tree in their garden home except this one. God told them that they would surely die if they ate from this tree."

"So maybe that's why the great Creator is angry with us and won't have anything to do with us," Mrs. Nalatu said.

"Well, yes and no," replied Mr. Tai. "Yes, God was not pleased when Adam and Eve disobeyed. God is angered by disobedience, and our disobedience keeps us separated from Him. But that doesn't mean He has left us alone and doesn't care about us. In fact, He still loves us very much. And He hasn't abandoned us."

Mr. Nalatu asked, "So if God hasn't forgotten the world He made, and if He is the great Creator, why does He allow gods like Lomoko of the volcano to get so angry and punish us?"

"Have some more tea," said Mrs. Tai as she filled each glass. "And do have some more banana bread."

"Thanks," said Teki. "I love your banana bread."

Then Mr. Tai continued. "After Adam and Eve disobeyed, God reminded them of their punishment. One day they would die. They could not live forever in the beautiful world God had created. And not only would they die, the earth would also be cursed. This meant that the earth that God created to be their perfect home would no longer be perfect. Instead, Adam and Eve would have to work very hard to make the earth produce the food God would provide for them."

Photo: Mila Zinkova

"Is that why we have earthquakes, hurricanes, floods, and volcanoes?" Teki asked.

"That's right, Teki. But that doesn't mean God is not still in control of His creation or that He doesn't care about us. Because God loves us, He still sends the seasons and the rains and provides everything we need for life. He is still a loving and good Father who cares very much for His creation."

"But what about Lomoko, the god of the volcano?" asked Mr. Nalatu. "He doesn't seem to care about us. He's very angry with us right now."

"God tells us in the Bible that there are no other gods," answered Mr. Tai politely. "The gods people worship are only the creations of men. God is the only God, and He is still in control of the earth, even the less-than-perfect earth."

"Well, even if there were no other gods, then the great Creator God must still be angry with us about something or he wouldn't let the volcano erupt," Mr. Nalatu said with a frown.

"I've only told you part of the story," replied Mr. Tai. "Yes, people disobeyed, and yes, God punished their disobedience. But God is also a God of great love and mercy. The imperfect world we live in now, where there is death and decay, is not the end of the story. In fact, there is a happy ending to the story. A very happy ending."

"I wish I could believe what you're saying," said Mrs. Nalatu hopefully. "But I can't imagine a really happy ending to the story. I think the best we can do is just keep trying to please the gods, or at least the great Creator. Then maybe He will be good to us and not cause the volcano to erupt."

"It might seem that way," Mr. Tai said. "But there is really nothing we can do to make God happy. The happy ending to the story has everything to do with something God did *for us.*"

"What is that?" asked Teki, who had been listening very carefully to every word.

"Well, after Adam and Eve disobeyed God, God told them about His plan to one day bring harmony back to His creation. He told them about a plan that would restore the relationship between people and Himself. This plan would also restore harmony within each person's heart, between people, and between people and the earth."

"What was the plan?" Teki asked, anxious to know the rest of the story.

Suddenly a loud knock on the screen door interrupted the breakfast discussion. "Mr. Tai, come quickly!" shouted one of the next-door neighbors. "The lava is no longer flowing toward the village. Some of it has already started flowing into the ocean near Coral Point. You can see the steam from here."

"That is good news," Mr. Tai said with a sigh of relief as everyone hurried out to the porch.

"It's good news for the village, but not for some of the corn fields," his neighbor said. "Another large flow is located directly above some of the fields on the upper slopes. I think your field may be in danger."

Mr. Tai turned to Mr. Nalatu. "Come with me, my friend. We need to drive up to our fields and see what's happening."

"May I go with you?" asked Teki.

"No, son," his dad said. "An area of flowing lava is no place for kids. You stay here with the others. And say your prayers to Lomoko. Are you wearing your lucky necklace?"

Teki didn't answer his dad as he turned and walked into the house with the others. He didn't want to believe in Lomoko or lucky necklaces. He wanted to believe in the God Kalani's dad was reading about in the Bible. He wanted to believe in a God who loved His creation and had a plan for restoring it to its original peaceful beauty.

Maybe this God would protect their corn fields.

"It doesn't sound good," said Mr. Nalatu fearfully as the two men drove up the mountain road toward their fields.

"No, it doesn't," replied Mr. Tai. "But God will protect us and provide everything we need. We'll drive to your field first since it's higher up on the slope, then we'll check on mine on the way back."

As they approached the upper end of Mr. Nalatu's field, they saw a massive wall of molten lava creeping slowly across the road. Everything the lava touched ignited quickly and burst into crackling flames.

"It's just a matter of time," said Mr. Nalatu hopelessly. "My field doesn't stand a chance against such a wall of fire."

As the two men stood watching at a safe distance, the molten red lava oozed slowly across the road and silently into the first rows of corn. The green stalks crumbled one by one as the wall of fire engulfed them. There was nothing the men could do but watch.

"It will soon flow into my field as well," sighed Mr. Tai. "There's no need to stay here now. Let's go home and tell the others. We can come back in the morning and see how much, if any, of the fields are left."

As the two men headed silently down the road back to the house, Mr. Nalatu broke the silence. "Before we left to check on the fields, you said that there was a happy ending to the story you were telling us. You said something about a plan the great Creator had for restoring His creation. Is that true? Happy endings are hard to believe when we see our corn fields being destroyed by the volcano."

"It's true, my friend," Mr. Tai said reassuringly. "When we get back to the house, I'll tell you the rest of the story. I'm sure Teki and your wife are anxious to hear it as well."

THINK ABOUT IT

» Why do you think Mr. and Mrs. Nalatu believe that the great Creator does not care about people or the world He created?
» How do you think Teki and his family will respond to the truth about the Fall and God's plan for redemption?
» Do you think the destruction of the corn fields will make Teki's family more likely or less likely to believe in the one true God? Why or why not?

WORDS YOU NEED TO KNOW

» **Humility:** An attitude in my heart that I am not better than any other person, each of whom is created in God's image

HIDE IT IN YOUR HEART

It's your sins that have cut you off from God. Because of your sins, he has turned away and will not listen anymore. (Isaiah 59:2, NLT)

All of you, clothe yourselves with humility toward one another, because, "God opposes the proud but gives grace to the humble." (1 Peter 5:5)

PANDORA'S BOX

Every culture has its stories. Sometimes these stories are fairy tales or folk tales, which everyone agrees are just fictional. A myth, though, is a special kind of story about gods, goddesses, and other supernatural beings. Some myths tell about something that could actually have happened long ago, like a great battle. Other myths explain how something came into being, like how the world was created. Still others try to illustrate a truth. The study of myths is called mythology.

The most famous myths come from ancient Greece and, later, Rome. The ancients told stories of gods and goddesses to explain things about the world, like why echoes happen. One famous myth is about Pandora, the first woman to be created. In the story, Pandora was given a jar—modern accounts say a box—but was told never to open it. Although she obeyed for a while, eventually she became too curious and opened the container. When she did, evil and sickness and pain escaped into the world. The only thing she was able to keep inside the jar was hope.

Can you see how parts of the story of Pandora are similar to the Genesis account of the Fall? In the Bible, Adam and Eve were instructed not to eat fruit from the tree of the knowledge of good and evil. When they did, they were no longer innocent, as God created them to be, and sin was released into the world.

The myth of Pandora may have been started by someone who had lost the knowledge of the Bible and was trying to remember the story of Eve. Or it may simply have been a story invented to explain why there is evil in the world. Regardless, the Bible says that sin and disobedience have separated people from God. Our only hope is to accept the salvation God has provided through His Son, Jesus.

PARADISE LOST

All the angels of heaven must have watched in awe as God spoke His creation, His master-piece, into existence (Job 38:4–7). For five days, He populated the heavens and earth with an array of marvels, each more wondrous than the last. Then on the sixth day the heavenly hosts beheld the crown jewel of God's creation: Adam and Eve. They alone were created in God's own image. The man and woman, their children, and their children's children would live in paradise and enjoy eternal, intimate fellowship with Almighty God.

Living in the twenty-first century, far removed from the pristine beauty of Eden, we cannot fully comprehend what perfection looks like. That's because none of us has ever seen perfection. The long, tragic history of the human race declares, all too painfully, that God's creation is no longer per-fect. Once upon a time, when time began, there was only life, beauty, light, and good. Now the world is full of stark contrasts: life and death, beauty and ugliness, light and darkness, good and evil. The earth that God made to serve and bless peo-ple still does, but only at the expense of our sweat and hard work. People's relation-ships are often marked by struggle and disagreement. And despite the fact that we do good things from time to time, we are forced to admit that evil is part of our human nature.

The Garden of Eden by Poussin

The problem of evil has baffled mankind's greatest thinkers throughout history. Some dismiss evil as nothing more than a myth created to explain human suffering. Others say that people are basically good and that evil is just an illness or weakness we will one day overcome. Others blame the evil that men do on the fact that some people have fewer resources and less education than others. Others go so far as to argue that the presence of evil in our world proves that a good and perfect God does not exist! Yet mankind's efforts to understand or minimize or eliminate evil have all come to nothing. We can only really understand the prob-lem of evil when we discover God's truth as revealed in His Word.

The Bible makes it clear that sin entered the world when people chose to disobey God. Tempted by promises of wisdom and power, we "exchanged the truth of God for a lie" (Ro-mans 1:25). We were given a choice between right and wrong, and we chose to do wrong. With this willful act of disobedience, we not only brought sin into the world, but we destroyed our perfect home, our perfect bodies, and our perfect relationship with our perfect God. Although we may find comfort in knowing that God loves us and still desires a personal relationship with His children, the Bible confirms that our sins cause Him to hide His face from us (Isaiah 59:2).

We must understand these terrible facts about sin:

1. We are all born into sin.
2. Our sins separate us from God.
3. Our sins multiply without God.
4. The wages of sin is death.

The subject of sin is not a joyful one. But it is absolutely essential that we see sin for what it is—a horrible, ugly thing that God hates with a holy, burning anger.

THE CONSEQUENCES OF SIN

Adam and Eve could never have imagined the horrible consequences of sin. They had never seen so much as a leaf wither and die, and so they couldn't even begin to comprehend the end of life. But the moment they chose to put their own desires first, ahead of God's commandments, death and destruction entered creation and became the way of all things. Both the earth and its people began an aging process that inevitably leads to death and decay, and the first couple's new sinful nature was passed on to every person who came after them. Tragically, the lake of fire became every person's eternal destination (Revelation 20:14–15).

Hell by Beccafumi

This brings us to the question that nearly everyone in the past two millennia has asked: Why would a loving God send anyone to hell? First, let's look at some of the consequences of sin. Then we will be better able to answer this question.

WE ARE ALL BORN INTO SIN

Even before we commit our first sin, we are born into this world as sinners. The Bible tells us, "When Adam sinned, sin entered the world. Adam's sin brought death, so death spread to everyone, for everyone sinned" (Romans 5:12, NLT). Every person born since the Fall has inherited a sinful nature, and every one of us has sinned as a result. Anyone who believes that he has not sinned is lying to himself:

For all have sinned and fall short of the glory of God. (Romans 3:23)

We all, like sheep, have gone astray, each of us has turned to his own way. (Isaiah 53:6)

If we claim to be without sin, we deceive ourselves and the truth is not in us. (1 John 1:8)

The Bible says, "There is no one who does good, not even one" (Psalm 14:3). That doesn't mean that no one ever does anything good. But people born with a sin nature—and that includes all of us—are not perfect. When we try to do a good thing, even with the very best intentions, our deeds cannot possibly measure up to the standards of a holy and righteous God:

All our righteous acts are like filthy rags; we all shrivel up like a leaf, and like the wind our sins sweep us away. (Isaiah 64:6)

Because our good works are nothing more than "filthy rags" in the eyes of God, you and I can do nothing to erase our sins. This is why "good people" don't receive a "Get Out of Jail Free" card—a free pass into heaven. You see, our best can never be good enough. Not one of us is born perfect, and no one can become perfect because of his or her good works. And only perfect people without sin can be allowed in the presence of God.

OUR SINS SEPARATE US FROM GOD

We must remember that God is holy—that is, He is completely and totally without sin. He is absolutely just and does only what is right and good. A holy God can fellowship only with those who are also perfectly holy. Why? Because sin cannot live in the presence of a holy God. Therefore, a holy God cannot fellowship with sinful people:

It's your sins that have cut you off from God. Because of your sins, he has turned away and will not listen anymore. (Isaiah 59:2, NLT)

[O Lord] your eyes are too pure to look on evil; you cannot tolerate wrong. (Habakkuk 1:13)

Any sin separates us from God. People try to differentiate between "big sins" and "little sins," but all sin is sin. And any wickedness cannot dwell with the Lord (Psalm 5:4). So when Lucifer rebelled and sinned against God, he was cast out of heaven and renamed Satan. When Adam and Eve sinned, they were expelled from Eden. And because every person since was born with a sinful nature, we each find ourselves separated from God.

Because we are separated from God, there is a vast emptiness inside each one of us that cannot be filled by anything other than God. The seventeenth-century French mathematician Blaise Pascal introduced the idea of what has since been called a "God-shaped hole"—a deep longing in our hearts for something more than this world can provide us. Some of us recognize this emptiness as a yearning to know God and to be restored to our place as His children. Others never recognize the source of this longing, and so they try to fill the emptiness with entertainment, money, power, fame, even drugs and alcohol. The tragedy is that they do not see that God, too, longs for people to know Him and sent His Son to provide us a way back to Him. And so they are left to indulge in their sins and suffer the consequences:

Yet no one calls on your name or pleads with you for mercy. Therefore, you have turned away from us and turned us over to our sins. (Isaiah 64:7, NLT)

OUR SINS MULTIPLY WITHOUT GOD

Cancer is a disease in which a group of cells in a person's body grows out of control and begins to intrude on and destroy healthy tissue, often leading to the person's death. Sin works like a cancer. When we sin, our sins lead us deeper and deeper into disobedience, causing increasingly more sinful behavior (Romans 1:18–32). Have you ever disobeyed your parents, then tried to cover up your disobedience by lying about it? You were trying to cover up one sin with another sin. You may have even found yourself telling bigger and bigger lies to cover up the previous ones! Sinful behavior is like a bad habit that becomes more and more difficult to break. Every sin comes with its own set of hidden traps that are easy to fall into but tough to escape from. The deeper we wander into sin, the easier it is to keep sinning until it looks like there's no way out.

Let's look at the example of Joseph and his brothers. Their story is told in Genesis 37–50. At first, Joseph's brothers were merely angry and jealous and unkind toward him because their father loved Joseph more than his other sons and gave him a beautifully orna-mented robe to show it. Then Joseph began having prophetic dreams in which he was shown ruling over his older brothers as their master. This made his brothers hate him all the more. But instead of repenting of their jealousy and pride, the brothers took it one step further and plotted to kill Joseph. Fortunately, the oldest brother, Reuben, talked just a bit of sense into them. So instead, they sold Joseph into slavery and then covered up their deed by telling their father he had been killed by a wild animal. What started as a few prideful thoughts and unkind words led to this horrible act and very nearly murder. (Years later, Joseph would end up ruling over his very surprised and very sorry brothers as the second-most powerful man in all of Egypt.)

Joseph's Bloody Coat Brought to Jacob by Diego Velazquez

This is how it always begins. Sin starts as such little things—an unkind thought, a stolen dime, a tiny white lie. We all like to think we are above selling a brother into slavery, but it began for Joseph's brothers the same way it does for you and me. Has your anger and pride ever led you to say or do something completely stupid that you later regretted? Do you need to stop reading right now and repent of a "small" sin that, unchecked, could grow into something much, much larger?

THE WAGES OF SIN IS DEATH

The apostle Paul was not one to mince words. He wrote, "The wages of sin is death" (Romans 6:23). When Adam and Eve sinned, death entered the world, and our sins have had deadly consequences ever since. At one point, God chose to wipe all but one man and his family from the face of the earth because the thoughts of people's hearts were "only evil all the time" (Genesis 6:5). Later, He burned the cities of Sodom and Gomorrah to the ground because of the sin rampant in those towns (2 Peter 2:6). Not only does sin often bring us closer to physi-cal death, but it causes spiritual death as well, pulling us ever farther from the source of all life, our Creator.

A holy God can have nothing to do with sin and sinners, but this does not mean He has abandoned us. As we have seen, God has promised to provide for every one of our needs. However, the people of this world no longer enjoy His divine presence, which once provided His children with perfect wisdom, guidance, and fulfillment. Instead, people are lost and con-fused, unable to fully understand the world around them. They can no longer think or reason without making mistakes in judgment. They find it harder to tell the difference between right and wrong, and so they do whatever "feels right," which is often wrong. And all the time they ignore the truth of God that is staring them right in the face! His attributes have been etched into everything He made, so people have no excuse for not knowing Him (Romans 1:20). Yet they refuse to worship Him or give Him thanks, so He leaves them to do things their own way. They continue to follow their wrong-headed impulses and indulge in bad habits and uncontrolled emotions, making themselves enemies of God (Colossians 1:21).

WARNING

MAY BE HABIT FORMING

Prolonged exposure can lead to death.

The truth is that God has not disowned people; people have disowned Him. They have run away from home, dragging along their fears and doubts like they were essential supplies. And like irritable children, they stick their tongues out at those who long to return home, saying it's stupid to believe in a God who would allow people to suffer. The Bible makes it very clear what happens next:

Since they thought it foolish to acknowledge God, he abandoned them to their foolish thinking and let them do things that should never be done. Their lives became full of every kind of wickedness, sin, greed, hate, envy, murder, quarreling, deception, malicious behavior, and gossip. They are backstabbers, haters of God, insolent, proud, and boastful. They invent new ways of sinning, and they disobey their parents. They refuse to understand, break their promises, are heartless, and have no mercy. They know God's justice requires that those who do these things deserve to die, yet they do them anyway. Worse yet, they encourage others to do them, too. (Romans 1:28–32, NLT)

When people sin, they understand that what they are doing is wrong and that the only just reward for their sins is death—but they continue to sin anyway! And they encourage others to do the same! They try to justify their actions by calling good things bad and bad things good (Isaiah 5:20). People try to minimize their sins through calling them by other names like "alternative lifestyles" or "the right to choose." Meanwhile, things go from bad to worse as people continue down the road to certain death:

People who are evil and cheat other people will go from bad to worse. They will fool others, but they will also be fooling themselves. (2 Timothy 3:13, ICB)

Situated near the small desert village of Darvaza, Turkmenistan, is the football-field-sized entrance to an underground cavern filled with natural gas. The gas was accidentally ignited in 1971 and has been burning ever since. Local residents call it "The Door to Hell," but this is a picnic at the beach compared to what hell will really be like.

WHAT ABOUT HELL?

Some people joke about hell and eternal damnation, while others casually use them as curse words. But the Bible tells us that hell is a very real and very terrible place of punishment. Jesus Himself talked several times about the eternal flames of hell. Speaking to the Pharisees, who kept God's law but had no faith or love for people, Jesus said, "You snakes! You brood of vipers! How will you escape being condemned to hell?" (Matthew 23:33). He said that hell is so awful that it's better to tear your eyes out than to go there:

> *"If your eye causes you to sin, gouge it out. It's better to enter the Kingdom of God with only one eye than to have two eyes and be thrown into hell, 'where the maggots never die and the fire never goes out.'"* (Mark 9:47–48)

Matthew 25:41 tells us that hell was prepared as a place for Satan and the angels who followed him. However, hell is also the final destination for those who choose to reject God's Son (Revelation 21:7–8). For you see, we do have a choice. Adam and Eve had a choice whether or not to believe God. Abraham was given the same choice. James and John had to make a choice between holding tight to their careers as fishermen or dropping everything and following Christ. Even the two thieves being crucified on either side of Jesus had a choice.

As you have learned, sin has introduced the world to every form of human suffering—pain, violence, disease, loneliness, murder, divorce, war, etc. These are the fruits of sin. And the greatest sin of all is to reject Jesus Christ as Savior. For God loved the world so much that He gave us His one and only Son to accept the penalty of death on our behalf (John 3:16). He said that if we will only believe and receive this free gift, then we will be His children once again and live with Him forever in a perfect place in perfect harmony with Him, with ourselves, with each other, and with all creation.

Jesus said, "The world's sin is that it refuses to believe in me" (John 16:8–9, NLT). Make no mistake: Those who choose to reject God's gift of salvation are choosing to pay the ultimate price.

MAKE A NOTE OF IT

Read Romans 1:28–31. Now list ten sins people commit when they do not think that knowing God is important. You may write the entire list if you wish. As you list the sins, search your own heart. Are you listing any sins that you need to confess and ask God to forgive?

WHAT SHOULD I DO?

When we understand that everyone has sinned and falls short of God's glory, it's easy to see that not one of us is better than any other person. Each and every man, woman, and child was made in God's image, and each was given unique gifts and abilities. We might be tempted to look at our own gifts and abilities and think we are somehow greater or more privileged than others. Yet we are all sinners who can be saved only by God's grace. **Humility** is an attitude that says, "I am not better than anyone else."

God requires His children to be humble (Micah 6:8). In fact, God will only fellowship with those who come to Him with a humble spirit:

All of you, clothe yourselves with humility toward one another, because, "God opposes the proud but gives grace to the humble." (1 Peter 5:5)

The high and lofty one who lives in eternity, the Holy One, says this: "I live in the high and holy place with those whose spirits are contrite and humble. I restore the crushed spirit of the humble and revive the courage of those with repentant hearts." (Isaiah 57:15, NLT)

What does humility look like? We need look no further than Jesus. Philippians 2:6–8 tells us that although He was God, Jesus did not insist on having the rights and privileges of His position. Instead He made Himself the servant of all people (Mark 10:45). He was "gentle and humble in heart" (Matthew 11:29). He fully submitted to the Father's will and always obeyed, even when it meant dying on the cross. We, too, are called to be modest, gentle, and submissive to authority. We cannot insist on our rights or privileges. If we are to serve our family, friends, neighbors, and those in need as Christ served us, we must never think of ourselves more highly than we should (Romans 12:3). In fact, just the opposite. Philippians 2:3 tells us to think of others as better than ourselves!

When we choose to humble ourselves the way Christ did, His blessings will follow. The Bible tells us humility leads to wisdom (Proverbs 11:2) and honor (Proverbs 15:33). When we humble ourselves and confess our sins to God, He is quick and gracious to forgive (Acts 3:19–20). And when we are humble, we will avoid the destruction that always comes with a prideful attitude (Proverbs 16:18). But if we become full of ourselves, thinking more of ourselves than we should—as Adam and Eve did when they believed they could become equal with God—then we are in for a certain and terrible fall.

MAKE A NOTE OF IT

Read the parable of the Pharisee and the tax collector in Luke 18:9–14. This is a story about pride and humility. Write about what Jesus is saying to you personally through this parable.

A PRAYER

Dear God, help me to remember the things I have done to displease you so that I may confess them to you. With all my heart, I want to turn away from my sins. Please forgive me for _____. And forgive me for _____. Thank you for forgiving my sins. Thank you, God, for sending Jesus to die for me so that I can know you as my Father. Help me to live each day in a way that pleases you. I love you, God. I pray this in Jesus' name. Amen.

EVERYONE HAS A STORY

Everyone's life is full of stories. Think about what you and a friend might talk about when you haven't seen each other in a while. You might tell stories about a family vacation or your Little League team. You might share stories about your family's move or about the birth of a new baby. We all tend to share with our friends and loved ones the small stories and the big stories of our lives.

Why is telling stories so important? Why do we enjoy telling our stories and listening to the stories of others? Maybe it's because we believe that most of the events in our lives are important. Even small stories, like how we were affected by a movie we saw over the weekend, are important. Certainly the big stories, like what a visit to another city or country meant to us, are important. We want people to know about us, and we want to know about others, and one of the most important ways we get to know people and they get to know us is through the telling of stories.

OUR STORIES AND OUR WORLDVIEW

You have learned from this book that a worldview is a set of beliefs through which you view and interpret life and the world and that this worldview guides your choices and behaviors. A worldview is a set of basic beliefs about God, the universe, people, truth, and right and wrong.

Now let's see how our worldview is related to the stories of our lives. As you know, people don't stop and say, "Let's see now—before I make a decision about how to act here, what is my worldview telling me to do?" No, for the most part you make hundreds, perhaps thousands, of choices each day without ever thinking about your worldview. And at the end of the day, you've lived out several more small stories about your life that you can share with others. Some may not be too interesting—just an ordinary day, we might say—while others may be very interesting, even exciting. Yet interesting or not, the daily stories of our lives are shaped by our deeply held beliefs.

As you might imagine, people with different worldviews write the stories of their lives very differently. A young Muslim girl, for example, although she has family stories and school stories and play stories like most children, will experience and tell her stories through Islamic belief glasses. Or a young boy who is told from an early age that God does not exist will live out his stories through naturalistic belief glasses.

Because some of the people around us have worldviews different from ours, our stories will also be influenced by their worldviews. This doesn't mean that we accept or adopt these other worldviews, but they can't help but influence us. Sometimes differing worldviews cause conflicts between people and between nations. These conflicts can result in dramatic and even painful stories for the people involved.

THE GREATEST STORY OF ALL

God's story is by far the greatest story of all, and we each live out the stories of our lives as smaller tales within His grand story. When we study God's story, we will begin to understand our own stories better.

God's great story is not fiction. It's about a real God who created a real world. And because God wants us to know the truth of His story, He had it written down for us in the greatest book of all time, the Bible. In the next and final lesson, we will imagine God's magnificent story as a drama—a play in three acts. As the curtain opens on the greatest drama ever written and we watch God's Great Story unfold, see how many truths about God, the universe, people, truth, and right and wrong you can identify.

THE HOUSE OF TRUTH: THE THIRD PILLAR

You are very close to finishing the first wall in the House of Truth. Once you have completed your House of Truth, you will have an excellent model showing the major beliefs of the Christian worldview. In this lesson, you erected the third pillar in your Wall of Fellowship:

BIBLICAL TRUTH 7:

Sin causes separation and disharmony between me and God.

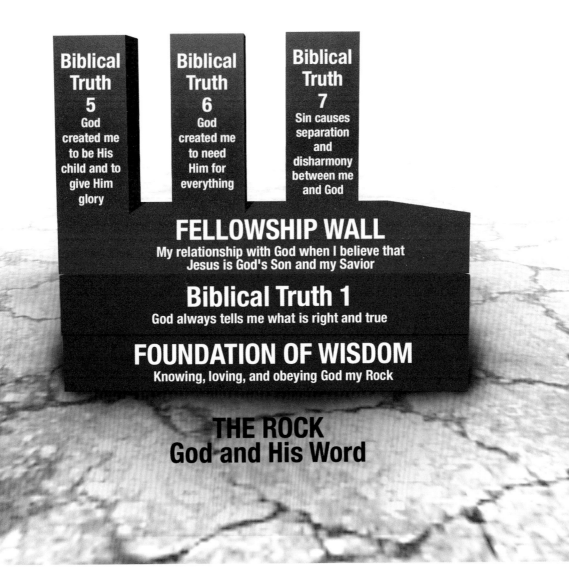

Biblical Truth 5
God created me to be His child and to give Him glory

Biblical Truth 6
God created me to need Him for everything

Biblical Truth 7
Sin causes separation and disharmony between me and God

FELLOWSHIP WALL
My relationship with God when I believe that Jesus is God's Son and my Savior

Biblical Truth 1
God always tells me what is right and true

FOUNDATION OF WISDOM
Knowing, loving, and obeying God my Rock

THE ROCK
God and His Word

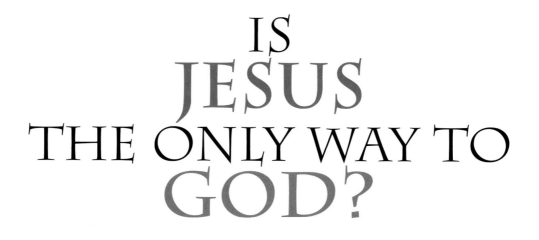

IS JESUS THE ONLY WAY TO GOD?

JESUS ANSWERED, "I AM THE WAY AND THE TRUTH AND THE LIFE. NO ONE COMES TO THE FATHER EXCEPT THROUGH ME."

JOHN 14:6

THE BIG IDEA

God created Adam and Eve to enjoy fellowship with Him forever—on one condition. Do you remember what that condition was? If you said obedience, you are correct. Why did God make fellowship with Him conditional on their obedience? As you have learned, He created Adam and Eve with the ability to make choices for themselves. And one of the choices they were created to make was whether they would obey or disobey God. By choosing to obey their Creator, they could show their love and reverence for Him. But in choosing to disobey God, they showed Him that they did not love Him as they should.

Adam and Eve knew immediately that their sin displeased God. So when they heard His voice in the garden, they tried to hide from God, something you know is impossible to do. Because God is absolutely holy, Adam and Eve could no longer have perfect fellowship with God or even remain in the garden. And as God had promised, they would no longer live forever on this earth—one day they would die and return to the dust from which God had made Adam.

If this were the end of the story, Satan would have accomplished what he set out to do by tempting Eve: He would have unraveled God's plan for creation. But this is not the end of the story. Despite the failure of Adam and Eve, God promised them that one day a child would be born who would crush Satan and his evil works. Jesus Christ would be that child.

Not only did God promise that Satan would be defeated, He showed Adam and Eve what was necessary to "cover" their sins. He did this by killing, or sacrificing, one of the animals He had created. God then took the skin from that animal and made durable clothing to cover Adam and Eve's nakedness. In this way, He covered their sin and shame. There was nothing they could do themselves to cover their sin. Only God could do this, and it required the sacrifice of an animal. This loving act of God showed Adam and Eve that He still cared for them and was not going to abandon them.

So what has God done to cover our sin and shame and to restore our fellowship with Him? The sacrifice of the animal for Adam and Eve was a picture of what God would one day do. But instead of sacrificing an animal to cover our sins, He sent His own Son to be our sacrifice. Jesus, the promised child, came to this earth to die for us. The blood He shed on

the cross provides the covering for our sins. When we choose to believe, when we have faith that Jesus is God's Son and our Savior and we repent of our sins, our fellowship with God the Father is restored. And this fellowship will be forever for all people whom God has called to be His children.

It is important to remember that just as Adam and Eve could not cover their sin and shame with fig leaves, we cannot do anything to cover our sins. Sometimes people try to hide their sins from others, but they can never hide them from God. Sometimes people try to cover their sin and shame by doing good works, in hope that God will forgive them and others will accept them. However, the Bible tells us that no amount of good works is enough to bring us back into fellowship with a holy God. Only God can save us from the punishment we deserve for our sins. There is nothing we can do to save ourselves—God has done it all as His free gift to us. This free gift is called salvation, and it is for everyone who will accept it. God's gift of salvation doesn't just save us from punishment; God also forgives and forgets our sins and does not hold them against us.

Of course, this gift of salvation is like all gifts: You have to believe the gift is for you, and then you must receive or accept it if you want to enjoy it. Has someone ever tried to give you a gift you did not want to receive? Well, some people do not want to receive God's gift of salvation. They don't believe it's for them, or they don't think they really need such a gift. Before you can receive God's gift of salvation, you must first believe that it's a real gift God wants to give you. You must believe that Jesus is God's Son and your Savior. This belief is

MANGO TANGO

Mangoes are a sweet tropical fruit, large and oval-shaped and yellow-orange when they're ripe. Mangoes grow in warm climates such as India, South America, and California where the ground doesn't freeze in the winter. Some mango trees are even hundreds of years old. Sometimes called the king of fruit, more mangoes are eaten fresh around the world than any other fruit!

Mangoes are very good for you, with lots of fiber and vitamin C. Ripe mangoes are used for fruit salads, salsas, and desserts like cakes, pudding, and smoothies. Mangoes are also used to flavor warm sauces for chicken and other meats. In some countries, unripe mangoes are eaten sprinkled with salt and chili pepper or sometimes made into a sour mango pickle.

To cut up a mango, first find the flatter sides of the oval. The almond-shaped seed inside should be sitting that way too. Cut the flat sides off, leaving about an inch-thick slab of fruit in the middle. Then trim the sides off the middle slab, leaving just the seed inside to throw away. Cut the remaining flesh into cubes like a checkerboard, being careful not to slice through the skin, then scoop it out with a spoon.

Now try this recipe to make refreshing Creamy Mango Sorbet:

- » 3 soft, ripe mangoes
- » ¾ cup sugar or honey
- » 1 cup half and half (or try vanilla yogurt instead)
- » 1 tray ice cubes
- » 1 large Ziploc bag

Have a parent help you cut the mango into cubes. Watch out for the big flat seed! Measure all the ingredients into a blender and mix for 2 to 3 minutes. Pour mixture into a large Ziploc bag and seal carefully. Freeze for 1 to 2 hours, squishing it once or twice so it freezes evenly. When it's ready, cut a corner off the bag and squeeze the sorbet into bowls for serving. Makes 4–6 servings. Enjoy!

called faith. However, just believing the gift is for you isn't enough either. You must accept the gift in your heart and want to change your life and start living for Jesus. You must be sorry for your sins and no longer do the sinful things you once did. This change of life is called repentance.

Remember, there's nothing you can do to earn your salvation. It's a wonderful free gift from God to you. It's a gift He gives out of the abundance of His grace. This means it's a gift of God's love and forgiveness that none of us deserves.

WHAT YOU WILL DO
» You will describe what Jesus did for us to restore our fellowship with God.
» You will define forgiveness and learn what God does with your sins because of Jesus.
» You will identify and define appropriate responses to receiving God's free gift of salvation.
» You will define *compassion* and be encouraged to demonstrate it in your relationships with others in response to God's compassionate gift of salvation to you.
» You will erect the fourth and final pillar in the Fellowship Wall—*Jesus died to restore fellowship and harmony between me and God.*

ISLAND PRAISE

"I sure hope the lava flow misses our cornfields," Teki said with a worried look on his face. "I've prayed to Lomoko, and I've prayed to the God you believe in, Kalani. But I'm not sure either one is listening."

"God hears our prayers," Kalani said with confidence as she finished her last bite of banana bread. "And whether our fields are destroyed or not, He will still take care of us."

"That doesn't make any sense," Teki retorted belligerently. "If God really cared about us, then He would send the lava away from our fields."

Kalani didn't answer and began helping her mom clear away the breakfast dishes.

"Kalani," said Mrs. Nalatu, "I'll help your mom clean up. Why don't you and Teki walk down the road toward our house. I saw a beautiful stalk of white ginger lilies beside the old stone wall. They would look beautiful on your table, and they'll help brighten the day for all of us, don't you think?"

"Oh, let's," said Kalani as she set a plate beside the sink then looked at Teki.

"Okay," Teki said reluctantly, "if you really want to."

As the two children headed down the road toward the beach, they could see in the distance the steam rising from the coastline where the lava continued to flow slowly into the ocean.

Photo: Mila Zinkova

"It's beautiful but scary at the same time," Kalani said as they stopped to watch the incredible sight.

"Yeah, it is," admitted Teki, still disturbed by the display of the volcano's power. "I sure wish our dads would hurry home and bring us news about the fields. I have a feeling it won't be good news."

"Teki Nalatu," Kalani scolded, frustrated at his stubbornly negative attitude, "try to see the good for a change. The lava hasn't destroyed any homes or our village. We're safe, and so is everyone else. Why can't you be grateful for that?"

He didn't answer but turned and started back down the road. "Where did my mom say those flowers were growing?"

Kalani knew it was no use trying to cheer him up, so she simply replied, "Beside the old stone wall. You know, just after the road curves down toward the beach."

"Oh, they really are beautiful!" exclaimed Mrs. Tai as Teki presented her with the freshly cut flowers. "And they smell so sweet! Thank you both very much."

As Mrs. Tai was filling a vase with water at the kitchen sink, she heard Kalani excitedly announce, "They're back!"

Everyone rushed to the front yard, anxious to hear the news. But before either Mr. Tai or Mr. Nalatu said a word, they could tell it wasn't good.

"It's all gone. Our whole field is destroyed," sighed Mr. Nalatu.

"And ours will be destroyed by morning," said Mr. Tai, trying not to let his disappointment show.

"See, I told you so," cried Teki as he ran to hug his dad. "Neither Lomoko nor the God you believe in, Kalani, is happy with us. I should have kept wearing my lucky necklace. Maybe we should have put more sacred lava stones in the field. Maybe I should have—"

"That's enough," his mom said, trying to hold back her own tears. "What's happened has happened. We can't fight Lomoko. He's much more powerful than we are. We can only try to please him more in the future. Maybe we'll be able to purchase some new land and plant another crop."

"Dad," said Kalani as tears began to fill her eyes. "*Why?* Why *our* fields?"

"We don't always understand why God allows things like this to happen, but we do know He is still God. And we know He's good and faithful to His children. That's the good news in the middle of this destruction."

Mr. Nalatu held Teki close, then said to Mr. Tai, "Just before we drove up to check on our fields this morning, you said something about the great Creator's plan to bring harmony back to His creation. We heard about no such plan from the stories of our ancestors. I think I'd like to hear your story. We need some good news right about now. At least I do. Would you share that with us?"

"Of course," said Mr. Tai. "Let's all sit on the front porch. The sun will set shortly, and I think with all the steam and vapor from the volcano still hanging in the air we shall have a beautiful sunset this evening."

Teki and Kalani sat on a straw beach mat, while their parents sat in the old wooden rockers Kalani's grandfather had made many years before. Coco the cat curled up near Teki's feet. Then Mr. Tai once again opened the family Bible to the book of Genesis.

"You remember this morning I told you that after Adam and Eve disobeyed God, everything changed," said Mr. Tai. "Their close relationship with God had been ruined because they had disobeyed Him. In fact, they tried to hide from God because they knew they were guilty. And because God is just,

He punished them the way He had said He would if they disobeyed. Their punishment was death. They would no longer live forever on this earth as God had originally intended."

"But you said this morning that God also punished the earth. You know—like He made it not very friendly anymore to Adam and Eve," said Mrs. Nalatu.

"Well, not exactly," replied Mr. Tai. "The earth didn't disobey God; Adam and Eve did. So God cursed the earth as punishment for Adam and Eve's disobedience. God created the earth to provide all their physical needs, and it still would do that. But now Adam and Eve would have to work very hard to get the earth to produce food for them. God caused thorns and weeds to grow in the ground for the first time, making man's work very difficult."

"See, I told you so," said Teki. "The Creator God was so angry, He decided to punish people forever until the day they died. And that's why the volcano destroyed our crops."

"Teki," Mr. Tai said gently, "let me explain the good news now. Yes, without understanding the good news, everything does look bleak. But God is a good and loving God. In fact, because He loves His creation so much, He announced a special plan to Adam and Eve."

"Well, what was the plan?" Teki asked.

"God told Adam and Eve that one day a child would be born," Mr. Tai continued. "This child would completely destroy God's enemy, Satan, who had tempted Adam and Eve to disobey. Not only would Satan be defeated, but this child would also provide the way to restore harmony between people and God and between people and the earth."

"Has that child been born yet?" asked Mrs. Nalatu. "I don't think so, or there would already be harmony on the earth."

"Oh, yes!" exclaimed Mr. Tai. "Not only has He been born, He's still alive today."

"Who is He?" asked Teki, his interest growing.

"The child is God's own Son. His name is Jesus. Many, many years after Adam and Eve disobeyed God in the garden, Jesus was born on this earth."

"Was He born like we are, with a real mother and father?" Teki asked.

"That's a good question, Teki," answered Mr. Tai. "God chose a special young woman named Mary to be the mother of His Son. By a miracle, God caused Mary to become pregnant without an earthly father. God is Jesus' heavenly Father, and Mary was His earthly mother."

"Did Jesus grow up without an earthly father?" Teki asked.

"No. A man named Joseph loved Mary and married her, and together they raised Jesus as their son."

"So are you saying that Jesus was born without the help of an earthly father? That sounds pretty strange," Mr. Nalatu said.

"Yes, it may sound strange to us, but it's true," said Mr. Tai. "Jesus is the Son of God the Father. Not only is He God's Son, but Jesus is also God. He and the Father and the Holy Spirit are three Persons united together as the one true God."

"So is Jesus God, or is He human?" Teki asked.

"He's both. Jesus is fully God, and He is also fully human. And because He lived among us as a human being, He understands what it's like to be human. While He lived on the earth He became tired and hungry just like we do."

"God let His Son be tired and hungry? Why wasn't God born in a great palace with servants that did anything He wanted?" asked Teki.

Mr. Tai grew more serious. "Although He is God, Jesus didn't come here to be a wealthy king and ruler. He was born in a poor village and learned to work as a carpenter. And while He was here, He lived only to serve and help other people."

"You said 'while' Jesus lived here," observed Mrs. Nalatu. "Doesn't He live here anymore? You said He was still alive. And why has He not restored harmony to the earth as you said He would?"

Mr. Tai smiled. "Let me back up just a little and explain. Do you remember Adam and Eve's punishment for disobeying God?"

"Yes," answered Teki quickly. "They began to die, and they had to work really hard to make the earth provide the food they needed."

"That's right. And that's why God sent His Son to live here on earth. You see, it was God's plan that His Son would take the punishment that Adam and Eve and all people since them, including us, deserved for their disobedience. And that's exactly what happened."

"When did all this happen? And how did God punish Jesus?" asked Mr. Nalatu.

"It happened about two thousand years ago," Mr. Tai explained. "When Jesus was old enough, He went about teaching people about God's love and His plan to restore harmony in the earth. Many people believed Jesus' message and followed Him. But many did not believe Him. In fact, some of them hated Jesus so much they wanted to kill Him. They succeeded, and He died like a common criminal, nailed to a wooden cross."

"Then God's plan failed." Mrs. Nalatu looked crestfallen. "He died before He was able to restore harmony."

"No, God's plan did not fail," Mr. Tai said with a reassuring smile. "God sent Jesus to die on the cross. Jesus took the punishment of death that each of us deserves for our disobedience. But because Jesus died in our place, now we don't have to die."

The Incredulity of Thomas by Benjamin West

"Wait a minute. Everyone dies," said Mr. Nalatu. "And what about Jesus? You said He's still alive today. Now I'm really confused. And what about the harmony you said Jesus was supposed to restore? I don't see harmony here on earth—just the opposite. We still have wars, hunger, earthquakes, volcanoes. Just look at our corn fields for proof."

Before Mr. Tai could begin to answer Mr. Nalatu's questions, Mrs. Tai interrupted. "Who would like something to eat? We've had a long day, and I'm sure everyone's hungry. How do tuna sandwiches, macaroni salad, and mango cobbler sound?"

"I'm hungry," Teki said quickly. "I think I can eat two sandwiches."

"May I help you?" asked Mrs. Nalatu, who really wanted to continue the discussion on the porch.

"No, thank you," Mrs. Tai said, smiling. "It will only take me a few minutes."

As Mrs. Tai left for the kitchen, Mr. Tai continued. "Yes, you're right. Everyone still dies. And yes, we don't see perfect harmony in the earth now. But let me explain. After Jesus suffered so much and died for us on the cross, He was buried. Now here is the really good news. After three days, God the Father raised His Son, bringing Him back to life. By doing this, He destroyed once and for all the power that death has over all people."

"I've never heard anything like this before," said Mrs. Nalatu with astonishment. "So where is Jesus now? And why do people still die?"

"After He came back to life, Jesus lived here on earth for only forty more days. Then He returned to live with His Father in heaven. But before Jesus left this earth, He made a promise: He promised that He would always be with us. And that is exactly what happened. To everyone who believes Jesus is God's Son, God gives the right to become His child. So yes, Jesus is still living today. He lives in heaven with God the Father, and His Spirit lives in the hearts of everyone who believes that He is God's Son."

"Are you saying that because Jesus died for us, God is no longer angry with us?" asked Mr. Nalatu. "Are you saying we can have a relationship with him now like Adam and Eve had in the garden?"

"Yes, that's exactly what I'm saying. And that's why it's called the Good News," answered Mr. Tai with a big smile.

"But you still haven't answered my questions about why we still die and why we do not have peace on earth," Mr. Nalatu said.

"Let me answer your question about death first." Mr. Tai opened his Bible to the gospel of John. "For me, these are the most beautiful words in the Bible. God tells us, 'For God so loved the world that he gave his one and only Son, that whoever believes in him shall not perish but have eternal life.' You see, our bodies still die. But just as God raised Jesus from death back to life, He will one day raise us back to life also. Jesus will someday return to this earth, and when He does, everyone who has become His child will receive a new body. And then we will live with Him forever and ever."

"Wow!" Teki exclaimed wide-eyed. "Forever? That's a long time."

"That's longer than a long time," agreed Kalani with a smile. "Just close your eyes, and try to imagine forever."

"But where will we live?" asked Mrs. Nalatu. "I don't want to live in the shadow of a volcano forever."

"And God doesn't want that for us," continued Mr. Tai. "When Jesus returns and gives us new bodies, He is also going to make a brand-new earth. Everything that's not perfect in our world will be made perfect. Then the new earth will be our home with God the Father, God the Son, and God the Holy Spirit forever."

"Then can we grow our corn?" asked Teki.

"Well, I'm not sure about that," laughed Mr. Tai. "But if there are corn fields there, I know one thing: The corn will be the most delicious you've ever tasted. And there will be no volcanoes or floods or droughts or anything else to ever destroy them. Whatever God has planned for us on the new earth will be more wonderful than anything we've seen or can even imagine."

"Sandwiches are ready," called Mrs. Tai from the kitchen. "Come on in if you're hungry."

After everyone was seated, Mr. Tai asked his wife to pray.

"Dear God," she began. "Thank you for protecting our lives and our homes from the volcano. And thank you for giving us good friends like Teki and his family. Thank you for sending your Son, Jesus, to take the punishment we deserve for disobeying you. And thank you for the promise of eternal life with you. Oh, and thank you for these tuna sandwiches and especially the mango cobbler. In Jesus' name. Amen."

"You've told us many things we've never heard before," Mr. Nalatu said after supper. "I want to believe this Good News, as you call it. But I'm not sure that it's really true. For generations we've been told the stories of the ancestors and of gods like Lomoko. Your story gives us more hope in our hearts than the stories from the ancestors, but I need to know if they are true or not."

"I understand," said Mr. Tai wisely. "I will pray that God will show you that what I've shared is true. Here, take this Bible home with you. You can read the story I've told you there. I suggest you read the story as told by a man named Luke. I'll place a bookmark at the beginning of that book so you can find it easily."

"Thank you," said Mr. Nalatu. "And thanks for inviting us to be with you today. Just being with your family has helped make this difficult day a little easier."

"Good night, Teki," said Kalani as his family got into their truck.

As Teki's family drove away, Kalani took her father's hand. "Dad, you know I believe everything you said today. But do you really think God is going to take care of us? The corn is ruined, the field's no good anymore, and—"

"Kalani," he said, giving her a hug, "God is going to take care of us today and tomorrow and the next day, just as He always has. I promise."

"But what are you going to do now?" she asked anxiously. "We don't have a corn field anymore."

"I'm going to help some of the other men harvest their corn this week," he replied. "And your mom's going to help some of the ladies prepare for the

Photo: Yvan leduc

harvest festival at church next Saturday. There's still corn growing in most of the fields, and in spite of the volcano, we're going to enjoy the harvest and thank God for what He has given us."

Each morning that week, Mr. Tai rose early and drove to his neighbors' fields. In spite of the damage to some of the fields, like his and the Nalatus', many others were ready for a bountiful harvest.

"We really appreciate your help this week," said a neighbor as they finished harvesting the last field. "You are coming to the harvest festival at the church on Saturday, aren't you?"

"Sure are," replied Mr. Tai. "We wouldn't miss it. And we're going to invite the Nalatu family as well. They lost their entire field, too, you know."

"That's what we've heard. Tell them that they are most welcome," said one of the men as he wiped sweat and field dust from his face. "And thanks again for all your help."

On Saturday morning, Kalani awoke to the aroma of sweet potatoes and sticky rice pudding baking in the oven. "What time are we going to the festival?" she asked as she walked into the kitchen.

"Good morning, my precious," her mom said. "We're going about noon. Your dad is already there helping some of the men prepare the fire pit for roasting the pig. We'll boil the fresh corn at the church and then—"

"Oh, Mom! Stop talking about all that food. I'm hungry enough already." Kalani laughed. "Is Teki's family coming to the festival with us?"

"We've invited them, so I hope they will come."

By noon, people began arriving, bringing more food than everyone could possibly eat. Large pots of water were set over outdoor fires for boiling the corn. With much fanfare, the men lifted the pig from the fire pit. As they removed the leaves of the ti plant in which the pig had been wrapped, the sweet smell of tender, smoked pork wafted through the air. Everyone spontaneously clapped their hands in anticipation of the first mouth-watering bite.

"There's Teki's family!" said Kalani excitedly. "They just drove up."

"Let's go meet them," said Mr. Tai. "We want to introduce them to our friends and make sure they feel welcome."

"I've brought some fresh mangoes," Mrs. Nalatu said nervously. "I hope it's okay."

"Oh, you didn't need to bring anything at all. But this will taste wonderful

with the pork," said Mrs. Tai. "Now we want you to meet some of our friends here at the church. And then we'll enjoy all this food."

The afternoon was filled with laughter as families sat on the lawn, enjoying smoked pork, corn on the cob, and more kinds of dessert than anyone could count. Of course, the volcano's eruption was a popular topic of conversation. But they talked most of all about the blessings of the corn harvest.

"May I have everyone's attention?" someone called in a loud voice. "May I have your attention, please?" As the crowd quieted, the pastor climbed the front steps of the church, and when he had their attention, he asked everyone to bow their heads for prayer. He began, "Father, we thank you for this wonderful day. We thank you for the harvest, for this island gold you have blessed us with. Thank you for protecting our homes and our village. Thank you for this food which you have given to us in abundance. May we always give you the glory for your goodness to us. In Jesus' name. Amen."

As Teki listened to the pastor's prayer, he thought to himself, *That's easy for him to say. His fields weren't destroyed. Where is this God's goodness to us?*

"Now we have a special announcement," the pastor said. "Will the Tai family and the Nalatu family please join me up here?"

With puzzled looks, both families made their way to the steps of the church.

"God has blessed this island richly. We have had a wonderful harvest despite the volcano. And now the members of our church family want to bless these two families who lost their fields this week. Together, we have purchased new fields to give to the Nalatu and Tai families. And the farmers in our church want to give ten percent of the money they receive from the sale of their own crops to your two families. They are doing this freely and with gratitude to God for His goodness to all of us."

The two families stood speechless on the steps. Mrs. Nalatu covered her face and began to weep. Teki grabbed his father's hand and squeezed it firmly. As he looked up to see his father's reaction, he saw tears begin to fill his eyes as well.

Mrs. Tai put her arm around Kalani as she, too, began to cry. "Oh my, oh my," she said. "What can we say?"

Clearing his throat and fighting back his own tears, Mr. Tai tried to speak. But all he could say was, "Thank you. Thank you all."

As the families stepped down onto the lawn, everyone formed a circle around them. Then the pastor opened his Bible and read: "'Let them give glory to the LORD and proclaim his praise in the islands.' Isaiah 42:12. God has truly blessed us, my friends. Let'sproclaim His praise here in our island."

Then with grateful hearts, everyone began to sing:

To God be the glory, great things He has done;
So loved He the world that He gave us His Son,
Who yielded His life an atonement for sin,
And opened the life gate that all may go in.

Praise the Lord, praise the Lord!
Let the earth hear His voice!
Praise the Lord, praise the Lord!
Let the people rejoice!
O come to the Father, through Jesus the Son,
And give Him the glory, great things He has done.

Teki, of course, recognized the song. But now, instead of hearing it secretly outside a church window, he was completely surrounded by the beautiful words and music. He closed his eyes and smiled as the words filled his heart with a different kind of joy than the first time he heard them.

As Teki's family drove home after the harvest festival, each of them was very quiet. Finally, Teki said, "Dad, Mom, I want to tell you something."

"What is it?" his dad asked.

"You remember when I walked home by myself from the cemetery, the day we took gifts to the ancestors?"

"Yes."

"Well, I didn't go straight home. When I reached the edge of the village, I heard the church bells ringing, just like we do every Sunday if we're near town. They were so beautiful, I walked to the churchyard so I could hear them better. At first I hid so the people going into the church wouldn't see me. But after everyone was inside, I sat under one of the windows. That's when I heard everyone singing the song they sang today. You know—'*To God be the glory, great things He has done.*' When I heard that song the first time, I didn't really understand what the words meant. I just knew I liked it. And the people sounded so happy while they were singing."

"They seemed very happy singing it this afternoon, too," replied Teki's mom.

"I know. That's what I'm trying to say," Teki continued excitedly. "The people at the church must believe the great Creator God loves them very much. Otherwise, how could they sing that song with so much joy? And how could they have so much peace even though the volcano could erupt again at any time? And why would the people at Kalani's church be so kind and helpful to her family and to us when they don't really know us?"

"Those are good questions, son," his dad replied. "I also have many questions after everything that's happened this week. Perhaps when we read the Bible that Mr. Tai gave us, we will find some answers."

Teki lay in his bed that night but couldn't sleep. He kept thinking of all the wonderful things that had happened at the harvest festival. But most of all, he kept thinking about the words of the song he had heard for the second time: *O come to the Father, through Jesus the Son, and give Him the glory, great things He has done.*

Finally, Teki closed his eyes and prayed, not to Lomoko as he usually did, but to the great Creator God. "I believe the words of this song are true. Please help my mom and dad to believe them too. I want our whole family to give you glory together for the great things you have done for us."

A gentle breeze rustled the curtain covering his bedroom window. Coco, who had been sleeping at the foot of the bed, snuggled up close to Teki's side. Teki yawned, pulled the sheet up under his chin, and fell into a peaceful sleep.

THINK ABOUT IT

» Why do you think God allowed both Teki's and Kalani's corn fields to be destroyed? What good things happened as a result?

» Why do you think the church community helped the two families? Why do you think they helped Teki's family even though the family does not know God?

» When we have the opportunity to share the Good News with others, what can we do to show the truth of what we say?

FANNY CROSBY

Have you ever worn a blindfold, maybe to play a game? Did you like not being able to see, or were you scared? Were you glad to take the blindfold off and be able to see everything around you again?

Fanny J. Crosby was born in 1820 in New York. When she was six months old, she caught a cold and developed inflammation in her eyes. Today, this condition is easily treated, but the nineteenth-century cure suggested to her family caused Fanny to become blind. Yet Fanny would become one of the most well-known people in the United States in her lifetime. This was because she had a special gift—poetry. One of her first poems was written when she was just eight years old:

> Oh, what a happy soul am I,
> Although I cannot see.
> I am resolved that in this world
> Contented I will be.
>
> How many blessings I enjoy
> That other people don't.
> To weep and sigh because I'm blind,
> I cannot, and I won't.

When she was fifteen, Fanny enrolled at a school for the blind. She remained there for twenty-three years, first as a student, then as a teacher. While there, she wrote many poems and was even asked to recite some of them in front of Congress!

Many of her poems were set to music as hymns, some of which we still sing today. Fanny wrote such favorites as "To God Be the Glory" and "Blessed Assurance." In fact, she wrote the words to more than 8,000 hymns and songs. Her hymns were so well known that she was invited to meet presidents and many famous people of her day. Sometimes the inspiration for her hymns came from a Bible verse or a phrase of conversation or even the music itself. Fanny kept writing hymns until she died at the age of ninety-four, joyful in the knowledge that the first thing she would ever see would be the face of Jesus.

WORDS YOU NEED TO KNOW

Forgiveness: An act of love that does not hold a person's sins against him, blame him, or try to get even with him

Grace: A gift of kindness that is not deserved

Mercy: A choice not to give someone the punishment he or she deserves

Salvation: God's free gift of saving us from the punishment we deserve for our sins

Faith: A belief and acceptance that Jesus is God's Son and our Savior

Repentance: A heartfelt sorrow for our sins that causes us to turn away from our sins and behave differently

Compassion: Acts of tenderness and love we give to those who are hurting

HIDE IT IN YOUR HEART

For Christ died for sins once for all, the righteous for the unrighteous, to bring you to God. He was put to death in the body, but made alive by the Spirit. (1 Peter 3:18)

Therefore, as God's chosen people, holy and dearly loved, clothe yourselves with compassion. (Colossians 3:12)

JESUS IS OUR BRIDGE TO GOD

Human history is the epic story of mankind's struggle for peace—peace with ourselves, peace with one another, peace with our surroundings, and peace with God. We have built magnificent cities that celebrate the highest in human achievement and give us the illusion of harmony, but sin and decay quickly take hold each time to disfigure and defile these monuments to our greatness. We have forged "unbreakable" treaties with our neighbors in order to mend fences and ensure lasting peace, only to call our soldiers to war a few months later. We have tried to combat evil with good laws and good intentions only to fail miserably because we could not change people's hearts. Our greatest artists and writers have tried to inspire people to feel and think and act in ways that reveal their better, more noble nature; yet many of these artists ended up heartbroken and disillusioned after discovering the truth that people are not "basically good" and can never be without help from above.

Some cultures have tried to patch things up with God (or gods or nature) by sacrificing crops, birds, livestock, or in a few extreme cases, one another. *Yikes!* Some people believed they could soften the anger of God (or gods or nature) through painful acts of self-punishment and even self-mutilation. Others believe that doing good works will move God (or gods or nature) to behave kindly toward us. This idea of a cosmic cause-and-effect cycle is sometimes called *karma*.

It doesn't take a very smart person to see that the world doesn't always work like it should. People sometimes hurt one another, and they often let each other down. Adults and, in many cultures, children work very hard each day but have little to show for it afterward. Fires, earthquakes, floods, and other natural disasters can wipe out entire homes and communities without warning. Indeed, the Bible tells us that because of the Fall the world became broken and people separated from one another and from God. The bad news is that without God all our plans and dreams and good works for restoring harmony are utterly hopeless. But

the Bible also tells us wonderful news of the one true God who does not change (Malachi 3:6) and whose plans do not change (Proverbs 19:21). God's eternal plan for creation is the same yesterday, today, and tomorrow. And despite outward appearances, the peace that people so desperately want but will never be able find on their own is already in the works! The author of this peace is none other than God's own Son, Jesus Christ.

God's eternal plan to redeem and restore His children and His creation is based on the life, death, and resurrection of Jesus. As we have seen, death is the only just penalty for sinning against a holy and righteous God. In order to spare His children from this punishment, God sent His only begotten Son to live among us on earth. While here He taught people about heaven, healed people of their diseases, and showed us what God is really like. Jesus never sinned, not once, yet He allowed Himself to be falsely accused, savagely beaten, publicly humiliated, then put to death on a cross:

> *He was wounded for the wrong things we did. He was crushed for the evil things we did. The punishment, which made us well, was given to him. And we are healed because of his wounds. We all have wandered away like sheep. Each of us has gone his own way. But the Lord has put on him the punishment for all the evil we have done.* (Isaiah 53:5–6, ICB)

Christ suffered for our sins once for all time. He never sinned, but he died for sinners to bring you safely home to God. He suffered physical death, but he was raised to life in the Spirit. (1 Peter 3:18, NLT)

In the Old Testament, God required the Hebrew people to regularly sacrifice a lamb without blemishes or flaws to cover their sins and satisfy His judgment. This was more than a ritual—it was a picture to help the people recognize the promised Messiah when He arrived among them. Jesus, the Messiah, became the Lamb of God. He lived a perfect life, without blemish or flaw, and was sacrificed to remove our sins once and for all time. The Bible tells us that "without the shedding of blood there is no forgiveness" (Hebrews 9:22). The blood of animals could cover people's sins but could not actually take their sins away. But the blood of Jesus—God the Son—would wash away the sins of the entire world!

Jesus' suffering was a terrible price to pay—more terrible than we can possibly imagine—but His sacrifice was necessary to build the one and only bridge that can lead us back to God the Father (John 14:6). Why? Why did Jesus give up His rightful place on a throne in heaven to be brutally killed on earth? The answer is one simple word: love.

Ghent Altarpiece by Cranach

God showed his great love for us by sending Christ to die for us while we were still sinners. And since we have been made right in God's sight by the blood of Christ, he will certainly save us from God's condemnation. For since our friendship with God was restored by the death of his Son while we were still his enemies, we will certainly be saved through the life of his Son. So now we can rejoice in our wonderful new relationship with God because our Lord Jesus Christ has made us friends of God. (Romans 5:8–11, NLT)

"For God so loved the world that he gave his one and only Son, that whoever believes in him shall not perish but have eternal life." (John 3:16)

Jesus loves you so much that He willingly made Himself a lowly man and let Himself be tortured and crucified. He was separated from the Father and the entire wrath of God poured out on Him, all so that you could find your way back to Him and live with Him in joyous harmony in a perfect world forever and ever.

But wait a minute! What happened when Jesus was killed? Didn't God's enemy win? Didn't Satan and his hordes of fallen angels break out the champagne and celebrate in demonic glee when they saw the Son of God hanging lifeless on a cross? No doubt they *thought* that victory was theirs. The Bible tells us what happened next. When Jesus died that Friday afternoon, darkness covered the earth (Mark 15:33) and a great earthquake shook the land (Matthew 27:51–52). Soon after, Jesus' body was prepared for burial and placed in a tomb by

grieving loved ones. Roman soldiers were posted at the tomb to prevent His followers from stealing the body and claiming that He had risen from the dead (Matthew 27:62–66). On Sunday morning, the third day, there was another violent earthquake. The guards shook with fear and fell to the ground as an angel, dressed in white, rolled away the stone from the entrance to the tomb. When Mary Magdalene and others went to the tomb at dawn to anoint the body of Jesus, the angel announced to them that Jesus was no longer there (Matthew 28:1–7). In fact, He had returned from the dead as He promised He would (Mark 10:33–34).

After His resurrection, Jesus appeared to many of His followers, some of whom did not recognize Him at first (John 20:10–16; Luke 24:13–35; John 21:1–14). In the next forty days, He appeared many times—once to more than five hundred people (1 Corinthians 15:6)! During this time He taught His followers about the kingdom of God, the Holy Spirit, and His own eventual return to earth (Acts 1:1–10). He also commanded them to tell people everywhere the Good News of His death and resurrection and what it would mean for all creation (Matthew 28:16–20).

It is important when you share the Good News of God's great sacrifice that you do not forget the resurrection of Christ. If Jesus had merely died, then indeed all would have been lost:

If Christ has not been raised, then your faith is useless and you are still guilty of your sins. . . . But in fact, Christ has been raised from the dead. He is the first of a great harvest of all who have died. So you see, just as death came into the world through a man, now the resurrection from the dead has begun through another man. Just as everyone dies because we all belong to Adam, everyone who belongs to Christ will be given new life. (1 Corinthians 15:17–22, NLT)

You see, in rising from the dead Jesus broke the chains of death once and for all. He took possession of the keys to death and hell (Revelation 1:18), "and having disarmed the [spiritual] powers and authorities, he made a public spectacle of them, triumphing over them by the cross" (Colossians 2:14–16). Satan was humiliated in defeat, enraged that his "victory" had proven to be his ultimate downfall. Now, because Jesus overcame death, the death we experience here on earth will be only temporary. When Jesus comes again, we will be given new, everlasting bodies. "In a flash, in the twinkling of an eye" we will be changed forever:

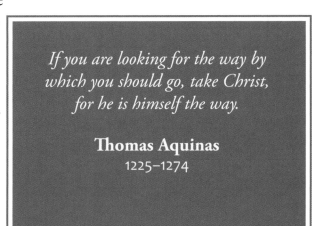

If you are looking for the way by which you should go, take Christ, for he is himself the way.

Thomas Aquinas
1225–1274

Then, when our dying bodies have been transformed into bodies that will never die, this Scripture will be fulfilled: "Death is swallowed up in victory. O death, where is your victory? O death, where is your sting?" (1 Corinthians 15:54–55, NLT)

MAKE A NOTE OF IT

Read the story of Jesus and His followers on the road to Emmaus in Luke 24:13–35. Why do you think Cleopas and his friend did not recognize the risen Savior? Now read 1 Corinthians 15. What do you think our resurrection bodies will be like? Could it be that Jesus' resurrection body was different enough that it kept His followers from recognizing Him at first? What happened that finally made Cleopas and his friend realize that this was Jesus? If Jesus came to you, how would you recognize Him?

GOD OFFERS US FORGIVENESS

One day, all who have given their lives to Jesus Christ will receive glorified bodies and spend eternity with Him in paradise. But how can that be? What about our sins? Yes, Jesus took our punishment for us, but isn't God the Father still angry with us? He is still a holy God. Haven't we disobeyed Him, and don't we sometimes still disobey? Is He simply going to forget what we have done?

Because of Jesus' sacrifice, God forgives our sins. He doesn't do this because we deserve to be forgiven. No one deserves to be forgiven, yet we all need **forgiveness** from God. Everyone has sinned and fallen short of His glory. And because every sin is ultimately an act of rebellion against God (Psalm 51:4) we desperately need God's forgiveness. If our sins are not forgiven, we will spend eternity suffering the consequences of our actions (Matthew 25:46).

But God is loving and merciful. In fact, He's eager to forgive us of our sins! The Bible tells us, "He is patient with you, not wanting anyone to perish, but everyone to come to repentance" (2 Peter 3:9). God wants to forgive us:

"I, I am the One who forgives all your sins. I do this to please myself. I will not remember your sins." (Isaiah 43:25, ICB)

What exactly does it mean to be forgiven? Forgiveness means that God no longer holds our sin against us. It means that He does not require us to be punished for our sins. He declares us "not guilty" as though we never sinned against Him. Perhaps most amazing of all, He has promised to forget our sin as if it had never happened!

"I have swept away your sins like a big cloud. I have removed your sins like a cloud that disappears into the air." (Isaiah 44:22, ICB)

He has removed our sins as far from us as the east is from the west. (Psalm 103:12)

"I will never again remember their sins and lawless deeds." (Hebrews 10:17, NLT)

God sees everything and knows everything—past, present, and future simultaneous-

The Prodigal Son by Rembrandt

ly—so how can He possibly forget something that happened? If God can forget about our sins, couldn't He also forget about a promise? What about you and me—could He forget that we are His children? No, God is not talking about an accidental kind of forgetting, like when you forget to brush your teeth or when your mom forgets where she put her car keys. He isn't capable of that. What God is talking about is purposely removing our sins from His memory; He is *choosing* not to remember our sins. Of course, the price for God's forgiveness is high, but He has paid that price Himself. Because of Jesus Christ's ultimate act of love, we can be free from the penalty and guilt of sin. God will no longer keep a record of our sins. Our forgiveness is total and complete.

So how should you respond when another person has hurt you or offended you in some way? The Bible says you must follow God's example and forgive that person (Matthew 18:21–35). You may be tempted to hold a grudge, but as Henry Ward Beecher once said, saying "I can forgive, but I cannot forget" is just another way of saying, "I will not forgive." Forgiveness should be like a cancelled IOU—torn in two and thrown away so that it can never be used again. Sometimes you will find it hard to do this, but remember what it cost God to forgive you. He paid a terrible price in order to purchase your freedom. The least you can do is to give up your pride and your hurt and your right to revenge in order to forgive the person who hurt you.

Forgiveness is the key that unlocks the door of resentment and the handcuffs of hate. It is a power that breaks the chains of bitterness and the shackles of selfishness.

Corrie Ten Boom
1892–1983

GOD'S MERCY AND AMAZING GRACE

Forgiveness is an act of love, mercy, and grace. **Grace** is an act of kindness that is not deserved or earned in any way. Let's say, for example, you agree to mow Mrs. Wilson's lawn for ten dollars. It's a hot, sunny day, and the work is hard but you do a good job. When you have finished and put away the mower and Mrs. Wilson pays you ten dollars, that is not grace. After all, that was the amount you agreed on, and the worker deserves his wages (Luke 10:7). But if, while you are working, Mrs. Wilson brings you a glass of ice-cold lemonade and a plate of cookies and invites you to take a break, that is grace. She looked out the window and saw that you were in need of refreshment. And although she did not owe you anything beyond the ten dollars you agreed on, she chose to give you a gift that would meet your need and make your job easier.

 Mercy, on the other hand, is an act of kindness in which a person does not receive a punishment he *does* deserve. Let's say, for example, that you and a friend are outdoors kicking a ball around, and one time you kick the ball so hard that it bounces into Mrs. Wilson's garden and ruins several of her prized begonias. Yes, it was an accident, but you are responsible for the damage. Mrs. Wilson has every right to demand that you or your parents pay to replace the broken flowers. She might even suggest that you mow her lawn for the next six weeks to cover the cost. Instead, she chooses to forgive you and replaces the damaged begonias at her own expense. That is mercy.

 King David, realizing the terrible sin he had committed by taking another man's wife, cried out to God, "Have mercy on me, O God, because of your unfailing love. Because of your great compassion, blot out the stain of my sins" (Psalm 51:1, NLT). God has every right to be angry when we disobey Him. His commands have been written down for us in the Bible, and we were all made to know the difference between right and wrong. We have no excuse, no defense, for choosing to do wrong. Instead, we must depend on God's mercy to save us from the eternal punishment we deserve:

> *God is so rich in mercy, and he loved us so much, that even though we were dead because of our sins, he gave us life when he raised Christ from the dead.* (Ephesians 2:4–5, NLT)

 You see, God chooses to show mercy to those who believe and does not punish them eternally for their sins. Now look closely at the second part of this passage. Not only does He choose not to punish us (mercy), but He actually gives us a gift we don't deserve (grace) instead! Because of the sacrifice of Jesus, God gives us the gift of eternal life with Him!

THE STORY OF KLAUS

Many years ago in a small mountain village in Germany there lived a young boy named Klaus. He was six years old. His family was very poor and they had little to eat, so Klaus was often hungry. Each morning, Klaus ate a small bowl of oatmeal before he headed off to the village school. Klaus's school had only one classroom for all the students from all the grades. First-grade students, fourth-grade students, and even high school students all sat together in one room. One teacher taught all the grades. Klaus loved his school and all his friends of different ages. He especially liked a high school student named Heinz who was tall and strong and acted like a big brother to Klaus.

Each day at lunchtime, Klaus quickly ate the small pieces of bread and cheese his mother had packed for him in an old sack. One day, as he waited hungrily for his friends to finish their lunches so they could play, he noticed a lunch sack on a bench behind the schoolhouse. He looked cautiously around to see if anyone was watching. When he thought no one was looking, he hurried behind the building. He tore open the sack and hungrily stuffed his mouth with two slices of cheese and a piece of bread. He knew that if someone saw him he would be in trouble for stealing, but he was so hungry he didn't seem to care. What Klaus didn't know was that his teacher was watching him through the schoolhouse window.

After lunch, the teacher called Klaus to stand in front of the class. She told all his classmates what he had done. Then she announced his punishment: He would receive six strikes across his back with a small tree branch. Sternly, she ordered Klaus to remove his shirt, turn his back to the class, and prepare for the beating.

All the students held their breath as they waited for the branch to fall on Klaus's back. Suddenly, a voice from the back of the room cried out, "Wait! Please wait!" As the teacher turned to see who had spoken, a tall, older student walked to the front of the room. It was Heinz, the friend Klaus thought of as a big brother. He spoke softly with the teacher. As Klaus stood shaking, he and his classmates strained to hear what the teacher and Heinz were talking about.

After several moments, the teacher turned to Klaus. "Put your shirt on, Klaus. Heinz has asked me to punish him instead of you. He wants to take your place for the punishment you deserve for stealing. I have agreed. Even though he did not steal the lunch, he will be the one to be punished for what you did. Klaus, go back to your seat."

The whole class gasped. They could not believe what the teacher had just said. As they watched wide-eyed, Heinz removed his shirt and turned his back to the class. Everyone sat silently as the teacher beat Heinz's back six times with the branch. They could not believe that an innocent person would be willing to take the punishment for a guilty person.

The story of Klaus is set in Germany over sixty years ago. It provides us a small though imperfect picture of what Jesus did for us on the cross. Of course, only Jesus was sinless, and only a perfect sacrifice can cover our sins. Why do you think one person would be willing to take the punishment someone else deserves? Write your response in your notebook.

God did not choose us to suffer his anger, but to have salvation through our Lord Jesus Christ. Jesus died for us so that we can live together with him. (1 Thessalonians 5:9–10, ICB)

God saved us and made us his holy people. That was not because of anything we did ourselves but because of what he wanted and because of his grace. (2 Timothy 1:9, ICB)

THE GIFT OF SALVATION

A few years ago, my wife and I attended the Masters golf tournament in Augusta, Georgia. The Masters is one of the world's most famous sporting events. We will never forget seeing golf's greatest players challenge what may be the most beautiful course on earth. And do you know how much I paid for the tickets to this event? Nothing! They were a gift given to me by a friend. These tickets weren't free; my friend had to pay for them. But I didn't have to pay anything. They were given to me as a gift.

Isn't it great to have a friend like that? Well, we all have a friend like that.

God saved you by his grace when you believed. And you can't take credit for this; it is a gift from God. (Ephesians 2:8, NLT)

People are made right with God by his grace, which is a free gift. They are made right with God by being made free from sin through Jesus Christ. (Romans 3:24, ICB)

God loves us so much that He gave us the greatest gift of all: **salvation**. The word *salvation* comes from the Latin *salvare*, meaning "to save." It means that God has rescued us from the awful consequence of our sins. Instead of an eternity in hell, He is offering us a perfect life in a perfect body in a perfect paradise forever with Him. This wonderful gift was not free; it was purchased with a price. Jesus paid the full price. What a friend!

You see, eternal life cannot be purchased for any amount of money. The richest man on earth will not be able to buy his way out of hell or into heaven. But a ticket to paradise is yours for the taking, completely free of charge. This is because Jesus Christ has already paid for you, for all of us, by dying on the cross in our place. By His sacrifice, He paid the price for all the sins we would ever commit and opened the gates to paradise to anyone who would believe on His name:

"Jesus is the only One who can save people. His name is the only power in the world that has been given to save people. And we must be saved through him!" (Acts 4:12, ICB)

[Jesus said] "I tell you the truth. Whoever hears what I say and believes in the One who sent me has eternal life. He will not be judged guilty. He has already left death and has entered into life." (John 5:24, ICB)

WHAT IS FAITH?

Admittedly, this sounds too good to be true. All we have to do is believe in Jesus? Yet the Bible is very clear that salvation is a free gift. We cannot earn our way into heaven. No amount of good deeds, good works, religious rituals, or being better than the average person is going to save anyone from eternal punishment. We must accept God's gift.

If your mother tells you she loves you and wants to give you a gift, what has to happen before you can enjoy the gift? First, you must believe her when she says the gift is for you. Then you must accept the gift and receive it. If you don't believe your mother really wants to give you the gift and if you don't accept it, will the gift be yours? No. It's likely your mother will return the gift to the store or perhaps give it to someone else. When God tells you that He loves you and wants to give you the gift of salvation, you must first believe that the gift is intended for you. Then you must accept His gift and trust that He will do what He says. This is called **faith**:

You love him even though you have never seen him. Though you do not see him now, you trust him; and you rejoice with a glorious, inexpressible joy. The reward for trusting him will be the salvation of your souls. (1 Peter 1:8–9, NLT)

Now faith is being sure of what we hope for and certain of what we do not see. (Hebrews 11:1)

But a person cannot do any work that will make him right with God. So he must trust in God. Then God accepts his faith, and that makes him right with God. (Romans 4:5, ICB)

WHAT IS REPENTANCE?

When a person is arrested for a crime and is brought before a judge, one of the first questions the judge asks is "Are you guilty or not guilty?" If you were the judge and the prisoner confessed his crime to you, would you pronounce him guilty or innocent? Imagine a judge telling a guilty criminal, "You're not guilty. You are free to go." How do you think the prisoner would feel?

When you come before a holy God, you are like a guilty prisoner standing before a judge. There is no need to call witnesses or present evidence or listen to testimony from forensics experts. Your judge, after all, is omniscient and omnipresent. He knows everything and sees everything, so He knows exactly what you've done and why you did it. Your accuser, the devil himself, is delighted—he wants to see you get what's coming to you. There is no defense that can justify what you've done, and you're truly sorrowful for having disobeyed the Father who loves you so much. So you choose to stand up, confess your sin to the judge, and ask for His mercy.

God smiles and says, "Not guilty. You are free to go."

The devil leaps out of his seat and screams, "But what about the sin?!"

God replies, "What sin? I've already forgotten it. Next case."

Acts 3:19 says, "Now repent of your sins and turn to God, so that your sins may be wiped away" (NLT). To repent means to be sorry for your sins and to confess them so that you can be forgiven. Repenting is an important way to show you believe in God's free gift of salvation. But repenting means more than just being sorry for what you have done. In the New Testament the word *repentance* is translated from the Greek *metanoia*, which means "a change of mind and heart." In the Old Testament, *repentance* is translated from two separate Hebrew words—one meaning "to feel sorrow" and one meaning "to return." So to repent means to be sorry, but it also means to turn away from the path of sin and return to God's way of doing things. Repentance, therefore, is a change in your heart and your way of thinking that causes you to act in a new way:

All must repent of their sins and turn to God—and prove they have changed by the good things they do. (Acts 26:20, NLT)

Being sorry in the way God wants makes a person change his heart and life. This leads to salvation, and we cannot be sorry for that. (2 Corinthians 7:10, ICB)

Does this mean that after you repent you will never sin again? No. Even God's children will not be free of sin until we die or Jesus comes back. But we can thank the Lord that when we confess our sins, our slate is wiped clean before God. He is not going to throw our old mistakes back in our face if we fall down and commit the same sin again. He is not going to hold them over our heads, and He is certainly not going to allow the devil to use them as evidence against us.

MAKE A NOTE OF IT

Why is it sometimes hard to forgive a person who has done something to hurt you? Are you more likely to retaliate, or do you simply hold a grudge against the other person? Are you currently holding a grudge against someone? In light of what God has done by offering you forgiveness in Christ, write a prayer in which you forgive this person for what he or she has done. Now offer this prayer to God and let go of the grudge. Do you feel any different?

WHAT SHOULD I DO?

If you see a person who is sad or hurt or in need, what should you do? First of all ask yourself, *What did God do for me?* Every one of us is guilty of sin and deserves to suffer eternal punishment. We are all in desperate need of a savior, someone to rescue us from this unimaginable fate. And so God had compassion on us and sent Christ to die as the payment for our guilt so that we could be called children of God and have a home with Him.

Compassion is an act of tenderness and love given to someone who is hurting or in need. Compassion flows from the Father over everything He has made (Psalm 145:9). God's compassion is an expression of love and sympathy for His creation, like a father has for his child (Psalm 103:13). He showed this most completely when He sacrificed His Son to rescue a sinful and hurting world. And so when we see a family member or a friend or neighbor who is hurting or needs help, we must

follow God's example and show compassion by offering comfort or even physical assistance to that person. The Bible says it this way:

Therefore, as God's chosen people, holy and dearly loved, clothe yourselves with compassion. (Colossians 3:12)

What does Paul mean when he says "clothe yourselves with compassion"? God commands us to have compassion for others because He had compassion for us. Compassion is part of who He is—it's a godly character trait. Now some people wear hats or T-shirts or jackets that show what school they attend. Others wear clothing displaying a team logo that shows their loyalty to a particular sports team. God wants us to "wear" compassion as a visible character trait that identifies us as His children. When you show compassion to hurting people, you are showing them what God is like. You might even invite them to join His team!

God commands us to follow His example by giving love and mercy to those who are helpless and harassed (Matthew 9:36), sick (Matthew 14:14), hungry (Matthew 15:32), and in prison (Hebrews 10:34). We are also commanded to show compassion to those who have hurt or harmed us (Luke 6:27). After all, we were all once enemies of God. If God is compassionate to you when you sin, how should you treat someone who has sinned against you?

A Prayer

Dear God, thank you for the greatest gift of all. Thank you for Jesus, who loved me so much that He paid the price for my sin to give me the gift of eternal life. Thank you that because of this gift, I can really know you as my God, as my Father, and as my friend. Help me to forgive others who hurt me, just as you have forgiven me. Help me to see when someone is in need and show me how I can help. In Jesus' name. Amen.

GOD'S GREAT STORY:
A COSMIC DRAMA IN THREE ACTS

Everybody has a story, just as everybody has a worldview. The Christian worldview is based on a unique story. That story is God's story, and His story is the greatest story of all. Because God wants us to know the truth of His story, He had it written down for us in the greatest book of all time, the Bible. In these final pages, we will imagine God's magnificent story as a drama—a play in three acts. As the curtain opens on the greatest drama ever written and we watch God's story unfold, see how many truths about God, the universe, people, truth, and right and wrong you can identify.

ACT I. SCENE 1:
GOD'S GOOD CREATION

Act 1 opens with the scene of creation and the words, "In the beginning, God . . ." (Genesis 1:1). This scene reveals the origin of the heavens, the earth, and everything in them. The six days of creation conclude with God creating His masterpiece, man and woman, and calling them to rule the earth as people made in His image. The scene is one of perfect harmony and includes everything that God created, both visible and invisible.

ACT I. SCENE 2:
HARMONY IN CREATION

In this scene, we see that God's good creation is all about relationships. God, who exists in perfect harmony as God the Father, God the Son, and God the Holy Spirit, has made His children to exist in perfect harmony with Him, with themselves, with each other, and with the earth. Adam and Eve walk and talk with God in intimate fellowship. They enjoy perfect peace and harmony as individuals, sinless and without blame, shame, or fear. They are in harmony as one flesh—husband and wife—ruling and reigning over creation together. And they enjoy perfect harmony with the physical earth from which God had created Adam. God intends for these relationships to remain in eternal harmony, a harmony that depends on obedience to His command not to eat from the tree of the knowledge of good and evil (Genesis 2:17).

ACT II:
THE FALL OF CREATION

God had created Adam and Eve in His image, and that included the ability to choose. If they could not make choices for themselves, they would never truly be able to love Him or love one another. He also gave them the ability to know good from evil, and at the same time He commanded them to choose good and not evil. By obeying Him, Adam and Eve would be able to show love to their Creator.

Then Satan arrives on the scene and tempts Adam and Eve to disobey. Tragically, they give in to his lie, and their disobedience instantly brings death and disharmony to all the relationships of God's creation. Adam hides from God, showing their fellowship has become broken; Adam's heart is filled with fear, showing he no longer has harmony with himself; Adam blames Eve for his sin, showing that their relationship, too, is broken; and to top it off God curses the earth as part of their punishment. Disharmony, death, and decay have become part of the created order, just as God had warned.

Act III:
Redemption and Restoration

Our first two acts fill just a few pages of most Bibles. So what happens in the remaining thousand or so pages? They are filled with the story of Act III. Just as things look darkest, God reveals His daring plan to make everything right again. He promises Adam and Eve that one day a Savior will come to crush Satan and his works and restore harmony to creation. This promise is repeated again and again throughout the Old Testament—in all, hundreds of prophecies are given to God's people telling about the coming King, who He is, and what will happen to Him.

Then Jesus appears, and He is everything that was promised and more. When God the Father says the time is right, Jesus sets out to teach the people about God and His kingdom. He heals many who are sick, blind, deaf, lame, or hurting. He even brings dead people back to life! But not everyone is happy about this. Some religious leaders are quite angry because Jesus refuses to follow their man-made rules. They plot to have Him captured and killed—and God allows it to happen!

But in a plot twist the enemy couldn't see coming, God raises Jesus from the dead on the third day and triumphs over the enemy once and for all. In Christ, all the relationships of creation are redeemed. Those who believe Jesus' words and choose to obey Him as God's Son and their Savior are restored in harmony with God, themselves, and others. They become new creations, and God lives in each believer at the moment he or she accepts God's free gift of salvation. But what about the earth? God reveals that He will create a new heaven and a new earth where His children will rule and reign with Him for all eternity.

For God in all his fullness was pleased to live in Christ, and through him God reconciled everything to himself. He made peace with everything in heaven and on earth by means of Christ's blood on the cross. (Colossians 1:19–20, NLT)

THE HOUSE OF TRUTH: THE FOURTH PILLAR

BIBLICAL TRUTH 8:

Jesus died to restore fellowship and harmony between me and God.

INDEX

HOW WILL SHE MAKE A DIFFERENCE?

The Bible tells us that in the last days, people will be selfish, abusive, ungrateful, slanderous, and without love (1 Timothy 3). She sees it every day on the TV programs she watches, in the news she hears, and in what she reads on the Internet. Will she grow up to become salt and light to the world or merely part of the problem?

Prepare your children to make a real difference in the lives of others by teaching them to see the world around them through the unerring lens of God's Word. Give them a strong foundation and clear biblical worldview with the **What We Believe** curriculum.

Beautifully illustrated and written in a conversational style, the What We Believe series makes the study of God's Word exciting and memorable for boys and girls of all ages. Through engaging stories and creative notebooking journals, your kids will develop a generous heart and courageous spirit to share the love of God with a world in need.

"Excellent, Bible-rich worldview curriculum."
World Magazine

"Absolutely wonderful!"
The Old Schoolhouse Magazine

"A fantastic and much-needed resource. I'm looking forward to taking my own kids through these valuable lessons."
Sean McDowell

Recommended by CHUCK COLSON on *BreakPoint*

apologia.
in partnership with
Summit
summit.org

IMAGE LICENSE INFORMATION

Creative Commons Attribution 3.0 Unported License
  Ralf Beier, 196-7
  Gisling, 148
  Forest & Kim Starr, 144-5

Creative Commons Attribution 2.0 License
  Eric Dufresne, 118-9

Creative Commons Attribution 2.0 Generic License
  lyng883, 20
  ideacreamanuelaPps, 102
  jasonb42882, 92-93

Creative Commons Attribution ShareAlike 3.0 License
  Mila Zinkova, 202-3, 222-3

Creative Commons Attribution ShareAlike 2.5 License
  blahedo, 141

Creative Commons Attribution-No Derivative Works 2.0 Generic License
  BrokenWing739, 132
  Spacemanbobby, 113

GNU Free Documentation License
  David Benbennick, 75
  Éclusette, 55
  Freestyle nl, 172-3
  Mbdortmund, 125
  Miraceti, 178
  Andreas Praefcke, 65
  TUBS, 34-5
  Yosemite, 89
  Yvan Leduc, 228-9